Be encouraged
and inspired,

Krin, Rachel, Kai, & Jacqui,
    We're really grateful for you all &
the time we've had together. Though
brief, it was meaningful & rich.
    May this story, written by Hannah's
Dad, bless & encourage you as you
walk on with the Lord.
    With full hearts,
        Joe, Hannah, & Elizabeth

The Caleb Years

...WHEN GOD DOESN'T MAKE SENSE

BY

DAVID P. INGERSON

Caleb was born with several undiagnosed congenital anomalies and endured ten major surgeries. His father writes the story, saturated with both pain and prayer, but remarkably without a trace of bitterness. His marvelous witness written with such skill, crafted in language honest and vivid, will not fail to deepen the faith and joy of all who trust God.

> **Eugene H. Peterson,** Professor Emeritus of Spiritual Theology, Regent College, bestselling author and translator of *The Message* Bible

David Ingerson's compelling portrayal of a father's heart agonizing for his suffering son, desperate for God's intervention, graphically demonstrates faith forged in the crucible. This is what utter dependence on God looks like, and a story that will challenge all of us.

> **Mark Batterson,** *New York Times* bestselling author of *The Circle Maker*

Military families understand adversity. When you add faith in Christ Jesus to the battle for a little boy's life, you define inspiration. In this great story Caleb and his family will become new spiritual heroes in your life that affirm the battle is already won.

> **Charles C. Baldwin, Chaplain, Major General,** USAF (Retired), former Chief of U.S. Air Force Chaplains

In *The Caleb Years,* David Ingerson has written a powerful book that will resonate with every parent and speak to the heart of every person who has suffered through tragedy and wrestled with their faith. His account is relayed with a depth of insight and authenticity that can only be known by one who has limped through the darkest of valleys and emerged with an iron embrace of the love and sovereignty of God.

The Ingerson family's story will inspire you to savor every precious moment with your loved ones, and it will help you develop the kind of eternal perspective that sustains and satisfies the human heart.

> **J. Michael Johnson, Esq.,** Constitutional law attorney, recipient of the Southern Baptist Convention "Champions for the Faith" and Family Research Council "Faith, Family & Freedom" awards

When God calls us to walk a journey beyond our human strength and to rely totally on Him, are we ready? *The Caleb Years* is such a journey that will reach into your deepest emotions. This is a must-read for any parent who is willing to say, "Your will be done, Mighty God." When God said, "My grace is sufficient," He meant it, and it is lived out in the lives of David and Kathy Ingerson in this book about their son Caleb. What an amazing journey that highlights the deep human emotions in a time of incredible stress.

Dr. Gordon Donoho, president/CEO, Christians in
Action Missions International

It is my distinct honor to commend this book to you, dear reader. I hope you are ready for an enriching journey. My beloved friend David has written a beautiful tribute to his valiant son Caleb, a powerfully honest psalm to his God, and what will prove to be an unparalleled blessing to you. With the remarkable detail of a medical journal, the visceral passion of a loving father, and the flourish that is uniquely David Ingerson, he invites you to taste the very real and intimate experiences of life and death, faith and doubt, hope and sorrow.

I am tempted to tell you that you will enjoy the trip, but more than that, you will be enriched. Read it with relish. You will empathize with David and Kathy, you will wonder at their God, and you will most certainly come to love their Caleb. We knew the fighter in the middle season of his fight. He graced our home and our church family. He warmed us with his smile. He frightened us with his prospects. And he inspired us with his life.

David's perceptive reflections in the final pages are the dessert after a wonderful meal. Laugh and cry like I did as I read *The Caleb Years,* then savor the wisdom.

Rich Bersett, pastor, Metro-East Christian Fellowship

What can test a parent more than watching their child suffer deeply? What can carry a family through excruciating circumstances except mountains of prayer, incredible friends, and oceans of grace? *The Caleb Years* is an incredible and inspiring story. I was sobered, saddened, and deeply moved. Having been friends with the author and his wife, Kathy, for several years, my respect for them soared as I read David's profoundly emotive account of the best of life in the biggest of trials.

Sam Kendrick, Integrity Men's Life Coach

What do you do when your entire world suddenly changes? David Ingerson writes a fast action play-by-play of how he coped with the emotional extremes experienced when his young son faced a prolonged illness from infancy. This is a must-read for those going through one of life's storms. For the rest of us, it is an inspirational message of faith that will prove invaluable should that storm arrive unexpectedly.

Scott Irwin, four-term city councilman,
Certified Financial Planner, Wharton School of
Business, Cannon Trust School honor graduate

David Ingerson has penned a truly inspirational story about incredible love and incredible faith in the most crushing of circumstances. All of us parents can relate to the excruciating pain that comes with seeing our children suffer. David and Kathy's story about Caleb's struggles and victories will resonate with all parents and will take you on an incredible faith journey. This is a must-read book that will greatly help you understand and strengthen your faith in the face of the very hardest of times.

Geoffrey D. Westmoreland, attorney, husband,
and father of two

David and I were stationed together at Scott Air Force Base during Caleb's fight. *The Caleb Years* is a great story of walking with God through severe times. David pours out his father's heart in this faithful account of his beloved son's incredible journey. The roller coaster of emotions sets the stage on which this unfathomable story unfolds.

Reading this fantastic account will surely prepare the reader to face similar trials of life head-on as David describes the challenges he and Kathy encountered while confronting the best and worst of the medical system. A tough but rewarding read for a very tough subject: the enormous trials of a wonderful little boy, his loving parents and how God saw them through it all.

Michael Stocksdale, Lieutenant Colonel, USAF (Retired)

Riveting. Reflective. Impassioned. The triumphant story of *The Caleb Years* delivers a hallowed prescription that drowns out the deafening sounds of heartache and despair by the overwhelming presence and power of God's love. The lessons of trials, testing, and tragedy clearly reveal and accentuate a higher purpose for living. The meticulous details of this breathtaking account reveal through a microscopic lens that the time we have should be used to glorify God. This is a must-read—especially for those who have or are still experiencing hurts that won't fade.

Bishop Henry L. Mariner Jr., pastor,
Hosanna Family Worship Center

This book is deeply moving. Many who have struggled with the unknowable answers to the nagging questions, "Why did this happen?" and "How could God have allowed this tragedy to befall us?" will find hope and help in this story.

The Caleb Years is for anyone who has ever found themselves in the midst of fiery trial, publicly uttering words of faith and victory while privately battling fear and doubt, anxiety and agony—a beautiful testimony to God's love and faithfulness as He delivers through the fire and a witness to His work in and through His children to accomplish His purposes.

Jeri Mazur, housewife, homeschool classical educator, mother of three

We've been close friends with the author and his family for many years. While we were familiar with the author's life challenges resulting from his son Caleb's medical struggles, we had no clue of the immensely powerful impact these stories would have when strung together in this book. In reading this story, we were moved to look at the struggles in our own life with a different set of eyes. Our faith and hope were bolstered as we read.

The story of Caleb's tumultuous birth and life struggles as well as his bright hope and victories reminded us of the Biblical character Job, who endured untold suffering and yet overcame. This is an amazing story that will build the faith of anyone who has endured tragedy. This book is a must-read and will encourage all of us when facing dark days to understand that there is yet reason for hope.

Arthur and Gloria Houston, playwright and producers of the stage play *We Shall Behold Him*

Gripping. Intriguing. *The Caleb Years* will grab you, the reader, and make you feel as I did—that you are a part of the story!

Patricia Schneider, middle school English teacher

Hope. That is the single word that best describes what the reader will take away from *The Caleb Years*. In his heartfelt and unabashedly honest book, David Ingerson offers us Hope that God is indeed present in our most difficult and darkest moments; when the pain we are experiencing overshadows all other realities, when life and God just don't make sense. But the Hope that David offers is not only a Hope that God is present but also a Hope that God feels our grief along with us and will bring us through to the other side, stronger with a faith and peace that we didn't know possible.

Max Davis, author of *The Insanity of Unbelief*

At times jarring and raw with emotion, the true passion and love of a father desperately seeking to protect his frail son is evident on every page. Written with the intensity of a man who has walked through deep pain and sorrow, David Ingerson leads us through to the other side, encouraging us to go on through the despair, to a place of peace and hope. I've known David since our time as cadets at the Air Force Academy, and this account is forged from the fires of real life...there is honest wisdom here for all. After reading *The Caleb Years*, I'm blessed—once again—to have been a part of the journey!

Henry Polczer, Colonel, USAF (Retired),
fellow Air Force officer, friend, and brother in Christ

What do you do when life doesn't make sense? How do you cope with impossible situations? In *The Caleb Years* you will see the true story of real people who walk through challenges that none of us want to face— and yet find a peace in God that is truly supernatural. David and Kathy Ingerson were part of Cornerstone Church during such a time in their life in which only God could see them through. As their pastor during that season, I was witness to the hand of God during life's darkest moments.

As you read this heart wrenching and inspiring story, you will observe this family demonstrate amazing love and determination for their precious son Caleb. I believe it will change you as it has changed me. You will walk away with a fresh perspective on life, love, family, and faith.

Mark Lehmann, senior pastor, Cornerstone Church,
Bowie, Maryland

The Caleb Years is one of the most inspiring books I have had the pleasure of reading, and believe me when I tell you that I have read a lot of books dealing with suffering and grief. Having experienced more than my share of emotional agony and heartache since I lost my daughter in a car accident fifteen years ago, I felt a strong connection to David's story. Many lives will be touched by reading this wonderful book.

David did an amazing job chronicling Caleb's journey. Although I didn't know Caleb, after reading this story I feel as if I do. I found myself on this emotional roller coaster, both rejoicing and crying. It's a story of love, faith, and trust—a story of listening to the voice of God and trusting in His Word. After every storm there is a rainbow.

Tracy C. Hester, bank branch manager, mother of two

This is a riveting, transparent, first-person account of a father's struggle to understand a loving, sovereign God while caring for his young son afflicted from birth with several severe medical challenges. You will agonize with David and his wife, Kathy, as they face crisis after crisis and walk a harrowing path they could never have imagined. Those dealing with similar hardships and all who face seemingly insurmountable obstacles in their life will find this book uplifting, encouraging, and inspiring.

Rob Woodruff, Colonel, USAF (Retired), former
Officer's Christian Fellowship staff representative at the
U.S. Air Force Academy

Wow! This is an incredible and impressive story that every father must read. You will be drawn into this true test of a father's faith, as I was.

Rod Pilgreen, investment broker

The Caleb Years is gripping. I couldn't put it down. I was flooded with emotions as I walked, ran, and pushed with the author and his family each step of Caleb's struggles. I identified with the author in so many areas and heard the cry of his heart echo deep within mine, bringing forth many parallel memories. Although it is filled with great pain, in the end, it is a book of hope! As I read the book, I felt as though I had the privilege of holding Caleb along with his parents and sharing in their hearts' cry.

Nancy McGreer, homemaker, mother of four,
nanna of eleven

When pain comes calling, we tend to shrink back and only tell of the victories. But I'm thankful that David lets us walk with him from within their raw and challenging Caleb years! As you read of this journey, you'll ache, cry, wince, laugh, and ultimately rejoice in God's grace. You'll learn practical ways to grow, survive, and minister during life's challenges. In the end, David wisely leaves the mysteries of God's ways mysterious and reminds us to trust our loving Father.

Jay Wesley Dawson, founder of Crossover International, an international ministry discipling men and training pastors in the U.S., Kenya, Nigeria, and Uganda

Reading about Caleb's "normal" life and the seemingly insurmountable medical odds makes our friend David Ingerson's book all the more surreal. How could a child so riddled with congenital anomalies be so beautiful and whole? How could a father and mother who researched and understood the medical sequelae cope with such frequent suffering of an adorable son? But God! Their lives intertwined with grief teach us to live on and face each day with the assurance of a hope-filled future.

Sapna S. McManus, M.D.

Parents' love for their children has no limits. Capturing Caleb's life, this story vividly depicts his parents' unconditional love enduring all. Faith and commitment to our children, like this author and his wife demonstrate, exemplify perseverance no reason can match. As you read, you'll find yourself cheering for these parents and will be inspired to likewise stand for your own children against any foe—even when all seems lost.

Elvir Mandzukic, M.Ed.

16 15 14 13 12   10 9 8 7 6 5 4 3 2 1

The Caleb Years: ...when God doesn't make sense
ISBN: 978-1-939570-14-7
Copyright © 2014 by David Ingerson

Published by Word and Spirit Publishing
P.O. Box 701403
Tulsa, Oklahoma 74170

DEDICATION

I dedicate this book to Kathleen, my bride of more than twenty-seven years and the most beautiful woman to ever grace our green planet. She has walked beside me, steadying and supporting me since I was a teenager. She vividly demonstrated an abiding love for family and love for God when I understood neither.

I dedicate this book to my other children: Sarah, Andrew, Hannah Joy, and Deborah. They walked though the Caleb years and beyond with poise and abiding trust in their parents and in each other.

I dedicate this book to our faithful parents, Joan Foster and Gerald and Donna Marion, and our many supportive family and friends who demonstrated unlimited love and sacrifice in real sustaining action.

Finally, I dedicate this book to you, our reader. May the stories in *The Caleb Years* inspire you with hope to not only endure but also overcome when painful trials challenge your life.

CONTENTS

Foreword

When David Ingerson emailed me the manuscript for *The Caleb Years*, I immediately downloaded but didn't open it for several days. Having been a published author and a public speaker for a number of years, it wasn't unusual for me to receive a prepublication manuscript seeking an endorsement or critique. *The Caleb Years* manuscript was different in that I knew and respected David. He and Kathy (his wife) were members of the congregation where I served and friends of mine. Still my schedule was full and a couple of weeks slipped by before I found time to open the file.

Since this was David's first book, I didn't know what to expect. I knew he was a man of many talents: a graduate of the U.S. Air Force Academy, a pilot, a retired Air Force officer, and a successful businessman—but that hardly qualified him to be a writer. Determining to keep my expectations in check, I began reading. To my surprise, I found David to be an unusually gifted writer. His attention to detail was amazing. His ability to share intimate information regarding Caleb's condition was emotionally wrenching without being maudlin. He captured Caleb's ebullient personality, providing snapshots of the child that glowed like a light in a dark place. I often found myself laughing through my tears. The tension between hope and despair, faith and fear was so real, I felt like I was living it with David and Kathy.

Having said that, let me say, *The Caleb Years* is no easy read. There's too much pain and suffering for that; the grief is too raw. Yet, when I finished reading it, I was filled with a painful hope and a stronger faith than I had known heretofore. David and Kathy had walked through the valley of the shadow of death; they had experienced the unspeakable without being destroyed. They had suffered, even died a little, each time they learned another devastating detail regarding Caleb's medical conditions, yet their faith remained strong. And when, against all odds, it seemed faith and medicine prevailed, their joy was cautiously optimistic. Unfortunately, it was short-lived as they were blindsided yet again. A tainted blood transfusion left Caleb with a full-blown HIV infection, a condition that they feared would eventually take his life. Now they faced a new temptation—they were tempted with anger toward a blood donor and medical system whose carelessness had likely sentenced their son to the very real possibility of a premature death. Once again their faith sustained them and they emerged from that experience, not bitter persons, but better persons.

If you are looking for pat answers, *The Caleb Years* is not for you. David and Kathy have no easy answers because there aren't any. Caleb's suffering is not a riddle to be solved, but a mystery to be entrusted to the wisdom of a loving God. What they offer is a faith that has been tested by fire, one that has been shaped on the hard anvil of life, one that has sustained them through all the anguish and grief of watching their son suffer so greatly.

Yet for all of that, *The Caleb Years* is essentially a book of hope. If you are walking through a dark place in your life, this is the book for you. God enabled David and Kathy to find joy in the most difficult times; the things they learned will guide you through the darkest night. He sustained them even when grief made it impossible for them to sense His nearness. Surely, He will do the same for you. They learned to trust His heart even when they couldn't understand His ways—with their help, you can too.

Thank you, David, for reliving the Caleb years in order to bring us words of wisdom, and more importantly, words of life. I know I speak, not only for myself, but for countless others as well when I say we are indebted to you. You have shown us how to live with unspeakable loss without losing our faith. And you have shown us how to find hope even when it seems all hope is gone.

Richard Exley, D.D.
author of *When You Lose Someone You Love*

Acknowledgements

My heartfelt thanks go to those who've helped bring this story to book form. I give a hearty thanks to my dear friend, pastor, and business partner Bishop Hank Mariner. Because of his strong encouragement to put my words into published print, I garnered the necessary courage to dare to so do.

To my publisher, Keith Provance, and his team at Word and Spirit Publishing, I extend my deepest gratitude for their support and guidance as well as patience as they listened to my tedious questions and ponderings too numerous to recount.

I am likewise grateful for my proofers: Marsha Kershner, Jacque Rolland, and Donesa Walker. They professionally and with strict attention to detail insisted each comma be properly placed.

Finally, to my mentor, pastor, friend, and accomplished author Richard Exley, I offer my most heartfelt gratitude for the numerous ways he encouraged and empowered me to bring this story to press. His fingerprints of support are imprinted on this book from front cover to back.

Introduction

Although this book tells the story of our family encountering unexpected trials surrounding the birth and medical needs of our fourth child, this is not a book principally written about my son or our family. This book is intended to serve as inspiration to you, the reader, who has encountered or certainly will encounter difficulties in your life that stretch you to the breaking point. These types of struggles will either result in your demise or serve to strengthen you and help you learn to persevere and overcome.

As I've contemplated these years and the disappointments and mental anguish so often experienced in the midst of them, I've come to understand that there can indeed be benefits to facing disappointments and suffering. As Eugene Peterson wrote in his book *A Long Obedience in the Same Direction,* "All suffering, all pain, all emptiness, all disappointment is seed: sow it in God and he will, finally, bring a crop of joy from it."[1]

I consider that if we will follow his advice and sow our sufferings, pain, emptiness, and disappointments by burying them at the foot of the cross of Calvary, we will indeed enjoy a harvest in due time. When and how that time of harvest and enjoyment will come, we may not know, but rest secure, it will come if you sow your sorrow in God.

One word of caution—be careful how much you listen to the advice of others when in a deep pit of despair. Oftentimes well intended and unsolicited counsel may not be just what you need. Therefore, it's up to you to be discerning. I agree with Peterson:

> When we suffer we attract counselors as money attracts thieves. Everybody has an idea of what we did wrong to get ourselves into such trouble and a prescription for what we can do to get out of it. We are flooded first with sympathy and then with advice, and when we don't come around quickly we are abandoned as a hopeless case. But none of that is what we need. We need hope…We need to know that suffering is part of what it means to be human and not something alien. We need to know where we are and where God is.[2]

During the Caleb years I came to know God in a way I'd not known Him during the simple, carefree days of my prior life. Now I walk with a more introspective step, knowing that just because I do not see the bright sun does not mean that it is not blazing above the clouds.

As you read *The Caleb Years,* may you determine to redefine the challenges you face in your own life as adventures. Although your adventures may stretch you, they will not break you if you resolve to never give up and with renewed hope determine to persevere and overcome.

CHAPTER 1

He's Going to
Be a Fighter

Ten minutes before six, I sluggishly awoke to the sound of my wife dressing in our small half bathroom. I reached out, stretched, and as I dropped my arms to the bed, I heard and felt a distinct splash. She heard it too.

"What was that?" I demanded to know as I bolted up, suddenly wide-awake.

"I had a dream," my wife of eleven years began. "I dreamed I was at the beach, floating on the water, riding the rolling waves up and down, surrounded by crystal clear water. Then I woke up and realized I really was surrounded by water."

"Does this mean...? Is i-it time?" I stammered.

"Yes. It's time." Kathy resolutely replied.

Due to my service in the U.S. Air Force, we'd been living on the lush tropical island of Okinawa, Japan, for over three and a half years. Often visiting the many beautiful beaches near our home at Kadena Air Base, we enjoyed watching the azure blue waves roll onto the beach. But the gently swelling waves of Kathy's dream

In the months ahead we would come to see the gently rolling waves in an altogether different way—as representing a tender, divine presence sweeping over us, buoying and carrying us along through treacherous waters

were different. Since her membranes had ruptured in the night, these waves signified what had happened to Kathy physically—the waters of childbirth broke as she slept.

In the months ahead we would come to see the gently rolling waves in an altogether different way—as representing a tender, divine presence sweeping over us, buoying and carrying us along through treacherous waters—waters through which we would not and could not carry ourselves.

The first thing I did after the waves swept over me was grab our telephone to call Sandy, a friend and fellow church member who had volunteered to stay at our home and care for our three older children when Kathy delivered the baby. For the past two weeks, Aunt Sandy, as she was affectionately known to our children, daily called asking, "Is it time?"

Since the baby was five days overdue, I was getting tired of the daily routine of repeatedly replying that indeed it was, "Not yet—time." This time I phoned her and simply said, "Aunt Sandy, it's time."

Aunt Sandy anxiously rubbed the sleep out of her eyes, hastily dressed, and speedily drove the short distance to our military family housing apartment. While waiting for Sandy to arrive, I called the naval hospital to notify them of the situation.

"Yes," the military charge nurse routinely replied, "if her membranes have indeed ruptured, you may bring her in." The military nurse's nonchalant demeanor did not match my more urgently excited state of mind.

"Oh, they ruptured alright," I insisted. "In fact, we woke swimming in the amniotic fluid."

After hanging up, I thought to myself: These medical personnel just don't get it—this baby is five days overdue and he is coming today!

After Aunt Sandy arrived, we set off for the naval hospital on Camp Lester, the very hospital where this baby's older sister Hannah Joy had been born nearly three years earlier. Although the drive was less than seven kilometers and the expected off-base traffic between the two military installations was light before six-thirty in the morning, the drive to the hospital seemed to take longer than it should have.

We found a parking spot near the main entrance and calmly walked into the stark white ship-shaped structure. The hospital mate who greeted us at the information desk seemed inordinately concerned when I told her my wife's membranes had broken and we needed to get to the labor and delivery deck, unavoidable terminology in a naval hospital. She anxiously insisted Kathy be transported to the fourth deck in a wheelchair.

Despite the hospital mate's obvious apprehension, now that we were in the familiar hospital, we calmed ourselves and lost any previous nervousness. We'd done this several times before. With three healthy young children, what could possibly go wrong?

Upon arriving on the labor and delivery deck, we noted the overworked staff abuzz with fast-paced activity. A distracted nurse automatically pointed to an empty labor room and told my wife to put on a hospital gown and get in the bed. The familiar tiled floor, sterile white walls, and sound of our footsteps echoing down the spartan halls brought back a wave of nostalgic memories of Hannah Joy's birth two years and nine months earlier.

For Hannah Joy's birth, we'd stayed home as long as possible after Kathy's labor began. I was at my office on a Friday about noon when Kathy called to ask me to come home and take her to the hospital. In response to her request, I asked how soon she thought I should be there. She replied as long as I came fairly soon, it would be fine. As often happens when distracted by work responsibilities, my idea of fairly soon and hers were not entirely congruent.

An hour and a half later, my concerned boss, a father of two himself, who had overheard my half of the aforementioned phone conversation, gently prodded me, "Don't you think you ought to be going? Aren't you going to have a baby today?" Glancing at my watch, I nonchalantly replied that perhaps he was right. Therefore, I casually set out from the office to collect my bride of eight years and head to the hospital for the third time to welcome into our home a new baby.

By the time I returned home to gather my wife and her overnight bag, she was pacing the room and panting between strong contractions. The look of concern on her face when not contorted in labor pains told me we'd better not delay any further. The short drive to the naval hospital frustrated me in that it seemed to take much longer than usual. The off-base Friday afternoon traffic was extremely congested on this small tropical Japanese island.

As we approached the symbolically seafaring hospital, Kathy—between gasps due to her intense labor contractions now less than three minutes apart—instructed me to, "Park...huh...at...the... huh...em...er...gency...hu...room...ent...hu...rance."

I objected, stating that the sign posted a three-hour parking maximum. My wife's pained response was final, "That...ll... huh...be...long...huh...enough...just...huh...PARK!"

As we rushed inside the ER, Kathy began experiencing another hard contraction and proceeded to squat to relieve her intense abdominal pressure. An ER medical technician shrieked, "Get this woman up to the labor and delivery deck, STAT!"

I huffed along behind the beefy hospital corpsman who hurled the wheelchair containing my roiling wife up the long alternating ramps to the labor and delivery deck. The harried charge nurse directed us to an examination room since all the labor rooms were full.

Upon examination, she screeched as she discovered Kathy fully dilated and the baby crowning. "Get this woman in the delivery room. She's ready now!"

They rushed Kathy into a large, brightly-lighted, sterile, green-tiled delivery room. Within moments, the half dozen buzzing medical staff had Kathy positioned on the delivery table. Suddenly, in the middle of a hard contraction her membranes ruptured, spraying amniotic fluid across the delivery room, dousing every-one in its path.

"Yea, Kathy! Go, Kathy!" I roared with exhilaration as I observed the amazed staff unsuccessfully attempting to scurry out of range of the spewing fountain of clear fluid.

Meanwhile, as the drenched medics regained their composure, Kathy shrieked, "I'm pushing—I'm pushing—somebody better come catch this baby."

Within minutes, a pink little girl, to be named Hannah Joy, emerged in one lightning-quick contraction. The attending doctor, who arrived just in time to be baptized in Hannah Joy's amniotic fluid, declared, "It's a girl. Official birth time, 15:46." As I heard this dramatic pronouncement, I immediately looked at my watch and noted I'd last observed the time as we entered the labor and delivery deck area at 15:35, just eleven minutes before the delivery. What an exhilarating lightning speed birthing experience that was. Surely this new baby's birth could not rival the excitement of Hannah Joy's ruckus arrival.

The next several hours were eerily mundane. As noon approached, Kathy still was not contracting and she was becoming increasingly restless. Given that the baby was now more than five days overdue, we thought it best to request Pitocin, a drug used to induce labor when our second child's membranes ruptured two weeks before his due date. Kathy's experience was that it worked effectively and rapidly. The attending obstetrician gladly agreed to prescribe the drug.

Although Kathy warned the distracted nurse, who administered the medication, to expect the Pitocin to work very quickly, the preoccupied nurse nonchalantly replied with mild disinterest, "Fine. We'll check you in a couple of hours."

Within minutes, Kathy's quiet uterus began to churn. More painful than normal labor, the induced labor would surely be over soon. As we attempted to notify the nursing staff that Kathy was progressing quickly, they let us know in no uncertain terms they were very busy and would come back to check on her the next hour.

A little more than an hour later, I pushed the call button again when Kathy suddenly climbed out of bed and began to squat and simultaneously exclaim, "Hey, I'm pushing. I'm pu-u-u-shi-i-ing."

When the nurse who responded to our call saw Kathy squatting, she took seriously our warnings to get ready. She unsuccessfully implored Kathy to wait for the doctor—"Don't push yet!"

"No! You don't understand," Kathy cried. "If you don't get a doctor in here immediately, you're going to deliver this baby."

"Okay, okay, I'll go find a doctor, but try not to push," the harried nurse pleaded as she ran out into the hallway to find a doctor.

After the nurse darted away, I tried to reassure my wife and soon-to-be mother of four that after watching her give birth to the other three children, I thought I could handle delivering our fourth baby by myself if necessary. For some reason my attempts at offering these comforting words didn't console Kathy as I expected they would. She merely cried, "O-o-o-h, get me a do-o-o-ctor! This baby's coming."

Moments later, the nurse returned and informed us a doctor was on his way. When I inquired who it was, she matter-of-factly replied that he was an ENT (Ear, Nose, and Throat) specialist who just happened to be in the hallway nearby when she went in search of a physician. "He's changing into his scrubs," the nurse nervously notified.

A few moments later, the hastily appointed delivery doctor walked in lightheartedly humming and began to scrub up. In response to my inquiry as to how many babies he'd delivered, the congenial doctor elusively replied that he'd assisted in delivering a certain number of babies while on an OB rotation during his residency program. The graying hair of this more than a little jovial doctor told me although his residency wasn't yesterday, he must be a well-experienced military doctor.

I mused that between the two of us, we had plenty of experience. Besides, I thought to myself, childbirth is one of the most natural things in the world. What could possibly go wrong?

Less than ten minutes later, on Tuesday, March 4th at 12:23 PM, our fourth child was born. The exultant ad hoc delivery doctor pronounced, "It's a boy." He then asked, "Do you know what you plan to name him?"

Since we'd named him over seven months earlier, there was no reason to delay declaring his distinctive name. I triumphantly announced, "His name is Caleb; Caleb Stephen-Alwin Ingerson. Caleb, in Hebrew, means bold one. And we believe he's going to be a fighter."

CHAPTER 2

Clinging to the Rock

No sooner had the doctor acknowledged my reply then he handed me the scissors to perform the time-honored fatherhood duty of cutting the cord, which for nearly ten months had tethered this child to his mother, providing life-giving nourishment, oxygenated blood, and waste removal. Now it was time for Caleb's 5 pound, 11 ounce body to function on its own, apart from the protective nurturing his mother's womb had provided.

As I cut the cord with more heartfelt elation than any grand opening ribbon cutting ceremony, the delighted delivery doctor gently placed Caleb in my arms to carry him over to the prewarmed incubator where the energetic medical technician would commence her initial assessments and treatments.

As I watched the tech merrily perform her standard examination, I suddenly had the most peculiar and irresistible urge to roll Caleb on his side so I could more closely inspect his rear end. It wasn't that I had any particular insight or reason to suspect anything amiss, nor had I ever, before or since, experienced such a strange prompting. Nevertheless, my curious urge was so compelling that it would not be satisfied until I performed the odd

As I cut the cord with more heartfelt elation than any grand opening ribbon cutting ceremony, the delighted delivery doctor gently placed Caleb in my arms...

inspection—until I took a closer look at the child's backside.

As strange as it felt, I reasoned the child was mine; if I felt a need to roll him over and take a look at his behind, then that was my prerogative. Besides, as his father, I surely had a responsibility to know if there was anything unusual about the child. Consequently, I gently rolled my newborn son over on his side and spread the cheeks of his little bottom. I was not prepared for what my eyes were to see. With more than a little curiosity, I made the following pronouncement: "Say, Doctor, this is curious; the garage door is closed."

Noticeably startled by my declaration, the doctor immediately dropped the needle he was using to suture my wife's birthing wound and replied, "Let me see," as he rushed over to take a look for himself.

After observing Caleb's anus had no orifice, the suddenly serious doctor barked to the nurse, "Go get Dr. Hall, now!"

Meanwhile Kathy was left alone in the midst of the messy chaos. As I glanced back at her, it was as if I could hear her silently mouthing, "Hello, what about me? I'm over here in a very vulnerable position, surrounded by blood and afterbirth, and that's my baby!" Even today, this ridiculous sight remains imprinted on my mind in a curiously humorous way.

Upon seeing the uncommon imperforate anus, the formerly cheery doctor was now all business. After the nurse rushed out of the labor room to retrieve Dr. Hall, the grim delivery doctor briskly told another technician to let the mother hold her baby but NOT allow him to eat.

In her dejected postpartum hormonal state, Kathy resigned, "Well, I guess I just won't nurse this baby."

I felt an immediate sharp stab and tightening in my chest as I contemplated the dreadful possibility that my son would not be able to breastfeed for several days, perhaps not at all. Dread swept over me like a giant deadly crashing wave as I realized Caleb would have no way to remove the toxins his body would produce in the normal functions of life—eating and digestion—until this problem was fixed. Because the umbilical cord had been cut, his mother's body could no longer take away the poisons his body would generate due to normal gastrointestinal function.

Consequently, I mustered my faith and boldly declared, "Okay, God, I won't eat until my son does!" What noble intentions I had. I would deny myself from eating as long as my son was denied food by mouth. Little did I know this casually concocted commitment would require an eighteen-day fast. How I would need to depend upon the buoying waves of God's ever-present help in the weeks ahead.

Within minutes Dr. Hall, one of four neonatologists stationed at the Camp Lester Naval Hospital Neonatal Intensive Care Unit (NICU), arrived to examine our newborn son. As the specialist poked and prodded the small child, I mused that it should only be a matter of days until Caleb was fixed and would be able to take food by mouth. Little did I know how unrealistic these expectations were.

After one short look at the child, Dr. Hall ominously warned, "We'll take a careful look at his heart."

To this grave pronouncement I challenged, "His heart! What do you mean his heart? Look at him, Doctor. He's pink. He's perfect. There's nothing wrong with his heart! Just one minor defect; I'm sure it can be repaired in no time."

The dead serious doctor merely nodded his head and added with portentous foreboding, "Analrectal malformations are sometimes associated with cardiac problems."

His declaration struck me square on the face like a board. My suddenly dizzy head was swimming with the brutality of this inconceivable pronouncement. More and more med techs, nurses, and doctors descended upon our delivery room until there was no room for more.

Without warning the disorganized mass of medical personnel whisked our little boy away, down the twisting, blurry halls to the NICU. I scrambled to keep up, trying to keep my eyes on the portable incubator that would become our son's home for the next three weeks.

Later I learned that until just a couple years prior to Caleb's birth, the only U.S. military medical facility in the Pacific region with a NICU was Clark Air Base in the Philippines. The 1991 explosion of Mt. Pinatubo accelerated the closure of that base and transfer of the NICU from the Clark Air Base hospital to this one on Okinawa. I later marveled when I understood the very devastating power of that volcano significantly contributed to our son's ability to survive in that it brought to our naval hospital the necessary medical expertise found only in a NICU.

As I exited the labor room behind the incubator and staff, I glanced over my shoulder at Kathy. As I caught her eye, I saw such a look of despair that I hesitated and started back to try to encourage her. But through her tears she shook her head and insisted, "Go. Our son needs you now."

I felt so helpless as I hurried out of the delivery room and caught up with the grim parade rushing our son to the formidable intensive care for newborns. My mind raced. My legs wobbled. I needed a source of strength. My mind fogged back to another time when I felt helpless and desperate.

Little more than two weeks after high school graduation, it was my second day of basic cadet training at the U.S. Air Force Academy. Life was whirling. During the frightening noon meal formation, the cadre of upperclassmen demanded we recite newly learned military facts and information. All morning long we'd been running, drilling, and performing calisthenics. The cadre roughly introduced us to the spartan basic cadet training (BCT) lifestyle, military history, policies, and procedures of the Academy.

The stern upperclassmen harshly grilled us, demanding we flawlessly regurgitate a multitude of newly learned information. They reinforced our learning by requiring we perform push-ups whenever we hesitated to answer correctly. It was impossible to determine if shouting was their chosen method of training or if they were simply relegated to shouting in order to be heard above the din of 1,560 basic cadets simultaneously being drilled, vigorously barking replies to the intimidating cadre with ample exclamations of "Yes, Sir!"; "No, Sir!"; "No excuse, Sir!"

While my body barely had the time and energy to satisfy the rapid-fire orders of the rabid cadre directing our Academy BCT, or Beast as it was affectionately known, my mind found time to reach beyond the bounds of the cadet area in the midst of the harrowing beastly experience. During the noon meal formation, I surreptitiously gazed from under the brim of my hat toward the top of the nearest Colorado mountain peak west of the Academy Cadet Area. Catching a glint from a shiny rock, my eye was drawn to an intriguing sight.

A large rock outcropping just beneath the summit of the peak, which I would later come to know as Eagle's Peak, cast an ominously vast shadow beneath the pinnacle. As my attention was drawn to the immensity of the rock, it occurred to me that it appeared to be precariously suspended—seemingly threatening to dislodge and come crashing down the mountain. The rocky outcropping seemed to be mysteriously balanced, almost as though it were held in place by some inexplicable supernatural force on the sheer face of the rocky mountaintop peak.

My pondering was suddenly, violently interrupted as a foaming-mouthed cadre member shouted, "What are you gazing at, Basic?"

"Nothing, Sir!" I heard myself immediately reply.

"If you're so bored you have nothing better to do than gaze around in formation, then you must need to do push-ups. Drop, Maggot!"

I scrambled down onto the terrazzo—the concrete cadet marching area—into a push-up posture, ready to pump them out. Apparently I'd not satisfied the upperclassman with the speed with which I dropped, for he jumped back up, exclaiming that I wasn't fast enough in that I did not beat him to the ground. "Get up, Maggot," he exclaimed.

As I quickly scrambled back up into my best at-attention posture, the chiseled upperclassman shouted, "Drop, Maggot!" and again immediately assumed a taunt push-up position more quickly than me. "Too slow; Get up!" came the now expected reply.

Three more times we went through this grueling exchange until I somehow beat him to the ground and assumed the push-up posture in a time with which he was satisfied. As we began doing push-ups, I called out the number, "One, Sir...two, Sir...three...

Sir…" Somewhere around "twelve, Sir," my mind left the sweaty terrazzo and raced back to the grand, ominous rock just beneath the summit of Eagles' Peak.

As my perspiring body pumped out push-ups on autopilot and my voice mechanically shouted the count, my desperate mind successfully sought the rock. When the upperclassman was satisfied I was nearly fatigued, he ended his shouting and the session of grueling push-ups. As he recovered to his feet, I scrambled to mine and on-command bellowed, "Air Force, Sir"

"Keep your eyes straight ahead and focus, Basic!" he yelled before turning away.

In the next moment, while my chest heaved for air and my heart raced from exertion, I stole a risky second glance at the rock. In a flash, my mind transcended the harrowing noon-meal formation harassment and rough demands of Beast. I mused that just as that rock somehow remained steadfastly in place despite its immense size and lack of apparent anchoring, so would I somehow depend upon the compelling hidden force that sustained it. Despite the horrific struggles of Beast, I would daily draw strength from that force to endure and remain.

Thus, I aptly, secretly named the rock Inspiration Point, for my daily glances not only connected me with the Unseen Force that securely held the rock in place but also reminded me of the Rock to which I could cling for mental and emotional strength to endure, remain, and succeed. I determined that as long as the rock remained, so would I. I would not be defeated; I would not give up. Four years later, Inspiration Point remained steadfastly in place, and the young basic cadet who daily snuck a peek, seeking inspiration from the peak, graduated and became a second lieutenant in the United States Air Force.

CHAPTER 3

Why Won't Anyone Look Me in the Eye?

Now, fifteen years later in the NICU at Camp Lester Naval Hospital in Okinawa, Japan, the former basic cadet again needed supernatural strength. I needed a stable rock upon which to draw stamina to steadfastly remain. I had learned of the Rock of Ages during my turbulent cadet years. I had learned to lean on the supernatural strength of that Rock when several times it seemed I was in danger of failing the stringent academic standards of the USAF Academy. Somehow, against the odds, against the stress and strain, I endured, remained, and overcame.

Now, I needed all the strength I could muster from that very same Rock. Little did I know in the days and years to come, I would falter in feeling for the Rock. I would reach for the strength of the Rock but would feel only its hardness, not its might. I would come to realize I couldn't fake or conjure up the strength of the Rock when I recognized only its hardness. There would also come a time when I would be numbed to the point where though I would touch the Rock, I would neither feel its strength nor its hardness.

When the fog of smoky haze surrounding me was so dense I could neither see nor feel, I would then fall onto the Rock. Though I sensed neither its power nor its hardness, I would only know I had stopped falling because I would somehow realize it was holding me. Then, with the hardness beneath me, holding me up, I'd comprehend I had no more strength and could do nothing. By and by, as the numbness began to thaw, I would again gradually begin to sense first the hardness and then the might of the Rock.

But that was for another day. That day would come. For now, I needed to trust one moment at a time. In the cataclysmic rush of the urgent and unexpected moment, it was easy to be swept along by a hidden buoying wave.

Once in the NICU, the activity was intense, emotions subdued, voices muffled and tense. Because the Pitocin had worked so effectively, Caleb was delivered quite quickly. Consequently, he was not sufficiently squeezed when passing through the birth canal to forcefully expel fluids from his lungs and windpipe.

Fluid flows freely when a baby is inside his mother's womb, but after birth these same fluids become a significant life-threatening hazard unless they are removed either during the normal birthing process or suctioned out of the trachea by medical personnel. Hence, the medical staff's first priority was to suction fluid out of Caleb's airway.

Many times the medical technicians and nurses vigorously endeavored to put the suction tube down Caleb's throat. Attempt after attempt they failed. After each failed attempt, they'd remove the tube and carefully examine it as though they were trying, even hoping, to find some expected defect in the tube. The pliable small plastic tube was labeled with sequential marks, each 1 cm, which the techs meticulously counted each time they withdrew the tube out of my little boy's throat. Each time they withdrew it, they'd step away from Caleb's incubator bed and talk among themselves, staring intently at the small tube as though they just knew it must be defective—yet dreading to acknowledge it was not.

I was the only person in the NICU who was not clad head-to-toe in medical scrubs. Like Saudi Arabian Muslim women dressed in abajas, only the eyes of the medical professionals were visible. Although no one allowed themselves to make eye contact with me, I carefully watched their eyes to try to detect some hint of what they were thinking. Even masqueraded behind such cumbersome medical garb, their eyes served as windows to their souls, failing to conceal their incredulity, betraying their anxious fears, sorrow, and pity.

Many times I longed to blurt out, "Why won't anyone look me in the eye? Why won't anyone talk to me? What's wrong with my son? Why are you all so afraid to look me in the eye?" Only later would I understand they were frantically working to try to save my son's life. But at the time, in my isolated ignorance, I felt so alone.

I was in a crowded room teeming with bustling, busy people, surrounded by strange beeping, flashing equipment, and yet I was alone. Caring for a chronically ill child can cause parents, whether together or apart, to feel alone and lonely, more lonely than they'd ever thought possible. Even the romantic love of a close married couple is often dimmed by the dark and lonely uncertainty of not knowing whether their child will live another day.

The medical staff finally gave up the struggle to get the small suction tube adequately far enough down Caleb's throat. Instead, they decided to intubate my son—to put a respirator into his trachea to ensure his breathing. Never having observed such an extreme medical measure, I was shocked at the horrific site as I observed the staff intubate my one-hour-old son.

I was panic-stricken. Although I couldn't comprehend the purpose of many of the things they were doing to my son, I understood that putting him on a respirator meant they feared he could not breathe on his own—a fear no parent takes lightly! Simultaneous to intubating my precious tiny son, someone inserted a penile catheter—ouch. That procedure I also didn't take lightly. The frantic pace of activity was numbing. I watched with amazement as a neonatologist inserted a central line into the remnant of the very umbilical cord I'd cut from his mother less than one hour previously.

In response to my look of perplexed dismay, the doctor briefly gave me his attention, reassuring me it was not only necessary but also quite convenient to use "the baby's" umbilical cord for a central line to administer medications as well as test his blood pressure and oxygen saturation. By this time my hapless son had so many peripheral and central IV lines with various systems monitors connected to him that he was beginning to look more like a science project than a baby who had just left his mother's womb naked, less than an hour ago.

"Why does everyone continue to refer to my son Caleb as 'the baby'?" I demanded to know. "Why won't anyone look me in the eye?"

Now confusion began to replace loneliness. To fight my mental chaos, I steeled myself to try to understand what was happening. With an adrenaline rush only a parent in this situation can appreciate, I determined to assert myself and take charge as a responsible parent should. I gathered my strength from somewhere outside myself—from some far away

Rock—and began to make mental notes and ask the doctors questions.

After what seemed like hours, the medical staff began to draw several important conclusions about Caleb's medical condition. Dr. Hall approached me to discuss the current results of their unfolding diagnoses. As though afraid he'd upset Caleb, he carefully invited me to join him a distance away from "the baby" in order to brief me on their latest grim news.

"Why does everyone continue to refer to my son Caleb as 'the baby'?" I demanded to know. "Why won't anyone look me in the eye?"

Dr. Hall responded by diverting his eyes from mine, ignoring my specific questions and beginning his description of my son's preliminary diagnoses. It suddenly occurred to me that the medical staff didn't expect Caleb to live. As this ominous realization swept over me, I understood that not using my son's name was their unintentional way of preparing themselves to deal with the anticipated death of this hopeless newborn patient.

This realization also explained why no one looked me in the eye. The medical staff wasn't cruel, unkind, or lacking in compassion—quite the opposite. Since they knew the child would likely not survive as well as expected I wouldn't understand that yet, they were nervous about giving away their fears before the doctor in charge had the opportunity to brace me for the near certainty that my newborn son's life would be very, very short.

Dr. Hall explained, as of that time, they'd confirmed Caleb had several serious, life-threatening congenital anomalies. His current diagnoses included the following:

1) An imperforate anus with, in all likelihood, an internal fistula or connective opening where one is not supposed to be, between his rectum and urethra.

2) An esophageal atresia with a tracheoesophageal fistula or EA/TEF. The EA/TEF was likely a type 2, which meant that instead of his esophagus being connected to his stomach, his trachea was. His esophagus ended in a blind pouch or atresia just a few centimeters beyond his larynx—the reason they were unable to put the suction tube down his throat. As I later learned the lingo and read the literature about the various congenital anomalies with which my son was born, I would later describe the atresia as akin to a capped off pipe.

3) Most serious of Caleb's problems was that the TEF resulted in a fistula, an open connection between his stomach and lungs, causing a dangerous potential for aspiration—lung contamination and blockage via his stomach. This situation was grave and urgent.

With each crushing blow of these overwhelming medical diagnoses, I was dizzied as though repeatedly slammed in the face with a board. I felt weak, so weak I feared I'd collapse on the floor. My mind, racing like a hamster running 'round and 'round his habit trail but going nowhere, desperately sought to comprehend the doctor's devastating words. The surreal nature of the situation made me feel dazed and completely unsteady. I suddenly understood how someone could get actively sick and vomit upon receiving extremely disturbing news.

I felt queasy and weak. My vision blurred. I could barely speak. As I contemplated the implications of my son's medical diagnoses, in that I had no medical training like my wife who was a registered nurse, the increasingly complicated medical jargon with which the doctors spoke was dizzying.

I fought panic as the devastating reality of my newborn son's unexpected congenital anomalies enveloped my mind. I nearly resigned myself to give up trying to understand and simply trust the doctors, but something about the grave pessimism and seemingly detached nature of their words instilled in me the realization that I was the one ultimately responsible for the care of my son.

I was the only one who truly had a personal vested interest in the life and health of this child. He was my son. It would be my responsibility to understand my son's medical conditions so I could direct his medical care. I must be responsible and take charge, but I had to understand to make correct decisions. I would need to study to understand his conditions. I determined to do that very thing.

CHAPTER 4

Non-Intervention Is Not an Option!

Just hours before—though it now seemed like days—as I left her in the delivery room, Kathy had weakly, yet desperately mouthed, "Our son needs you now."

My mind was reeling as Kathy's words echoed through the chaos. As Caleb's father, it was my responsibility and mine alone to make the life-and-death medical decisions that would be required. No doctor could make such decisions for me.

I would have to understand my son's medical conditions so I could make vital decisions. To do this, I would need to educate myself. I would need information. I would need understanding. I would need stamina. I would need to consider all aspects and implications of my son's medical treatment options.

I would need to question the doctors any time I didn't understand. I would need to read and study all complexities of my son's diagnoses. I'd have to process the information by carefully considering all the options and possible side effects of each procedure and medicine. I would need the mental and physical strength I understood was only available by leaning on the Rock.

> I understood that the strength I needed would only come through faith—the kind of faith that's only known in soulful desperation, the type of faith that cannot be faked or conjured up.

Although I felt so weak and inadequate, in that desperate moment, I realized my son needed me. He needed me to be strong. He needed me to make decisions regarding his medical care. I could abdicate that duty to no one. I silently reached out to the Rock and prayed for strength to stand with a sudden, quiet desperation and determination I'd not known before. Somehow I sensed strength from the Rock.

I understood that the strength I needed would only come through faith—the kind of faith that's only known in soulful desperation, the type of faith that cannot be faked or conjured up. It is a faith that says although you know you can't go on, you must and you will. It's a faith that is utterly dependent upon the Rock. I knew I needed that kind of faith.

I couldn't let my son down. I felt as though I would either collapse from mental and emotional exhaustion or the Rock of Ages would have to hold me up. Exercising faith meant I had no other choice than to trust and do what needed to be done. I didn't know how, but I would do what had to be done.

As I somehow mustered strength from the Rock, I began to fire question after question at Dr. Hall:

- What's involved in the surgery needed to repair my son's EA/TEF?

- What is the procedure for repairing his imperforate anus? How soon can it be undertaken?

· In the meantime, by what mechanism will his waste be disposed?

· How soon will Caleb be able to eat by mouth? (I had a vested interest in this issue.)

· Can we get him treated and stabilized within the next ten days so I can go ahead with my plans to travel to the Philippines?

The only unequivocal answer to any of my questions was Dr. Hall's reply to my last one about the feasibility of accomplishing the needed medical procedures within the next ten days. In that number of days I would depart for the Philippines with a group from my church on a mission trip for which I'd been planning and preparing more than six months. His curt reply was sobering.

"Not if 'the baby' is to live, and you want to see him through this first of many treatments."

Little did I know it would be many more than ten days before I'd be available to do anything other than sit at my son's bedside, hoping and praying for his healing.

Midway through Dr. Hall's attempt to answer my many questions, he was joined by the three other neonatologists assigned to the Lester NICU. One of the doctors interrupted our intense question and answer session to inform me that arrangements were being made to fly "the baby" via a Medical Evacuation Flight (AIREVAC) to Tripler, the Army Medical Center in Hawaii. There, better medical care would be provided due to the presence of many specialists who were not available on Okinawa. I was encouraged—finally we were starting to make reasonable progress toward taking care of Caleb's medical needs.

Another of the three neonatologists added that we were expecting a Navy pediatrician from a military hospital in mainland Japan to conduct an echocardiogram on "the baby." He explained that an echocardiogram uses technology similar to ultrasound to examine the condition of the patient's heart.

This Navy pediatrician, who just happened to be on Okinawa for a few days of temporary duty, had been trained to read echocardiograms during his pediatric residency. Therefore, the neonatologists had arranged for him to conduct this important diagnostic procedure since there was no pediatric cardiologist available on Okinawa.

Within three hours of Caleb's birth, the Navy pediatrician arrived at the NICU and without even looking at me, commenced setting up his equipment and conducting Caleb's first—first of hundreds—echocardiogram. I felt so alone in this vast room with dozens of blue and green scrub-clad people buzzing about. Many crowded around to stare intently at the monitor. It seemed I was the only one who saw nothing other than a snowy, random haze on the TV-like screen.

For what seemed like hours, all eyes followed the painstaking progress of the doctor as he moved the echo probe back and forth, back and forth, over little Caleb's tiny chest. I mused they'd need to use lotion to help heal the chafing his instrument was sure to induce on this child's tender chest by his incessant back and forth, back and forth movement. I wondered how many times he could run back and forth over the very same few inches of my son's chest.

Since I was unable to make sense out of the fuzzy black and white clouds on the monitor, I tried to read the expressions of the poker-faced doctors. I nervously shifted my weight back and forth from foot to foot, afraid my sighs of anxiety and fatigue would distract the doctors who continued to intently stare at the messageless screen, searching for something that wasn't there. Finally, well beyond the time I could bear, the doctor completed his examination and handed the equipment to the medical technician for clean up.

Without looking my direction, the doctor slowly moved away from the echocardiogram equipment and motioned for me to follow him to a spot strangely out of hearing range of "the baby." The deliberate but grave tone with which the doctor began his words sent chills down my spine. As I braced myself for the mind-numbing news I anticipated, I feared my legs would not hold me.

Because this diagnosis was so very significant, before the doctor began his measured speech, the NICU staff sent for "the baby's" mother. As Kathy, still exhausted from drug-induced labor, was wheeled into the NICU, the emotional trauma of having her newborn son stripped from her arms just after birth was apparent on her face. As the med tech wheeled her chair past "the baby," Kathy reached over the clear plastic incubator and longingly touched her sterile, spread-eagle son. As though awakened from slumber, he writhed against the discomfort of the respirator tube, lines, and wires connected to his tiny body. Kathy looked away, unable to watch her son cringing in pain while she was unable to hold him and give maternal comfort.

The desperation on this traumatized mother's face was glaring as she looked away from her pitiable son. Our eyes met—hers pierced my soul. Her eyes silently screamed to make sense of what was happening. In a flash, they told of her yearning to understand how we would endure. I looked away—I dared not maintain eye contact more than a moment or my eyes would lose their focus, blinded by salty waves of sorrow.

The doctor began his sluggish discourse by quietly saying he was very sorry, but he had some very bad news. While mechanically talking to the yellow legal pad balanced on a sterile steel clipboard, the doctor spoke so slowly I wondered if we were locked in slow motion. As he spoke, he methodically made an illustration of Caleb's heart, explaining as he drew.

"Your baby has a severe congenital defect known as Hypoplastic Left Heart Syndrome (HLHS). Although approximately 1,000 babies are born each year with this most serious cardiac defect, few survive beyond a few days. HLHS is characterized by severe malformation of the left heart, resulting in insufficient blood flow. An HLHS heart has a tiny left ventricle, a tiny mitral valve, and a tiny aorta. The left ventricle, the systemic ventricle, normally pumps oxygenated blood to the entire body after the oxygenated blood comes into the heart from the lungs via the pulmonary vein, through the left atrium, then through the mitral valve. The mitral valve is the valve that directs the oxygenated blood from the left atrium to the left ventricle in preparation for being pumped out to the body.

"Babies with HLHS get sufficiently oxygenated blood through a temporary natural shunt called the patent ductus arteriosus, or PDA, which connects the pulmonary artery to the aorta, thus connecting the left and right heart, comingling oxygenated and non-oxygenated blood. In the womb there's no distinction between the pulmonary and systemic blood supply because the mother's circulatory system supplies the oxygen the baby needs. Normally, within two to three days after birth, as the newborn's lungs oxygenate their own blood, the PDA closes and the left and right hearts are then distinctly separate. HLHS babies can only be kept alive if the PDA is forcibly kept open using a medicine known as prostaglandin."

Being an action-oriented man, I immediately asked the doctor what treatments were available to repair this defect. The doctor again turned to talk to his legal pad and slowly spoke as he wrote.

"There are three treatment options available for HLHS babies:

1) Norwood,

    This is a multi-step surgical procedure known as the Norwood Procedure. It involves three open-heart surgeries: one immediately, another at approximately six months of age, then a third at approximately two years of age.

2) Non-intervention, and…"

    The doctor's voice trailed off as he unsuccessfully tried to hide his emotions. Visibly shaken, he finished his answer by silently writing.

3) TRANSPLANTATION.

Kathy gasped and insisted, "A heart transplant is out of the question." She shuddered at the gruesome prospect of needing to wait for an infant heart to become available—waiting for another child to die.

I aggressively added, "Non-intervention is not an option. Therefore, there is only one course of action: the three-staged surgical procedure." In my mind it was simple. There was no need for further discussion other than to begin plans to accomplish the firmly decided treatment plan—the Norwood.

CHAPTER 5

I Shall Not Die but Live

The neonatologists wanted to be sure we understood this relatively new surgical treatment plan was palliative only and would not cure our son of heart disease. The Norwood procedure, developed approximately fifteen years earlier, if successful, would enable our son to live for an indeterminate time, perhaps to adulthood, albeit with a less-than-normal heart.

"What physical limitations would my son have?" I wanted to know.

"It's too early to conjecture," the doctor ominously replied. "He has to make it past the first two surgeries before such questions can be addressed."

The ominous implication was that if our son lived beyond six months as well as lived through the second open-heart surgery, then and only then could we contemplate his future. The full impact of this chilling forecast would strike us later as the long hours and hazy days attending to our son's medical care wore on. But, for now, there was no time to linger and discuss the many probing questions swirling through my mind. We had to act and act fast to save our son's life.

> I was becoming keenly aware that no one is responsible for this child's life other than his parents.

The doctor dryly informed us that this latest diagnosis required we immediately transport "the baby" via an urgent AIREVAC flight to a hospital equipped to handle a case as complex as our son's. There was no such facility in the Pacific region. In fact, the former plans to take Caleb to Trippler Army Medical Center in Hawaii were superseded by the immediate need to transport this medically complex patient to the mainland USA.

As quickly as this Navy pediatrician appeared to perform the echocardiogram, he disappeared—the first of dozens of physicians we'd meet just once over the course of our son's medical care, discuss his opinion, and then never see again. I was becoming keenly aware that no one is responsible for this child's life other than his parents. As his father, it was my job to take this responsibility seriously. It's amazing how this stark realization can empower an otherwise powerless parent.

Dr. Hall, the attending neonatologist, returned to inform us that the University of California at San Francisco (UCSF) had been selected as the most suitable hospital nearest our paradise-lost island of Okinawa, Japan. At UCSF, our son Caleb, with his extremely complex series of medical needs, would get the support he needed. The urgent AIREVAC would depart Okinawa the next morning at 0615 hours with a flight plan that would include a fuel stop at Hickam Air Base, Hawaii.

Since cabin air pressure decreases as aircraft climb, even in pressurized aircraft cabins, expanding gases in passengers' and crewmembers' bodies must escape. Given Caleb's misconfigured gastrointestinal (GI) system, which included no connection to the outside other than a misplaced fistula between his trachea and capped off lower esophagus, the doctors voiced concern that "the baby" would not be able to adequately vent gases as the barometric pressure of the aircraft cabin decreases during its climb to cruising altitude.

Therefore, surgery was required to insert a means by which gases could be drawn out from Caleb's GI system. Within six hours of his birth, this child with a malformed, defective heart was placed under anesthesia and subjected to the surgeon's deft healing knife.

While Caleb was in surgery, over thirty concerned friends from our church descended upon the hospital to offer support. Their commotion caused such a disturbance that the charge nurse on the postpartum deck asked them to leave. In response, Glenn Kennedy, our pastor, and I corralled our friends down to the cozy hospital chapel on the first floor, the administrative deck of the hospital. Although there was no sign posted within the chapel indicating the room's maximum capacity, it was surely stretched to its limit that evening.

Not knowing what else to do, our intimate group began to sing gentle songs of faith and worship. The harmonies and prayer that ascended from that dimly lit room were as powerfully moving as any I'd experienced in my thirty-six years. In the midst of such transcendent worship, I sensed a depth of passion and desperation I'd never known before. In that moment I experienced God's compelling presence in the face of excruciating agony as I cried out to Him on my son's behalf.

At one point, I knelt in the middle of the room with my beloved friends all around. As I began to weep, I fell straight down to the carpeted floor with my face buried in the rug and with great sobs cried out, "Oh, God, give my son a new heart. Oh, God, my son needs a new heart. Heal my son, oh God, oh God, oh God."

In that tiny, crowded chapel, whether it was my friends gathered there or Someone Else touching me, I cannot say. But one thing of which I was certain: though in the greatest mental anguish of my life, I felt somehow buoyed and lifted above the din of my pain and fear. I cried out for that same Rock of Ages from whom I'd drawn strength as a cadet. I cried out to Him and silently declared He would bring glory to Himself through the life of my son.

After about an hour, Glenn led me out of the cozy, dimly lit chapel; into the stark, overly bright hallway; and up the military stairwell to wait outside the sterile operating room for the surgeon's initial report. Visibly fatigued, Dr. Hall emerged from the operating room and began to inform me of the surgeon's progress. He had traded his hospital scrubs for bicycle gear. Although it was not long before midnight, this doctor would ride his bicycle home after relaying the surgeon's news to this disheartened father. His brief report was initially encouraging, but he had more to say.

"The surgery has gone quite well, better than anticipated. The surgeon has completed placement of a gastric tube, or G-tube, which will be used to extract air from the baby's stomach during the AIREVAC flight tomorrow.

"Since he's tolerating the anesthesia so surprisingly well, the surgeon has decided to construct a loop colostomy, enabling the baby to eliminate solid waste. The procedure should be done within the next hour to an hour and a half. Then the patient will go to the recovery room where the staff will be able to take you in to see him as he wakes up."

After fielding several of my eager questions, Dr. Hall turned his attention to the details of the transport to UCSF. He advised that the attending neonatologist at the UCSF NICU had agreed to accept our son as a patient, but due to the critical and complex nature of his many congenital defects, the doctor was inclined to recommend non-intervention. The crushing blow of Dr. Hall's incredulous message took the wind out of me. These words were shocking and completely unexpected.

I steeled my confidence for a fight and blurted out, "How can this doctor agree to accept our son as a patient but recommend we simply let him die?"

The bedraggled, distracted doctor muttered something unintelligible and turned to his bicycle gear. As he secured his helmet for the ride home, he assured me that we were not obligated to accept the doctor's recommendation. We would have to weigh the doctor's advice and then make our own decisions regarding our son's medical care.

Although my wife and I were in the same waiting room, we felt so alone—so separate in our own mental chambers of terror, awash in our own confusion and fear. The numbing incredulity I felt was surreal. If my mind had been a computer, it would have locked up and ceased to function; the data did not compute. It did not make sense. In my mind, a doctor would not, could not accept a patient and then recommend to let him die without intervention.

Likewise, in my mind, a healthy married couple with three healthy children would not conceive and give birth to one with so many life-threatening defects. None of this made sense. How could we make sense of this scattered data that did not compute? What were we to do? How could we endure? Where would we get answers? What would happen next? Who could help us? Could we help ourselves?

Dr. Hall turned to cycle home. It was the last time we would see this doctor who had been so instrumental in our son's life since he emerged from his mother's womb. Although our pastor was at my side offering comfort and support, it seemed I would have to face the uncertainty of my son's life alone. The doctor left me standing long-faced and lost in a world of confusion and uncertainty. As I watched him walk to the stairs, I felt so alone—so isolated from everyone around me. Although Caleb was our fourth child, the gravity of my responsibility as his father felt ominously solemn.

In my adult life, I'd not been particularly interested in the medical field, nor was I well read regarding medical issues. I'd been quite healthy as had all my children. As a pilot, I tried my best to avoid the hospital and doctors as much as possible.

Hence, I was not particularly comfortable with the prospect of needing to make life-and-death medical decisions. The few times over the years I'd needed medical care, I didn't hesitate to blindly accept the recommendations the experts made for me. With Caleb's urgent and critical medical needs, I was entering a new level of medical complexity and gravity with which I had no experience.

I suddenly realized I could not depend upon anyone else, not a doctor, not a nurse, not my pastor, nor anyone else to make the seemingly impossible medical decisions Caleb's care would require. Caleb needed me to fight for him. I would have to arm myself with relevant medical information so I could make informed decisions about my son's medical care—even if it meant choosing to refuse the doctors' recommendation, which in this case we understood to be non-intervention.

Meanwhile, back at the small hospital chapel, Clement, a special friend and fellow church member, had an important message he wanted to give me. Coming to Okinawa from his homeland of Ghana, West Africa, Clement was studying to earn his masters degree at the University of Ryukyus. We'd become close friends as I'd weekly picked him up at his apartment along with several other Ghanaians to drive them to attend church.

Pastor Glenn brought Clement to the surgery waiting area where we nervously awaited further word regarding Caleb's progress during the loop colostomy portion of the surgery. Clement related to me that he sensed God tell him I was to claim for my son the promise found in the book of Psalms, chapter 118, verse 17, which says, "I will not die but live, and will proclaim what the Lord has done."

We thanked Clement for his sensitivity and concern as well as assured him we would consider his words. Little did we know just how much we would consider his words in the days, months, and years to come.

CHAPTER 6

Be Magnified, Oh Lord

Within two hours after Dr. Hall cycled away, a bedraggled surgeon emerged from the operating room, tugging at her surgical hat and mask. The pediatric surgeon explained Caleb had weathered this, his first surgical storm, surprisingly well.

She began, "He now has a G-tube that will allow his stomach and intestines to be deflated in-flight during tomorrow's AIREVAC flight as well as a loop colostomy for solid waste elimination. Now the real challenges begin. He's being moved to the recovery room as we speak. As soon as he's stable, the nurse will take you in to him."

Then, as suddenly as the exhausted military doctor appeared and briefed us on our son's condition, she simply walked away, never to be seen by us again. Within forty-five minutes a nurse led Kathy and me to the recovery room. I pushed her wheelchair as together we went in to see our little fighter after his first victorious battle. As he awoke, he struggled against the discomfort of the respirator tube, which would not be removed for another three weeks.

There is no more pitiful sight than to observe the anguish on a mother's face as she helplessly watches her newborn son contort his tiny face and body in silent screams as he writhes against such a serious encumbrance as a respirator—and she is not able to pick him up to hold and comfort him. As I felt the all too familiar sting of salty eyes, I turned away so as to not completely lose my composure.

Kathy mustered her strength surprisingly well. She resolutely reached over the side of the incubator, gently touched the arm of her lonely son as she'd done hours before, and boldly prayed for calm and rest for the child. After he calmed down, the nurses pushed his incubator back to the NICU, and a medical technician pushed Kathy's wheelchair back to her postpartum hospital room—in the opposite direction.

With my friend and pastor, Glenn, at my side, I accompanied my little fighter to the NICU. Glancing over my shoulder, I couldn't help but notice Kathy's forlorn expression—her hunched shoulders gently shuddering as her head hung down. In her confusion, she tried to grasp why she, the new mother, could not hold her newborn son. Trying to make sense of the senseless, she couldn't comprehend why she and her newborn departed in opposite directions.

I silently screamed, "Why? Oh why must my wife suffer such emptiness and lonely longing? Why can she not hold and comfort her newborn son?" Little did I know the depth of agony her empty arms then felt were no match for the extremes they'd feel in the years ahead.

Once back at the NICU, it occurred to me that due to the non-stop activity since Caleb's birth nearly twelve hours ago, I had failed to make the obligatory birth announcement phone calls to our family in the States. I prayed for strength and headed for the bank of international pay phones. The first call I made was to my mother. Since her answering machine picked up, I merely left a message indicating I'd call back later.

Next, I dialed Kathy's parents. Given that Caleb was already five days overdue, Kathy's parents were eagerly anticipating the customary phone call. Kathy's father was in the barn attending to his evening milking chores. Because he had a phone which rang simultaneously in the farmhouse as well as the milk house, both grandparents excitedly picked up the call.

As soon as they recognized my voice, they expectantly inquired, "David, it's so good to hear your voice. Do you have good news for us? Has our newest grandson been born yet?"

I gulped a large mouthful of moist, raw emotion and replied, "Uhmm...yes...Caleb was born about twelve hours ago..."

"Well, tell us about him. How much does he weigh? How long is he?" my mother-in-law interrupted.

I relayed the traditional height and weight information but tried to continue my discourse by adding, "But you should know he has some medical problems."

As much as I tried to disguise it, I could not. From the haltingly ominous tone in my voice, it was obvious something was gravely amiss. My forthright statement jarred the suddenly concerned grandmother. She urgently asked, "David, what's wrong? Is he okay?"

Fighting tears and the onslaught of untamed emotions, I flatly stated, "He has several significant congenital anomalies that are life-threatening, not the least of which is a seriously malformed heart."

Their unexpected, immediate, and uncontrollable sobs were difficult to endure. After we cried together for more than a few moments, we were unnaturally able to secure our emotions and begin a lucid conversation. I described Caleb's birth defects as best

I could, explained he'd already had one surgery, and explained he likely faced many, many more.

"What can we do to help?" Grandma asked in a suddenly very professional manner.

"You know we'll be praying for little Caleb and will have the praying elders of our church lifting little Caleb and you up to the Lord this very night," added Grandpa.

"Thank you," I replied. "I'll let you know when we learn more. For now, please understand that we're headed to San Francisco tomorrow via an urgent medical air evacuation flight ordered just for Caleb. We'll call you from California."

Next, I successfully phoned my mother. Not wanting to endure another emotional roller coaster, I began the conversation by saying, "Mom, Caleb was born earlier today, but he has some serious medical problems." That hasty preamble nearly ended my first faulty attempt to communicate with my mother about my son.

After several moments of forced congratulations, she weakly but matter-of-factly asked what his problems were and what would happen next. I welcomed her ability to congratulate yet remain focused on the medical problems without panic. I briefly explained Caleb's complex medical problems, described how he'd already successfully weathered one surgery, explained about the AIREVAC to the West Coast via Hawaii, and promised to call from California.

I'd barely pronounced the word pray when all three children, as though racing for a Jeopardy buzzer, in unison thrust their hands out to touch the child.

With the emotionally draining phone calls complete, Glenn and I settled in to keep our nocturnal vigil beside Caleb's incubator. What an encouragement this good friend was during that longest night. Soon after midnight, Sandy, the dear friend who'd volunteered to watch our children during Caleb's birth, telephoned me at the hospital and suggested, "David, don't you think I should wake the older children and bring them to the ER to meet their little brother —just in case they don't get another chance." The gravity of her dark words was stunning, but I knew the wisdom behind them was sound. Hence, at approximately 2 o'clock in the morning, Aunt Sandy arrived at the hospital NICU with the three older children.

Despite the combination of the remarkably early hour and the strange hospital surroundings with all its eerily blinking and beeping machinery, the children were astonishingly calm but excited about meeting their new little brother. Although the nursing staff made a valiant effort to suit up each child in scrubs and surgical masks, two-year-old Hannah Joy just couldn't tolerate the adult-sized surgical mask. Hence, I held her so as to keep her a reasonable distance from her fragile new brother. Never had I seen a more poignant scene as these six-, four-, and two-year-old siblings stepped up on stools and tenderly peered at their baby brother in the Plexiglass incubator.

As only children can, they inquired about the myriad of medical equipment surrounding and connected to their little brother. Curious, but not worried, six-year-old Sarah took notice of Caleb's colostomy while her four-year-old brother, Andrew, wanted to be assured Caleb's tubes would be removed prior to his coming home. As they adoringly looked at this special child, I asked the children if they wanted to pray for their little brother. I'd barely pronounced the word pray when all three children, as though racing for a Jeopardy buzzer, in unison thrust their hands out to touch the child. They'd observed adults laying on hands for prayer. Although it hadn't yet been a topic of teaching in our home, apparently they understood loving touch to be a vital way of connecting.

In awe, I humbly and quietly bowed my head and offered a simple prayer, asking God to heal our little boy and grant him sweet rest through this, his first night outside his mother's womb. Satisfied they'd accomplished their intended objective, the children climbed down from the stools and confidently strode out to Aunt Sandy. In utter amazement at the children's simple acceptance and lack of dismay at seeing their baby brother attached to a dozen peculiar medical lines and leads, tubes, and machines, I asked God to give me such confidence—childlike trust and faith. I would sorely need it in the days to come.

After Aunt Sandy took the children home, Glenn and I finally had time to talk—really talk. For over three years I had been an active member of our church. I served alongside Pastor Glenn in numerous capacities. For five months I'd trained a team that was poised to go to the Philippine Islands on our church's annual medical/dental mission trip. I had been his confidante and best friend as we'd met weekly for an early morning breakfast for over two years. During our weekly meetings, we offered spiritual counseling and accountability to each other.

We had grown extremely close. Glenn considered me his right-hand man. At one particularly emotionally charged moment, Glenn hugged me and told me he loved me. With tears in his eyes he said, "It's not supposed to end this way."

Later that night, Glenn and I drove to his house to deliver medication he'd picked up for his then youngest daughter, Mercy. When Glenn came out of the house, he brought the written words to the song, "Be Magnified, Oh Lord," by Lynn DeShazzo. He said his wife, Sue, felt divinely directed to give the lyrics of the song to us so we could sing them to our son. It was to become for us, Caleb's song.

Be magnified, oh Lord.
You are highly exalted.
For there is nothing You can't do.
Oh, Lord, our eyes are on You.
Be magnified.
Oh, Lord, be magnified.
Oh, Lord, be magnified.[3]

Our desire, truly, was that the Lord God would be magnified through Caleb's life. We expected we would surely see the child's dramatic healing and deliverance from his many medical maladies. We were to learn, however, that even when our expectations are not always met, God can nonetheless be glorified in and through our lives, if we are willing and cooperate.

CHAPTER 7

Congratulations
Can Wait

Leaving Glenn's home, we drove to our on-base apartment, arriving at 3:15 AM so I could pack a bag for San Francisco and try to sleep for an hour before returning to the naval hospital at our 0500 hours report time to board the AIREVAC.

Kathy's best friend, Carleen, had previously gone to our home at Kathy's direction to pack a bag for her. Carleen even surrendered to picking through our dirty laundry to gather an adequate supply of clothes for our hastily planned trip to the States. After packing my duffle bag, I sat down at my computer to send an e-mail regarding Caleb's situation and promptly fell asleep.

At 4:15 Sandy climbed the stairs to my room and woke me so I could get back to the hospital for the flight. I got up and dressed to go. As I rushed through the kitchen and out the front door, I realized I'd forgotten to pack any music. I glanced to my right and noticed a package on the countertop. Kathy's mother, Donna, had sent a baby gift along with one small gift for each family member. For me, there was a single cassette tape, *The Very Best of Heart*

> Without another word, I leaned into the ambulance and watched the door on my life in Okinawa close before my very eyes.

Cry. Not wanting to delay our departure any longer by taking the time to carefully select other music, I hastily grabbed the tape and pressed through the door.

Glenn and I arrived at the ship-shaped hospital at 0515 hours. The medical team was assembled and busily preparing little Caleb for the transport. Thirty minutes later Kathy was wheeled to the NICU just as we were leaving to load the ambulance for the drive to Kadena Air Base. As I stole a quick glance her way, the languishing look on her face caused by distress from having to leave our other three children for an unspecified time was agonizing.

In her mind, it didn't make sense that she, a newly minted mother of four, had to leave her three other children, all under the age of seven, to be separated from them by 6,000 miles of vast ocean. It was unnatural, surreal.

Since the ambulance would take us straight to the AIREVAC-configured C-141 parked on the flight line from where we would depart for California via Hawaii, Glenn accompanied us only to the rear door of the hospital entrance. After we boarded the ambulance, as the med tech reached out to close the heavy swinging doors, Glenn stretched out his hand to touch and pray for us one last time.

I would savor that touch in the months ahead. We stood and wept for each other for what seemed like several minutes. Without another word, I leaned into the ambulance and watched the door on my life in Okinawa close before my very eyes.

Watching Glenn's forlorn face as the ambulance doors slammed shut was heart-wrenching. I sensed such great love and great anguish. I heard his words ringing in my ears: "It's not supposed to end this way." We were leaving our warm, supportive family on our cozy, familiar island for the cold unknown of the big city where reportedly, the doctors didn't think our son's life was worth saving.

Boarding the aircraft was a traumatic ordeal as we watched the medical team lift our little son's incubator from the ambulance to the ground and then onto the aircraft. The portable incubator looked so cumbersome and very heavy with its enormous battery pack and extensive medical equipment intended to keep little Caleb alive. I marveled that it took such sophisticated equipment to keep this newborn child alive outside his mother's womb.

Before his birth, sustaining his life was so simple—such a contrast. I wondered at the simplicity and protective power of the human womb. Our son's many medical maladies, which would now so hamper his life, were not only unknown but also of no consequence while inside the protective, nourishing body of his mother. But within moments of leaving that womb, these same medical conditions became life-threatening.

It's astonishing to contemplate how a child like this could thrive inside his mother's body, but outside the womb, as soon as his first breath was taken, his life would be in jeopardy. The raging debate over abortion often comes down to the argument over when a baby can survive outside the womb. For us, the question was moot. Although our son was able to breathe without artificial aid immediately after birth, it wasn't long until the doctors realized that without urgent medical intervention, Caleb would not long survive outside his mother's body. And he was five days overdue.

As I pondered Caleb's situation, I wondered how anyone could believe it reasonable to pinpoint a certain gestational age at which a baby is capable of living independent of his mother's womb. And based on that arbitrary gestational age establish the maximum age at which a baby can lawfully be deprived of his life—aborted. The very thought was incredible to me. By using this preposterous standard, one may argue my son could have been legally aborted up until he was delivered, five days overdue. Given the herculean efforts to which the medical community was going to save and promote our son's life, such thinking seemed outrageously inconsistent.

Some who support allowing selective abortion argue the issue is simply a matter of a woman having control over her own body. Although Caleb, like all pre-born babies, was summarily connected to and dependent upon as well as nourished and protected by his mother's body for more than nine months before his birth, he was not part of her body anymore than he was a part of mine. Once the sperm and egg met, a distinct new person came into being. Any other view makes no sense.

Caleb was our son from the moment of conception, a distinct creation formed by the hand of God. Hence, Caleb's many congenital anomalies were his challenges that we, as his parents, were obligated to address. We would not shrink from our obligation, no matter the cost.

We were airborne, on our way to California by 6 o'clock in the morning, the day after Caleb's birth. The AIREVAC crew, consisting of eight flight and medical personnel, had flown to Okinawa from mainland Japan earlier that very morning. In addition to the fully augmented crew, the personnel assigned to care for our son included a dedicated medical team from the naval hospital in Okinawa. This designated team included a neonatologist, a flight nurse, and a medical technician.

Although I did not appreciate the significance of this large a contingent of personnel, I later learned that this three person medical team was assigned to the mission because the NICU doctors feared our son would not survive the trip without the support of heroic intervention.

The flight was one of the most emotionally grueling episodes of my life. In a fatigued pit of despair and desperation, I alternated between weeping and sleeping all the way from Okinawa to Hawaii and then to California. Between sessions of weeping, I walked over to the incubator to check on my son. He seemed to be sleeping very soundly. He looked so peaceful inside the thick Plexiglass bubble of the incubator.

If I hadn't known the grave state of his medical condition, I would have thought he was a normal, healthy child, save for the many various wires and tubes running in and out of his body, connected to a variety of humming, beeping, and bleating medical machines and monitors.

One of the crewmembers, the loadmaster, took particular interest in us. It must have been obvious that I'd been weeping. On one occasion he came over and spoke to me.

After learning of our son's grave medical situation, he expressed his deep concern. Through my numbness and tears, I encouraged him to put his faith and trust in God and thereby be assured of eternal life. Although he gently replied he did not personally believe in God, he enthusiastically thanked me for taking the time to explain my faith to him.

This concerned loadmaster assured me that his mother was a strong Christian and although he himself did not yet believe, he would be sure to call her and ask her to pray for our little Caleb. I found myself musing that although my relationship with Glenn was not supposed to end the way it did, perhaps a relationship between this young man and the Rock of Ages was supposed to begin this way.

Given that the AIREVAC flight took place less than 24 hours after she gave birth, Kathy was still quite fatigued from the labor and delivery. She spent the majority of the long flight sleeping in a gurney the crew had situated for her.

When she wasn't on the cot, she would sit in a wheelchair beside our son's incubator, both strapped to the cargo floor of the transport plane. While watching Kathy during one of her visits to Caleb's incubator, my mind was suddenly transported back to the days before Caleb's conception.

Several months before Kathy's birthday the previous year, while tucking our three-year-old son, Andrew, into bed, he confided with an impish smile, "Mommy's going to have a baby. He's going to be a boy baby. He's going to be my baby brother, and I'm going to play with him."

I incredulously asked him where he got that information. In reply he simply flashed his characteristically mischievous smile, closed his eyes, and fell fast asleep.

On Kathy's birthday that June, she blew out her birthday candles and made a wish: "I want to be pregnant again! I want to have another baby born before my birthday this time next year."

This heartfelt aspiration, more prayer than wish, she kept to herself until one month later, unbeknownst to me, she conducted a home pregnancy test to confirm what she already knew. She was pregnant. I was elated since we had eagerly anticipated a fourth child for some time.

Upon announcing the impending birth to the children, big brother-to-be, Andrew, smugly smiled, as only an innocent three-year-old can, and declared, "I knew it, Mommy!"

Saturday evening, just one week later, as I packed my bags in preparation for traveling to the States on Air Force business, Kathy told me her hormone level had dropped dramatically and as a result, she was bleeding. I dropped my nearly packed suitcase and asked what this meant.

She deadpanned, "I'm miscarrying."

Immediately alarmed, I asked, "How long has this been going on and why haven't you told me about it sooner?"

She ignored my question and replied, "Because it's so early in the pregnancy and I've experienced a miscarriage once before, I know what to expect and am certain there will be no worrisome complications."

As I struggled to understand why she'd not informed me sooner, she flatly said, "It's over."

Not satisfied that it was over and unwilling to sit idly by and do nothing, I alerted our church prayer chain. I expected it should have been simple to request our friends pray for Kathy and the baby; however, because we'd not yet informed anyone outside our immediate family that we were expecting, the first thing I had to contend with when telephoning friends was their enthusiastic congratulations.

Again and again I impatiently retorted, "Thanks, but congratulations can wait; we need prayer—now! Please pray for our baby."

After finishing packing and spending over an hour making phone calls, I confidently went to bed, satisfied I'd done my duty, all I could. The next morning I departed for the States for eight days of temporary duty, a.k.a., a business trip. Meanwhile, Kathy was relegated to deal not only with her own physical symptoms but also with our church friends' overattentiveness. Surely, as they told her, they were only trying to help.

CHAPTER 8

God, Don't Let Mommy's Baby Die!

The next morning Kathy and the children drove me to the airport in Naha. From there my early flight, with a six hour layover in Osaka, Japan, departed for St. Louis. After dropping me off, Kathy and the children proceeded to our Sunday morning service at Kadena Community Church.

During worship, two ladies and one of the church elders escorted Kathy into our pastor's office where they prayed for her and the baby. As they prayed, one of the ladies, Rachel, forthrightly declared that God had spoken to her about our child. He was a child of promise and he would not die. Kathy was unable to accept these words because she thought she'd already miscarried the baby.

After the service ended, some of the ladies took our children from Kathy's care and sent her home with strict instructions to go to bed and rest, in order to give time for healing. This grew into a very trying time for Kathy. She wept as she lamented that she didn't understand what was happening. Nevertheless, she decided to comply with their instructions, at least for a day or two.

Meanwhile, midway through my six hour layover at the Osaka Airport, I phoned Kathy to check on her and see how she was feeling. Although I was deeply disturbed that there was little I could do to encourage her when she reported to me the traumatic events of the morning, I tried to reassure her, explaining she should not fret but instead rest and patiently wait. If it was indeed God's word to Rachel that the child would live and not die, then it would come to pass. Kathy was understandably upset at the prospect that God would speak to someone else about the child in her womb instead of her.

The next couple of days were emotionally draining as each morning the ladies came and took the kids for the day. In the evening they brought them home and promptly deposited them in their beds, giving Kathy strict instructions not to get up with them in the middle of the night. "If a need arises," they instructed Kathy, "call one of us and we'll be right over to attend to the issue."

Hour after hour Kathy sat in bed and stewed. She was so confident she'd already miscarried the baby. She muttered to herself, "These ladies must all be totally crazy."

Eight days later upon my return from the States, Kathy was still confident she'd miscarried as her symptoms continued. Curiously, at each meal our oldest daughter, six-year-old Sarah, prayed, "God, don't let Mommy's baby die."

Curiously, at each meal our oldest daughter, six-year-old Sarah, prayed, "God, don't let Mommy's baby die."

One evening when Sarah prayed, I looked over at Kathy and asked what she'd told the children. She answered, "Nothing at all."

These perceptive children had picked up their information by overhearing the adult conversations around them. We smug adults often overlook the powers of observation of our children, sometimes to our harm.

Finally, after numerous requests from friends, Kathy submitted to a pregnancy test at the base medical clinic. The positive result so alarmed her that she asked the doctor to call me at my office. "Your wife is threatening to abort," the doctor advised me.

Ready for a fight, I angrily retorted, "My wife would never abort a baby!"

"Oh, no, it doesn't mean she mentally wants to abort her baby," the doctor explained. "It simply means her body is trying to reject the pregnancy."

Instantly, my heart began pounding. Despite my suddenly hyper-elevated heart rate, with amazing calm, I asked the doctor what the next step would be. The doctor indicated he had scheduled an ultrasound for the next morning.

I took off from work the next morning in order to accompany Kathy to the naval hospital for the procedure. The surroundings were strangely familiar, reminding me of the labor and delivery deck where our daughter Hannah Joy had been born just over two years ago.

Although we were both apprehensive and expected the worst, the reminiscence brought a smile to our hearts as I remembered Hannah Joy's rapid birth. I recalled how I'd apologized to the labor and delivery staff for taking so much of their time—eleven minutes—before Hannah Joy was born with a gushing torrent as Kathy's membranes broke, baptizing all in its path just moments before the lightning fast delivery.

Although this was her fourth child, it was Kathy's first ultrasound. We found ourselves apprehensive not because of the unknowns of the procedure but because of our concerns over Kathy's continued bleeding and decreased hormone level. Remarkably, as soon as the doctor positioned the internal probe for the transvaginal ultrasound—more of a stressor to me than Kathy—I was able to see the telltale movement of the baby's heartbeat!

"Hallelujah," I declared. "Rachel was right. This baby truly is a child of promise and he will not die." After seeing the clear evidence of life, a viable heart beating in the tiny fetus, we spent the rest of the morning in a swirl of celebratory elation.

After the ultrasound, Kathy and I went to the Officers' Club buffet to spend some much needed time alone. With deep gratitude, we thanked God for sustaining the life of this child even when we'd thought there was no hope.

After finishing our meal, we lingered and discussed God's miraculous provision. While we had doubted Him, our faithful friends had remained steadfast, believing in the miracle of life. Little did we know how much we'd come to depend on their faith and loving support in the months ahead. We ended our tender time together by naming this child.

As Kathy and I recounted the roller coaster emotions we'd experienced over the course of the previous several weeks, we shared what we were learning through the ordeal. Having appreciated the life and character of Caleb from the Old Testament and fancying it a splendid name for a strong valiant son, I told Kathy I believed God would have us name this child Caleb. I believed our son was going to have a similar character as that of the Hebrew hero of old, who conquered giants even in his old age. Kathy enthusiastically agreed.

Together we chose Stephen-Alwin for his middle name. He would be filled with the Spirit of God like Stephen, as recorded in the Book of Acts, and he would seek to glorify God like Alwin Marion, his faithful and beloved maternal great grandfather.

Thus, just eight eventful weeks after his conception, we named our son Caleb, which in Hebrew means bold one. After the harrowing early days of the pregnancy, we sensed this child was a fighter. We culminated our time together by writing the following letter on a napkin.

Thursday, July 18th

Caleb Stephen-Alwin,

Today you are eight weeks old; you have a strong heartbeat; you have a different spirit. Today God got our attention. He has reminded us to pray—raising our children to be great, striving always for greatness. We commit ourselves anew to the task.

Signed: Daddy and Mommy

Six weeks later a Bible teacher from mainland Japan conducted a weekend seminar at our church. During the course of the weekend, at a men's only session, he instructed the men to pair off by twos in order to pray for each other. He told us to pair up with someone we did not know. By the time I looked around to find a partner, I was the only one left standing alone. Consequently, the speaker reached out his hand to pair with me.

He instructed us to pray for discernment and then share whatever impression we understood pertinent. My turn came first. After praying for my partner, I reminded him of the importance of daily prayer and Bible reading—a rather safe or convenient word from God.

"Thanks for that," the speaker politely replied. How sophomoric, I thought—who am I fooling? Then it was his turn to pray for me.

After praying for a few moments, he opened his eyes and looked straight into mine. Originally from Canada, Ron and his wife had lived as missionaries in Japan for twenty-three years. Hence, I was quite surprised when he declared, "I see you in a hurricane."

I scoffed and gently chided, "Ron, you've lived in Japan twenty-three years. You know as well as I do they're called typhoons in the Pacific region."

Not at all flustered, he replied that although he did not know what it meant, he was certain God wanted to prepare me to face a storm of some kind. Although he didn't understand why, hurricane was the word that came to mind while praying for me. "One thing is certain," he said, "whatever the hurricane represents, when it comes, you must be steadfast and trust in God to deliver you. Nevertheless, be not dismayed for you shall be delivered, and God will be glorified through the storm."

As I marveled at whatever this strange warning could mean, I breathed a prayer: "God, in all things, I long to see You glorified in my life and the life of my family, even if it is at times difficult and painful."

Six months later I was vividly reminded of Ron's stark utterance as our AIREVAC encountered unexpected turbulence during our flight from Hawaii to our final destination on the West Coast—where tropical storms are referred to as hurricanes.

The next several months of the pregnancy were uneventful. So uneventful we forgot about Kathy's early, not uncommon first trimester difficulties. While riding in the car, our seven-year-old daughter, Sarah, suddenly prayed, "God, don't let Mommy's baby die!" Kathy, nearly full term, glanced at me as we both wondered why our little girl would be praying such a prayer after so many months of uncomplicated pregnancy. We would soon find out.

CHAPTER 9

A Testimony of Our Friends

By the end of February that next year, we'd spent over five months preparing and training our short-term mission team. The team would travel to the Philippines in mid-March for a medical/dental mission. During our church worship service on Sunday, March 3, our mission team was assembled before the altar for a commissioning prayer. As a trainer and intended leader of the team, I was among those for whom the commissioning was conducted.

As the team returned to their seats, a church member, Andy, pulled me aside and told me he sensed God gave him a special message just for me. Andy explained that while we were praying, God showed him I was going to be humbled, humbled even by a little child and all my authority stripped from me. Although his words seemed harsh, I was excited because Glenn and I had been actively seeking a new leader to replace me since I was due to rotate back to the States by June of that very year.

Inspired by Andy's message, I imagined while on our soon-to-depart mission trip, one of the men in our group would step out and pray for a sick little child. This moment would signify that this individual was the one who would replace me and accept the authority I'd held as lead evangelist. Andy's message was good news, I thought. Little did I know the child through whom I would be humbled and stripped of my authority would come not from the Philippines but from my very own body.

The AIREVAC made a fuel stop at Hickam Air Base, Hawaii, where our dear friend Patty Gray was stationed as an Air Force chapel manager, an administrative chaplain's assistant. Patty had been a close friend of the family since I'd attended pilot training, nine years before. Patty's devotion to our children over the years had earned her the title, Aunty Patty.

As soon as the aircraft taxied onto the Hickam parking ramp, a USAF chaplain with flight line access met and informed us that Technical Sergeant Gray was waiting inside the air terminal, asking to meet with us. We assured him we wanted her granted access to us as soon as possible. Arrangements were made for her to join us as we waited in a quarantined passenger area. After the harrowing transfer of Caleb's incubator from the aircraft electrical system to its own battery power, he was wheeled into the passenger terminal where more medical personnel awaited to stabilize him.

When our eyes met, they filled and overflowed with salty sorrow.

Due to Aunty Patty's unending hospitality, Hickam Air Base, Hawaii, had been a home away from home for Kathy and the children many times during our nearly four years on Okinawa. The famously lush beauty of Hawaii is rivaled by few other places on the green earth.

Whenever Kathy gathered our children and boarded a space-available flight to Hawaii, Aunty Patty somehow always seemed able to locate a large house that needed a sitter and borrow a van to transport our family around the pleasant tropical island.

The sheer, green-covered mountains presented a spectacular backdrop against which Kathy, Patty, and the children created many fond memories. This brief visit, however, was different. This visit had a backdrop of nothing other than the beeping of medical monitors connected to our precious newborn son. We may have been in Hawaii, but we felt like we were lost in a cold, austere hospital waiting room with no idea what would happen next.

I'll never forget the forlorn look of love and anguish displayed on Aunty Patty's face as she came into the room and met our new son. When our eyes met, they filled and overflowed with salty sorrow. There's something about seeing someone as close as Patty, as close as flesh-and-blood family, that suddenly brings out unexpected deeper emotion during times of intense stress.

Although he slept most of the time, whenever Caleb did awaken, he seemed intent upon trying to free himself of the many foreign tubes and wires to which he was tethered. Aunty Patty sat with and encouraged us while the aircraft was serviced.

After about thirty minutes, we were informed the aircrew had discovered a mechanical malfunction; consequently, our departure would be delayed while they sought to rectify the problem. For the next three hours, Aunty Patty enjoyed bonding with our precious little boy as he lay in his protective incubator. Thankful for the time to hug, weep, and pray with Aunty Patty, we soon re-boarded the aircraft and departed the lush isle of Hawaii.

Our C-141 arrived at Travis Air Force Base within 36 hours of Caleb's birth. Exhausted but anxious to complete our trek to the

UCSF hospital, we were disappointed to learn of yet another delay. The ambulance and transport team would not be ready to transfer Caleb to their incubator for another four hours. In the meantime, Dr. Allgood, an Air Force pediatric cardiologist stationed at the David Grant Medical Center at Travis, would conduct Caleb's second echocardiogram.

While observing his second, just like during his first echocardiogram, I felt totally ignorant and impotent, like a dog watching TV, staring at the formless images on the echo screen. Nonetheless, when the procedure was completed, Dr. Allgood relayed her detailed diagnosis, which would prove to be helpful as the days unfolded at UCSF.

Finally, the transport team arrived and prepared Caleb for the trip to UCSF. Informed by the ambulance driver that Kathy and I could not both fit in the ambulance, we decided to rent a car to follow them to the UCSF Medical Center. As Kathy waited and watched the medical staff stabilize Caleb and prepare to transport him, I rode the Enterprise shuttle to their complex just outside the base to obtain a car.

During the short jaunt to the rental office, the driver asked me what brought me to the area. I told him. His facial expression revealed he was not prepared for my answer. With grave compassion he began, "I'm so sorry to hear about your son; I hope he's going to be all right."

I weakly assured him that God would be glorified in our son's life. I had called Enterprise from the hospital and arranged to rent the least expensive car, a subcompact, for $199 per week. However, upon arriving at the rental office, we discovered the only subcompact available had not yet been cleaned since its previous rental.

"I don't care about the dirty condition," I insisted. "I need to get back to the hospital right away so I can follow my son to San Francisco. I can't wait for it to be cleaned. I'll take it dirty!"

As I stepped into the vehicle, the Enterprise employee gasped when he saw the condition of the car. "Wait! I can't send you out in that filthy car," he exclaimed.

Since I didn't have time to wait for his staff to clean the car, he offered me the only other car available, a large four-door sedan, his full-size luxury model. To my protestations that I couldn't afford the more expensive car, the Enterprise associate replied he would charge me the subcompact price since it was their mistake—not mine. Having shared with him about our son's dire medical situation during the shuttle from the Travis hospital, I was pleased to tell him I would take the larger car as a blessing and thanked him. As I drove back to the hospital so Kathy and I could follow our son's ambulance to the city, I sensed God's presence sweeping us along as a wave sweeping the beach.

As we approached San Francisco, Kathy and I were over-whelmed by an unusual sense of foreboding. We together wondered aloud as to the possible cause of such an ominous feeling: What dangers would our son have to face? Would we have to fight a difficult battle convincing the medical staff that we would not entertain non-intervention? What other perils could possibly await us?

We were aware that during the AIDS scare of the early 1980's, some in this area had earned a reputation for reportedly ignoring the warnings of the perils of the deadly HIV virus. In fact, I understood that even at this time, thirteen years after the height of the AIDS epidemic, reportedly, some still failed to take suffi-cient steps to mitigate the significant risk of infection. Although we boldly prayed as we drove our rental over the famous Bay Bridge, we could not shake the menacing dread that hung over us.

No sooner had we arrived at the 15th floor Intensive Care Nursery (ICN) at UCSF when the charge nurse's telephone rang for their newest patient's parents. The call came from Adele, a dear friend and former neighbor on Okinawa, in whose home we conducted weekly Bible studies until her family left the island two years previously. Their family had moved to Moffett Field, just one hour south of San Francisco. She learned of our arrival at the hospital by reading a forwarded e-mail that described our son's birth as well as explained we were headed for San Francisco. What an encouragement it was for someone we'd not seen or heard from in over two years to reach out to us.

Within the next several hours, we received numerous calls from across the United States, Canada, and Japan—literally from around the world.

Over the next several days so many friends and family called that the nursing staff became unsettled by the flurry of phone calls and asked us to curtail them. The phone calls may have been bothersome to the nursing staff, but to us they were a testimony of our friends and the caring community in which we'd lived during our years on Okinawa.

CHAPTER 10

My Heart's Cry

The first three hours at UCSF were spent re-evaluating Caleb's heart condition. The 15th floor ICN was surrounded by windowed walls from waist to ceiling. The view of San Francisco was breathtaking. From the station where Caleb's incubator was located, we had a lovely view of the famed orange-red Golden Gate Bridge. As I looked out over the hilly streets of San Francisco and the San Francisco Bay, I marveled at the serenity and beauty that belied the turmoil roiling inside my heart. I looked over at my son and marveled how he appeared to be so at peace despite the many doctors, nurses, and other medical personnel continually poking and prodding him.

Caleb's first of many nurses noticed the faraway look in my eyes and instructed me to be sure to get out and enjoy the city. Spending 24/7 at our son's bedside would accomplish little other than tire us to the breaking point. She said the beauty of the city should be enjoyed as the view from the ICN windows suggested. After all, she reasoned, we'd need to recharge our batteries. If nothing else, she recommended we enjoy some of the many fine ethnic restaurants in town. Obviously, she knew nothing of my forced fast.

That first day two echocardiograms, several chest X-rays, and various tracheoesophageal studies were conducted to confirm the diagnoses that preceded Caleb's arrival. It was obvious the medical team wanted to compile a complete assessment of Caleb before proceeding any further.

While we understood such invasive examinations were necessary, it was terribly stressful that the doctors and medical technicians all summarily ignored us. No one seemed willing to discuss the result of their analysis, not to mention look us in the eye. It was harrowing to stand by without any acknowledgement from the teeming medical staff that was poking and prodding our little boy.

Alone in our world of exhaustion and confusion, no one from the hospital seemed willing to extend a hand of welcome. Physically fatigued from lack of sleep and mentally spent from the turmoil of the past two days, we fiercely longed for the expected meeting with the team of UCSF doctors.

Finally, when we knew we could endure no longer, the time for the expected meeting with the attending physician, Dr. Sola, arrived. This is the same physician of whom Dr. Hall in Okinawa had ominously warned us. Although Dr. Sola had agreed to accept Caleb as a patient, he felt medical intervention would likely not be warranted due to the complexity of Caleb's case.

In other words, as far as we knew, this doctor was going to recommend we not seek to save our child. We understood he was going to recommend we employ compassionate care, which meant we would take Caleb home in order to let him die peacefully over the next several days. Not only was non-intervention not an option but also returning home to Okinawa was out of the question. Given my impending stateside transfer, we did not even know where our next home would be.

Although we had anticipated and dreaded this meeting, Kathy and I, along with a social worker, assembled with two doctors: the attending staff physician, Dr. Sola, and his British assistant, the senior third year neonatology fellow. While we were convinced we should give our son the best chance to live as normal a life as possible, we were unprepared for what these doctors would tell us.

As soon as the meeting commenced, Dr. Sola began to explain all the intricacies of Caleb's medical conditions. While he kept referring to the highly complex nature of Caleb's many congenital defects, he made no reference to his initial opinion, as reported to us by Dr. Hall, that intervention was not warranted.

Finally, after listening to his extensive assessment, I could wait no longer to address our most pressing question. I passionately blurted, "Is the UCSF medical team prepared to offer Caleb their most enthusiastic support and intervening treatment?"

With wide eyes, the doctor surprisingly exclaimed, "I assumed that is why you came all the way from Japan."

Before we could answer, the British senior fellow spoke up. He wanted to be sure we understood that if we did choose to go forth with the intervention route, we might eventually end up with much heartache and an invalid child who would be forever in and out of hospitals, or worse. In his thick British accent, the senior fellow declared, "He might even turn out a vege-table all 'is life!"

He insisted on knowing if we were willing to accept that likelihood. His seemingly negative perspective and strong English accent led us to dub this man the scoffing doctor. We would hear more from him later.

"Doctor, our son's name is Caleb. In Hebrew that means bold one, and he is a fighter. Therefore we believe God would have us join our son in an all out fight to give him every chance for life."

I answered by explaining, "Doctor, our son's name is Caleb. In Hebrew that means bold one, and he is a fighter. Therefore we believe God would have us join our son in an all out fight to give him every chance for life." We explained that although we understood, as much as anyone could, the serious implications of our decision, non-intervention was not an option.

To this, the social worker, who purportedly was there to represent our interests, promptly chirped, "We're so glad to hear you say that. The hospital staff needs to know what your philosophy is since many parents have different ideas about what type of care their children ought to receive." Thus commenced Caleb's medical care at the UCSF medical center.

Because the time zone in Japan is sixteen hours ahead of the American West Coast, by the time evening rolled around, we had endured the longest day of our lives. Dog tired, we readily accepted a hospital room supplied by the ICN staff. We welcomed the chance to sleep, even if on uncomfortable twin-sized, plastic-covered hospital beds.

The very next day, our UCSF social worker, with an incredulous expression exclaimed, "You have a room at the Ronald McDonald House. I've never known anyone to get a room in such a short period of time. You get to move in tomorrow. That's incredible—unheard of."

"Yes," Kathy quickly replied, "It's because I prayed and asked God to give us a room."

"Do you think it's a sign?" the social worker mused as she gently rolled her fingers over the large crystal necklace she wore.

Kathy told her, "Yes, we do believe it's a sign, a sign of the love of a personal God who cares about His children, even about the small details of their lives. The God of the Bible is not a metaphysical force. He is a personal God who cares deeply for His children." The social worker seemed satisfied but unconvinced.

Once we moved into the Ronald McDonald House, in that our room had its own phone and answering machine, our daily calls from friends and family around the world multiplied. We were encouraged as many called to declare that they were praying not only for Caleb but also for us.

On our third night in San Francisco, Caleb underwent his second surgery. Dr. Rusty Jennings, former naval submarine officer and Annapolis Naval Academy graduate, performed the operation to close the fistula, the connecting hole, between Caleb's esophagus and trachea. Caleb tolerated the anesthesia well enough that Dr. Jennings decided to connect Caleb's esophagus to his stomach during the same operation.

After the surgery, he told us the fistula had been securely closed but the esophagus was not as easy to repair. He assessed the surgical connection as adequate. He explained it was connected under mild pressure due to the moderate two-centimeter distance that separated the two ends of the esophagus.

We praised God for yet another victory in the battle to bring Caleb to sufficient health. Notable were Dr. Jennings's words that we needed to wait at least seven to ten days before, in his professional opinion, it was medically prudent for Caleb to go through his next operation, open-heart surgery.

Days later, while intently listening to *The Very Best of Heart Cry* as we drove to and from the hospital, we marveled at God's detailed provision. We realized that this, the only cassette tape in our possession, which so effectively inspired and encouraged our hearts, had come to us in the most peculiar way.

Kathy's mother had heard this tape playing in an Ann Arbor, Michigan, bookstore while shopping the previous summer. She thought of me and decided to purchase and send the tape in her Christmas package that fall. She sent the tape in a larger box, which contained a shirt she intended to give me. Several days later, after realizing she'd inadvertently switched her husband's shirt and mine, she called Kathy in Okinawa and advised her to ship my gift back, stating she would send a new package later with the proper shirt. Unaware there was a cassette tape tucked inside the box with the shirt, Kathy dutifully returned the entire unopened package to her mother.

In the meantime, Kathy's mother, Donna, sent the correct shirt in a separate package, which must have literally crossed the returned package in the mail. When Donna received the unopened package with the cassette, she simply held onto the tape, intending to send it at a later time. This she did three months later, just one week before Caleb's birth. The package arrived the day before Caleb was born, just in time for me to grab the unfamiliar cassette out of the freshly opened package and drop it in my hastily packed overnight bag as I pressed through the door in the wee hours of the morning to catch the AIREVAC flight to Travis.

We marveled as we noted each song on the tape contained heart-centric lyrics. The gripping songs served to soothe our anxious minds in a gently encouraging fashion. These lyrics well represented the most significant medical focus of our precious son's precarious life. The heart-centric themes were to absorb our rapt attention moment-by-moment for months to come.

CHAPTER 11

A Soothing Balm

We arrived in California Wednesday morning, just over thirty-six hours after Caleb's birth. For most of the first week we kept a nearly 24-hour vigil beside Caleb's high-tech incubator in the ICN. Finally, by Saturday, utterly exhausted both emotionally and physically, we succumbed to the nurse's pleas to take a midday nap at the Ronald McDonald House, a ten-minute drive from the hospital.

A surprise phone call interrupted our nap. Judy, a San Francisco resident and mutual friend of Meg, our missionary friend in Okinawa, called to introduce herself. Meg had notified this Japanese friend of Caleb's birth and associated medical problems as well as told her we had been sent via urgent AIREVAC flight to San Francisco.

Two days later, during a weekly prayer meeting with three other ladies, Judy believed she and her friends should go to visit Caleb and his parents. As she contemplated the prospect, Judy determined she would not mention it but wait for confirmation. No sooner had she thought this when one of the other ladies verbalized in prayer, "Lord, it would be wonderful if we could visit the dear parents of little Caleb."

Judy excitedly told the other ladies, "That is exactly what I've been silently praying." They all agreed it must have been God who simultaneously put it in all their hearts to visit us. When Judy described this interaction and asked if they could come visit us, tired as I was, I dared not refuse. Little did I know how I would welcome this contact with fellow Christians. We arranged for their visit the next day, Sunday afternoon.

Carefully orchestrating complex medical intervention can be extremely difficult. It is also oftentimes exceedingly more challenging when the patient is a child with as many serious medical challenges as our son. Therefore, as Caleb's father I understood part of my role was to ensure that the complex scheduling of his medical treatment strategy was coordinated effectively.

Nevertheless, on our first Sunday morning in San Francisco, finding a good place to worship was my primary goal. As I intently searched for a church in the Yellow Pages, an advertisement adorned with streamers and confetti piqued my interest. Upon calling for directions, I was amazed to learn the church was just six blocks from the Ronald McDonald House.

Although we lived on the small island of Okinawa where parking was often at a premium, we were nonetheless accustomed to the privilege of parking our car in a lot adjacent to our church building during worship. This city church in San Francisco met in a vintage building obviously designed before nearly every American family owned their own car. Hence, we circled the church three times, intently searching for an open parallel parking space within less than three blocks of the church. After all, we'd only driven six blocks from our temporary home to get there.

By and by, we finally observed someone pulling out of a nearby parking slot that we vigorously accepted as ours and hustled to the worship center. The singing had already begun. Immediately, as Kathy and I entered the sanctuary, we knew we'd come to the right place. There was dancing, clapping, and much rejoicing. Kathy and I were primed for offering a genuine heartfelt sacrifice of praise. In our bodies we'd never been more exhausted, but our spirits within us yearned to sing and dance like never before. The reckless abandon with which we worshipped was invigorating.

After the sermon the pastor invited those with urgent needs to come forward for prayer. Understanding our genuine need, Kathy and I eagerly made our way to the front. After a brief prayer with his hand on my shoulder, Pastor Brian directed a couple, LaRoy and his wife, Leverse, to pray with us.

As we explained the reason we were in San Francisco, we sensed such warm compassion in this godly couple. We felt such love surrounding us in their embrace and prayer. After a passionate, tearful prayer, Leverse lifted her head and spoke directly to Kathy. She quoted a verse from the Old Testament but was uncertain of the specific reference. "I will not die, but live, and declare the works of the Lord."

We were greatly encouraged as Leverse's words echoed the sentiments spoken not only one week ago by our fellow church member and friend, Clement, but also more than seven months previously by Rachel during the early stages of Kathy's pregnancy. LaRoy and Leverse pledged to help us in any way they could.

In the weeks ahead they proved true to their word as they called us several times. They also visited us in the hospital more than once and even took us out for dinner at one of the many fine ethnic restaurants for which San Francisco is so well known. Kathy enjoyed a fine meal. I simply visited with our new friends

> After such an invigorating, uplifting morning, I felt as though I was invincible. I would soon learn I was not.

and longed for the day when my son would eat by mouth, and I would likewise do the same.

We left the Hosanna Celebration Center that first Sunday morning with renewed strength for the protracted battle that lay ahead. Our appreciation for the family of God, scattered the world over, grew that memorable morning. I remembered the lyrics of the old song that declare what a friend we have in Jesus. Yet I was increasingly appreciating what a friend we have in the friends of Jesus.

After such an invigorating, uplifting morning, I felt as though I was invincible. I would soon learn I was not. As Kathy took a much needed nap at the Ronald McDonald House, I drove to the hospital to check on Caleb. He was still heavily sedated and breathing with great artificial sighs as the mechanical respirator forced oxygen into his lungs. His intubated appearance was pitiful in that the heavy sedation induced a form of medical paralysis in order to keep him still and allow the delicately repaired esophagus to heal.

As I silently prayed over my helpless son, his nurse nonchalantly mentioned that a cardiothoracic surgery fellow had been there earlier in the day and informed her that Caleb was scheduled to be the first case in the operating room the next morning. With a sudden sharp stab in my side and immense consternation, I immediately recalled Dr. Jennings's words about the importance of waiting at least seven to ten days until it would be prudent to proceed with the next surgery.

Anger, fear, and my blood pressure instantly shot to the ceiling. I adamantly demanded I would need to hear directly from the general pediatric surgeon, Dr. Jennings. I also informed the nurse in no uncertain terms that I needed to speak directly with the cardiothoracic surgeon to confirm he'd coordinated directly with the general surgery department. Although the nurse tried to assure me the aforementioned doctors had in fact consulted, I made it quite clear I was not satisfied. The nurse mumbled that she'd see what she could do.

For the next two hours I stewed over the dilemma of having been told two entirely contradictory things by the two surgeons who medically held Caleb's life in their hands. As the afternoon wore on, I became increasingly agitated. I felt that if something didn't happen to help calm my anxious fears, I would soon lose control. "Please, God," I prayed, "help me. I'm about to lose it! I don't know if I can take this any longer. Please provide me some way to remain calm and wait for the doctors to contact me as I've requested."

I anxiously sat at Caleb's bedside, contemplating the seemingly contradictory medical decision to proceed with his first open-heart surgery the next morning. In the midst of my impatient musing, Caleb's nurse startled me by suddenly saying, "You have visitors."

As I walked outside the ICN, I wondered who could possibly be there to visit me. No sooner had I rounded the corner outside the carefully guarded, clean environment of the ICN when I saw several Asian women, briskly walking toward me with a large bow-wrapped basket in hand.

"Oh, hello. Konichiwa (Good Afternoon)," I happily exclaimed as I recollected Judy's phone call from the previous hazy day. "Gomen nasi (I'm sorry), I'd forgotten about your planned visit," I apologized. "Kathy, my wife, is not here. She's at the Ronald McDonald House taking a much needed nap."

As we made hasty introductions, Judy assured me they understood Kathy needed a nap, and they were very happy to have caught one of us at the hospital. We made our way to a visitors' room to get acquainted. These precious ladies brought a large basket of goodies with fresh fruit, dried fruit, nuts, trail mix, cookies, flowers, containers of juice, and various pieces of inspirational reading material. The basket was topped with a large attractive bow and encouraging card.

What a marvelous gift they brought. It represented significant time and loving energy expended for my wife and me, two people they'd never met. For the next two and a half hours, we visited as old friends, speaking of our mutual faith in God and declaring that all would result in glory to Him. Our meeting was a soothing balm to my worried, weary heart— truly a bright answer to my hastily offered prayer for help.

CHAPTER 12

Son, What Can I Do for You?

Though we'd just met, I immediately felt as though I'd known Judy and her friends a long time; they felt the same. The ladies listened intently and offered gentle encouragement as I explained how discouraged and distraught I'd been the two previous hours. They were so compassionate and calm. Their courage and cheerfulness was contagious. As I described each detail of providential provision during this trying time, I sensed a fresh wave of God's love and uplifting strength. In that so many had so gently cared for us in so many ways, we couldn't sufficiently express our gratitude.

The ladies hung on each word of each story as I explained about the prophetic psalm Clement shared with us in the naval hospital in Okinawa and about the early days of the pregnancy when Rachel had confidently declared that Caleb was a child of promise and would not die. They were as convinced as we that God had confirmed this promise when they heard how Leverse had shared the same verse with Kathy that very morning at Hosanna Celebration Center.

They marveled with me at God's providential loving care as I explained how our dear friend Aunty Patty had been able to see us and meet Caleb during our refueling stopover in Hawaii. They rejoiced with me as I explained how we were renting a full-sized car at the subcompact price as well as how our hearts were touched with the music of our sole cassette tape, *The Very Best of Heart Cry,* as we drove the short distance each day between the Ronald McDonald House and the hospital.

They likewise testified to how they'd been led to come visit. They were so excited about the work of God in our midst; their enthusiasm was contagious. After visiting for some time, I took them in one at a time to see Caleb. Each looked upon him with such loving concern that it boosted my courage to know someone I knew so little cared so much.

We spent a rich time of prayer together in that intensive care waiting room. As those women prayed, an overwhelming sense of God's presence lifted my heart and melted my anxious fears. At that time, I couldn't have comprehended how often intensive care waiting rooms would serve as ad hoc prayer rooms in the days and years ahead.

When we finished praying, I told the ladies I was no longer anxious about the impending surgery. I would wait on God and trust Him to protect and provide for my son. As my visit with the ladies concluded, I marveled that amidst believers in Jesus Christ such a connection of comfort and compassion is readily possible, even with people entirely unfamiliar to us, from such diverse cultural backgrounds.

After the ladies departed, I returned to Caleb's bedside. His nurse immediately informed me that Dr. Jennings was available and waiting for my call. I phoned and spoke directly to him as he enjoyed a round of golf across the San Francisco Bay in Oakland.

Understanding how urgently I'd needed to speak with him, he assured me he was happy to talk with me.

The surgeon explained that he and Dr. Hanly, the cardiothoracic surgeon, had spoken face-to-face Saturday morning. They agreed that while there is increased risk to proceeding with open-heart surgery so soon after his repair of Caleb's tracheoesophageal (TE) fistula, they had no choice. Caleb's heart function was not stable enough to risk waiting. The risk of operating so soon after his TE fistula repair was dramatically outweighed by the dangerous risk of delaying the vital cardiac surgery.

With gratitude, I politely thanked him for taking my call. I strongly sensed the prayers of Judy and her friends during their brief visit had enabled me to calm my heart and mind before speaking to the surgeon. I reflected that as much as we depend upon and appreciate the medical community for their expertise and support, it is not the doctors but rather God, manifested through His servants like these faithful ladies, who grants us strength to carry on in the midst of such emotionally trying times.

That night yet another disappointment wracked my nerves, challenging me to stay calm in the midst of the storm. I had not spoken to a UCSF cardiologist or cardiothoracic surgeon about our son's diagnosis and treatment plan. And yet, each hour brought us closer and closer to the time the surgeon's knife would open my son's chest.

It had been nearly a week since Dr. Allgood, the USAF pediatric cardiologist, performed Caleb's second diagnostic echocardiogram at the Travis hospital. She had reported to me that while Caleb's left ventricle was indeed smaller than it should be, it was larger than the classic HLHS left ventricle. This analysis caused her to suggest there might be some other treatment less drastic than the anticipated three-staged Norwood.

The Norwood treatment plan incorporates three open-heart surgeries staged over a two- to four-year period, during which time the heart is literally replumbed, forcing the right pulmonary ventricle to do the job of the left systemic ventricle. The procedure involves disconnecting the major veins through which the body's blood is transmitted to the heart and reconnecting them directly to the lungs. The result decreases the heart's overall workload in that the newly configured heart pumps blood directly to the body, bypassing the lungs.

As we discussed Dr. Allgood's diagnosis with her the previous week, I asked what she understood were the chances for an alternate procedure less invasive than the Norwood. As a cardiologist, not a surgeon, she was unable to make a reasonable recommendation other than we must insist the surgeon discuss any other options prior to commencing the Norwood. Once we started down this surgical path, there would be no turning back.

Her words haunted me with a chill I could not shake. Constantly hoping personnel from cardiology and cardiothoracic surgery would sit down with us and discuss Caleb's diagnosis and treatment options, I was daily disappointed and frustrated due to the lack of communication.

I therefore determined the surgeon's knife would not touch my son until I spoke to the lead cardiothoracic surgeon, face-to-face. I needed to consider Dr. Allgood's diagnosis and inquire if there was any chance of salvaging the left ventricle since Caleb's was reportedly somewhat larger than those presented in classic HLHS. I had explained this objective to numerous hospital personnel. All offered a sympathetic ear and assured me that the surgeon, Dr. Hanly, would not perform the surgery until he'd consulted with us as Caleb's parents.

It was Sunday evening, the night before our son's first open-heart surgery, and I had not yet spoken to a UCSF cardiologist or cardiothoracic surgeon. I was growing increasingly uncomfortable.

Later that evening, after Kathy returned from napping at the Ronald McDonald House, a cardiothoracic surgery resident finally came to obtain our signatures for the surgical release forms. The resident was unable to address my many questions about Caleb's larger than classic HLHS left ventricle. I sat dumbfounded as this cavalier resident nonchalantly explained that the surgeon, Dr. Hanly, would speak to us either before or immediately following surgery. I interrupted and clearly stated, "I must speak directly to the surgeon before he commences surgery."

"Alright, in that case," he told us. "Not to worry. I'll not only pass on your concerns to Dr. Hanly but also I'll ensure one hundred percent that Dr. Hanly will speak to you before he begins the operation." Unsettled by the resident's cavalier attitude on this topsy-turvy day, we returned to the Ronald McDonald House with the prospect of speaking with Dr. Hanly before surgery still ominously pending.

My mother, so deeply affected by the tragic news of Caleb's birth defects and subsequent medical needs, immediately scheduled a flight to San Francisco. Since she and my stepfather were wintering in Las Vegas, the short flight to San Francisco was easy to arrange. She planned to fly to San Francisco on Monday and return to Vegas on Thursday, just before Caleb's first cardiac surgery. This schedule, she thought, would provide ample time to visit before the stress of Caleb's first cardiac surgery. This was not to be the case.

Sunday, as we finalized plans of her visit, I explained, "Mother, Caleb's surgical schedule has changed. If you fly in tomorrow, you'll be arriving while he's in surgery."

"So be it," she replied.

Earlier that night as I gazed at my pale, still son, I well identified with his helpless, paralyzed condition. I found myself wondering: Son, what can I do for you? What should I do for you? How can I do anything for you? I feel helpless. I feel paralyzed. In my despondency and despair, I realized we needed to brace ourselves for the battle. At just one week of age, Caleb would undergo not only his third operation but also, and more importantly, his first open-heart surgery.

I involuntarily prayed, "Lord, I feel so alone, so helpless. I don't know what to do. I fear I can't stand the pain, the pressure, the confusion. This shouldn't be happening. My son should not have to suffer so. This is not right. This is not normal. This makes no sense. Please help him. Please help me. Oh, God, I need to feel Your presence and power! I feel so weak; please calm my aching heart and languishing mind."

I expected Him to send soothing waves of His presence to envelop me in His peace. Yet, despite my impassioned prayer, I felt nothing. I remember thinking it was my job to somehow comfort my wife, but she conveniently fell asleep before I could gather my troubled thoughts and force myself to go to bed to try to sleep. But sleep would not come.

CHAPTER 13

Thankful to Give Back

The next morning we arrived at the hospital—not rested, but braced for the battle—just in time to see our son whisked away and wheeled down to the operating room. A sudden lump in my throat hindered my breathing. I sensed a panicked tightening in my chest as I realized I'd not yet spoken to the surgeon.

Just then, the cardiothoracic surgical coordinator came to lead us to the surgery waiting area. She took us down an elevator notably dingier than those we normally used, labeled, STAFF USE ONLY. As the creaking car descended from the fifteenth to the sixth floor, I felt my heavy heart sinking deeper and deeper until it seemed beyond my reach, hidden in a heavy and hazy fog.

As the elevator finally stopped on the sixth floor, I shook off the haze and tried to keep up with the surgical coordinator as she led us out of the elevator and past the stark white halls of the Pediatric Intensive Care Unit (PICU), Caleb's home for the next two weeks after his heart surgery.

As she led us to the surgical waiting area, I asked who would assist us in ensuring Dr. Hanly would consult with us prior to opening Caleb's chest. She assured me she was the appropriate

As the creaking car descended from the fifteenth to the sixth floor, I felt my heavy heart sinking deeper and deeper until it seemed beyond my reach, hidden in a heavy and hazy fog. person to whom we should address our concerns. She also confided, "If Dr. Hanly has time prior to going into the OR, he'll surely stop by to see you."

That was the last straw. "No!" I defiantly declared. I informed her in my most professionally polite but assertive voice that not talking to Dr. Hanly before the procedure was unequivocally unacceptable. "I absolutely insist on speaking to Dr. Hanly before my son is opened up." This young professional was unable to conceal her apprehension as she attempted to remain confident and convince me, and perhaps herself, that she would be sure to make that happen.

For the next hour and a half, I paced and fervently prayed for help to remain calm. The coordinator passed by us numerous times. I took each opportunity to stop her and check the status of my son. Each time she nervously reported, "Dr. Hanly has not yet gone down to the OR, but as soon as he does, I'll be sure to let him know that you are very interested in seeing him."

Finally, at 9:40, just twenty minutes before I needed to leave the hospital to go pick up my mother at the airport, I was informed the surgical team had completed their preparations to place Caleb on the heart-lung bypass machine. I could tolerate waiting no longer. I grabbed the telephone reserved for family members and called the coordinator's pager. Within minutes she appeared and nervously asked if everything was all right.

"No! It isn't," I brashly insisted. In no uncertain terms I told her, "I refuse to tolerate any further delays. I demand to see Dr. Hanly immediately."

After assuring me she'd do what she could, she hurriedly turned and walked off. Within minutes both the chief cardiologist and Dr. Hanly appeared and led Kathy and me into a nearby conference room. In order to accommodate us, the doctors quickly emptied the small room by unapologetically excusing another parent who'd been directed to wait there to meet with his child's doctor. They explained they had a higher priority and surely their doctor would understand.

The cardiologist and surgeon willingly listened to my questions and impressions. They were quick to apologize for not sitting down with us earlier; they assumed another cardiologist had already visited with us and answered our questions. I made sure they understood that at no time had any cardiologist from this medical center given me—not even once, not even in passing—the official UCSF HLHS diagnosis for our son. I further explained, "I've watched nearly twenty echocardiograms conducted on my son in the long six days we've been at this hospital. Not once has any cardiologist or echocardiogram technician offered us any information from the studies they've conducted."

The doctors were visibly shaken and assured me they'd not let it happen again. I focused our discussion on the possibility that the left ventricle might be large enough to warrant salvaging with some alternate procedure versus proceeding with the traditional Norwood. Dr. Hanly commended me for my accurate in-depth understanding of the diagnosis and proposed treatment. He explained he would not completely rule out an alternate procedure until he had the chest open and could see the heart with his own eyes. "At this point," he said, "based on what our echocardiograms show, the possibility of doing anything other than the Norwood is in the realm of the miraculous."

I quickly replied, "I happen to believe in the miraculous!" His silent response betrayed he hadn't expected such a reply from a numbly distressed parent of a newborn with congenital heart failure.

Dr. Hanly went on to explain, "Although it's true the left ventricle is somewhat larger than we had at first expected, the mitral valve, which conducts blood flow from the left atrium to the left ventricle, is so tiny nothing can be done to salvage or repair it." Satisfied I'd done my best and had to leave the result in God's hands, I shook hands with the cardiologist and surgeon and bid Dr. Hanly God's strength.

We returned to the chilly green waiting room where I immediately left my wife and set off for the San Francisco airport to pick up my mother. The surgeon proceeded to the OR to commence the procedure on my son while the cardiologist returned to his routine. Routine—when would life for us return to routine?

As I drove to the airport, my numbed mind tried to remember what a normal schedule and routine felt like. It had only been a week since my son's traumatic birth, and already I could sense myself feeling detached from nearly everything around me. Detached from everything I knew normal or routine, I felt lost. I felt a dizzying dullness I'd never known before. Reality, colors, tastes, and smells seemed to have dimmed and lost their vivid edge.

As I drove, my mind wandered back to what seemed like the distant past. The afternoon of Caleb's birth felt like it was locked in some fuzzy ancient history. I wondered at all that had happened during the past week, all that made it feel like his birth had occurred eons ago. The gap in time was dark and void.

My musings were too confusing to grasp, so I drove on, focusing on the job I had to do. I had a duty to perform. I had no choice but to focus on my duty. I had to drive this car to the airport and back to the hospital. I had to get my mother at the airport and get back to the hospital.

Under such intense stress, I knew I would not survive unless I somehow focused on doing my duty, my immediate duty, to drive the car safely to the airport and back to the hospital, albeit as on autopilot. I instinctively understood that my son needed me. He needed me to remain alive, which meant I must not distractedly drive my rental off the bridge. What more I could do to really help him, I did not know.

Seeing my mother at the airport was strangely painful and uncomfortably awkward. She and I are both emotional people who often do not conceal our feelings well. This was a time I did not want to succumb to sloppy emotionalism. I had to remain strong for my son, or so I thought. For my mother, this apparently made no sense. I had unwittingly prepared myself for our tense meeting. With each stressful step from my rental car to the air terminal, I gradually hardened my heart toward my mother or anyone else who would show too much emotion on this effusive battlefield of agony.

As I approached the terminal, we unexpectedly met at the arrival curbside. As soon as our eyes met, I diverted my glance from hers. With an endearing look of love, my mother stepped briskly toward me, obviously intent upon giving me a strong hug to deeply communicate her love and support. Although her face shone with intense concern for her pained son, she likewise looked like she could burst into tears at any moment. Her countenance was so tender, so haltingly motherly.

Although I sensed it not the right thing to do, I nevertheless hardened myself so as to not lose my composure and begin to uncontrollably cry. Unable to bear her strongly emotional look of love, I diverted my glance and refused her eye contact. I offered this loving mother a cold, curt half-hearted hug. Although I knew she longed to communicate her love and concern to me with a warm and soothing embrace, I wasn't strong enough to endure it. So I rejected her overture. I grabbed her suitcase and briskly strode back toward the garage where I imagined I could hide the turmoil and angst in my heart once back in the rental car.

I would later regret refusing her that moment of mothering. I would realize too late that in refusing her the privilege of mothering me, I was in a sense rejecting her love. I would later understand she and I both needed that warm, unashamed embrace of two wounded people, but I refused her. I could not bear it, or so I thought.

At that time, I did not understand the balm such emotions could offer. I thought I was not strong enough to handle the scene. Instead of allowing my grief and hurt to surface, I cloaked them in suppressed anger manifested by an assertive, even aggressive demeanor. While my behavior may not have been the most appropriate manner of dealing with the stress of the situation, it afforded me plenty of energy with which I would later fight the system when it seemed as though no one was listening.

Back in the surgery waiting area, we began our sentinel duty. Although the decor was subdued and comfortable with overstuffed armchairs and love seats, we found no relief from our tension. We simply couldn't relax. As the waiting room staff prodded us to try to rest, we alternated between pacing and trying to nap. "Please just relax," they opined over and over. "Why don't you try to get some sleep? Take a nap."

Though they meant well, their recommendations affected no relief. I tried to be congenial, but I found my mind unable to concentrate, wandering amidst imagined predictions of potential life-threatening complications.

Adele, our friend and former neighbor from Okinawa, and one of her friends joined us in the waiting room during surgery. Adele's friend brought her one-year-old daughter, Jessica, on whom Dr. Hanly had operated the previous year. This kind mother came to offer solace and comfort with the solidarity only the parent of a newborn requiring open-heart surgery can appreciate.

During the time of her daughter's surgery, she received such immense emotional and practical support from friends and family, she still felt overwhelmed with a compelling sense of gratitude. In that she deeply desired an opportunity to give back in appreciation for all that was done for her, she brought us a large bow-brightened basket filled with a variety of snack foods and treats. She even brought a stuffed animal for Caleb.

Although this mother understood from her own experience what would likely bring us comfort, she worried we'd not welcome her overtures of support and love. She even nervously wondered if we'd resent her daughter's presence and apparent good health. Quite the contrary, although we may not have shown it, watching her energetic child play brought us a comforting sense of hope. We soon became fast friends.

As the long day came to an end, we marveled that this young mother thanked us for the opportunity we had given her to serve us and give back.

CHAPTER 14

We Vowed Not To Give Up

The long day stretched longer than we could have imagined. We alternated between pacing the halls, napping, sitting and talking, and playing with one-year-old Jessica. Finally, after eight hours in the OR, the surgeon emerged to report the surgery had been successful and routine. Routine? How could anyone refer to open-heart surgery performed on the ping-pong ball-sized heart of a one-week-old newborn as routine? And yet, after actually holding my son's heart in his hand, this surgeon brashly reported the eight-hour procedure as routine.

After giving his brief but triumphant report, the surgeon noticed the one-year-old girl and said hello to her as only a pediatric surgeon would. Adele's friend seized the moment and thanked Dr. Hanly for the surgical repair he'd performed on her daughter just one year ago.

Suddenly, in utter amazement, the surgeon asked the child's mother if he could take a look at her daughter's chest scar. She readily, proudly allowed him to do so. With wide eyes of deep satisfaction, Dr. Hanly gently probed beneath Jessica's blouse and with a confident look of satisfaction, tenderly tickled the energetic child before returning her to her beaming mother.

The moment was precious. Here was the West Coast's most famous pediatric cardiothoracic surgeon, aptly nicknamed Dr. "Golden Hands" Hanly, happily marveling at his own one-year-old handiwork in the most unlikely place, the surgical waiting room. It was a crowning moment on a day of curious confusion. We silently breathed a prayer of thanks for the relief of a good report.

Within forty-five minutes, our son was transported to the PICU. In that the PICU was on the sixth floor in a separate wing of the hospital, our spectacular view of the Golden Gate Bridge was no longer visible. We traded it for a newer, brighter wing of the hospital. Since only two at a time could visit in the PICU, Kathy and I took turns escorting my mother, Adele, and her friend into the laboratory-like mass of wires, machines, monitors and stark white beds to see Caleb.

Caleb's chest was covered with an immense pile of white gauze bandages, resembling a medieval soldier's bulky armor; we affectionately dubbed it Caleb's breastplate. The surgeon explained Caleb's thoracic cavity had been left open with a piece of clear Gore-Tex stitched over it to cover the internal organs. His chest needed to remain open for several days to facilitate the massive drainage of fluids, which naturally occurs following the trauma of cardiothoracic surgery in such a tiny newborn.

In little chests like Caleb's, if the thoracic cavity is closed before a sufficient amount of fluid drains, the excess pressure caused by a build up of fluid surrounding and pressing against the heart would eventually cause the heart to stop—an unnerving prospect. Hence, Caleb's chest remained open. The surgeon estimated closing Caleb's chest within 48 to 96 hours if everything progressed well.

While we realized the necessity of planning for and taking action to prevent such a dire complication, we did not want to think about the possibility of Caleb's heart suddenly stopping—we shuddered at such a prospect. Therefore, we spent the balance of the day making victorious phone calls, informing family and friends that Caleb's surgery had been a success.

Dozens of people sent us daily encouraging e-mail messages, indicating they were praying for us and our son. Although many requested we send them updates of Caleb's progress, we did not have the means available to so do. Consequently, we prayed for a way to send e-mail messages to our many concerned family members and friends.

The following morning my brother, John, called to offer his emotional support and electronic expertise. He was a computer geek in the days before anyone thought to affectionately refer to those with his skills as geeks. Well I remember the wrenching sound in his voice as we spoke on the phone. He lamented that he, Mr. Fix-it, couldn't fix our son; therefore, he wanted to do whatever he could to help.

Although his obvious love communicated by the fact that he was hurting along with us was more than sufficient, he refused to be idle. Hence, he arranged for a laptop to be shipped to us at the Ronald McDonald House. What a marvelous gift it was as we were then able to send daily updates to our following of several hundred, thereby keeping them abreast of Caleb's progress not only initially but also for the next several years.

At the end of each long day, we collapsed on our bed at the Ronald McDonald House. We would hit the play messages button on our answering machine and weep for joy as we listened to message after message of support and encouragement. These messages were songs of deliverance sung by our many supportive friends and family. The power of their simple but heartfelt words bolstered our confidence in the day-by-day battle for our little fighter.

Support from friends came in ways other than phone calls and e-mails. Our church family from Okinawa surprised us by depositing an unexpected $2,000 into our checking account to help us cover unforeseen additional expenses—and unforeseen expenses piled up like we could not have anticipated. We were flabbergasted by this unsolicited assistance.

Out of thankful hearts, we offered a tithe, a gift of ten percent, to another family staying at the Ronald McDonald House. This weary husband and wife had traveled to San Francisco from an Indian reservation on which they lived and worked as tattoo artists in northern California. They were in San Francisco supporting their fourteen-year-old son who had been severely burned in a campfire accident.

We placed the monetary gift inside the cover of the paperback *More Than A Carpenter* by Josh McDowell and slid the book under their door as we departed for the hospital the next morning. Another Ronald McDonald House guest witnessed the family find the $200 gift later that morning. She described how the husband excitedly jumped up and down after opening the book and counting the discovered money. He proclaimed, "This is the best day of my life. Nothing like

As he came down from his third or fourth enthusiastic leap for joy, he exuberantly handed her one of the twenty dollar bills.

this has ever happened to me before!" As he came down from his third or fourth enthusiastic leap for joy, he exuberantly handed her one of the twenty dollar bills. In his enthusiasm he unwittingly gave away a tenth, a tithe of his gift!

Nearly every day we encountered opportunities to encourage and support others who were enduring unbelievably trying times. We had the privilege of praying with several Ronald McDonald House guests for their own sense of solace as well as for the health of their chronically ill children. Many lifted up their heads after a prayer, whether brief or long, and brightly declared they again felt the strength to go on.

One such young mother, whose child's bed was next to our son's, had endured over four months, sitting and hoping, at her newborn son's incubator. She was so weary some days; she could barely trudge to the hospital from the Ronald McDonald House.

One day, after passing her in the hallway just outside the 15th floor ICN, we noticed she appeared particularly tired. We asked how she was doing. She responded by looking down and saying she wasn't sure how much longer she could endure. Her husband was thousands of miles away, and she was alone in the big city except for her son, a preemie, who'd been unresponsive for months with little meaningful progress. Not knowing what to say that would be of any genuine help, we humbly offered to pray for her son's recovery and for her continued strength.

That night, as our hearts broke for this young mother, we knelt at our bedside, bowed our heads, and offered a simple prayer. We asked God to bring relief to our beleaguered fellow mother of one so young and yet so ill.

Several days later we encountered her in the hospital cafeteria. She appeared energetic and cheery. We excitedly asked, "How are you doing? How's your son doing?"

"Oh, my son is doing so much better today and I feel like a new woman. Thank you so very much for praying for him."

On another occasion, we enjoyed the opportunity to discuss the value of family and spiritual issues with a visiting physician from Israel, a pediatric cardiothoracic surgery fellow named David. Like us, he and his wife had given special Hebrew names to each of their four children based on Old Testament scriptures. He was intrigued that we'd done the same thing.

We explained the significance of Israel to those who are believers in Y'shua—Jesus. Before Caleb was transferred from the PICU back to the ICN, we gave David a gift basket with Hebrew worship music and one of my favorite books, *Y'shua: The Jewish Way to Say Jesus.*

The next day when Dr. David saw Kathy across the PICU, he hastily excused himself from his meeting with another patient's parents and made a beeline over to her to thank us for the thoughtful gift. We marveled at how dramatically the doctor demonstrated his appreciation for our small gesture. Our hearts were greatly encouraged. Despite our cultural differences, we'd connected with him in a meaningful way.

We paused and gave thanks to God for such encouraging encounters. They served to strengthen us as we vowed not to give up but to continue believing for our own son's healing and meaningful future.

CHAPTER 15

Embracing the Unknown

One evening while Kathy was speaking on the pay phone to our friends in Okinawa, the aunt of a ten-year-old cardiac patient overheard her praying. The lady boldly approached Kathy after her phone call and desperately asked, "I'm sorry, but I couldn't help overhearing you praying on the telephone. Are you a Christian?"

As Kathy emerged from the cramped phone booth, she confidently replied, "Yes, I am."

"Oh, won't you please help us? My brother is so terrified. He won't even go into his ten-year-old daughter's hospital room. She's being returned to the OR after open-heart surgery because they can't get the bleeding inside her chest to stop. I'm so afraid we might lose her, and he's too scared to go see her before they take her back to the OR. Please come pray with us."

Kathy quickly agreed to accompany the lady but located me first so I could join them. Just before the OR staff whisked the unconscious pasty-faced ten-year-old back to the operating room, we hastily gathered in the hallway outside the PICU, made quick battlefield introductions, and began to pray. As I put my hand on the man's shoulder, I felt him shake with sobs of fear and apprehension underneath his black Harley-Davidson imprinted T-shirt.

During our brief prayer, his stance stiffened as he wiped his sweaty palms on his faded Levis. No sooner had we said "amen" then he boldly strode into the PICU, just in time to touch his daughter's hand as they began to wheel her hospital bed into the elevator and down to the OR for a second opening of the young girl's chest that day.

The sight was more poignant than any made-for-TV hospital drama. This rough, tough Harley rider whose knees previously buckled at the prospect of seeing his precious ten-year-old princess with her unusually wavy, shiny black hair hidden under the sterile blue-green disposable cap atop her head, mustered his courage and reached out to touch his daughter's clammy, pale white hand. This tough guy boldly kissed her on her pallid cheek and whispered a precious, "I love you."

We turned away from the scene and gazed out the mini-blinded window. We peered across the courtyard, seeking to not hinder this tender moment with our own leaking eyes.

Over the course of the previous week, this man's wife had been distraught to the point of immobilization by her husband's fear and refusal to enter the PICU. His fear had consumed him, rendering him unable to offer the strong paternal support such dire moments called for. His refusal to enter his daughter's hospital room caused his wife to question God and reject any offers of assistance or counsel from her sister-in-law.

Several days after we prayed with this distressed father, we learned from his sister that he had begun to display new boldness and joy since that evening. She described how he now confidently stepped in to see his daughter each day and how her niece was recovering remarkably well from the second surgery.

While Caleb's medication-induced paralysis continued, we daily sang, prayed, and read the Bible at the bedside of our unresponsive son. We believed the sound of our voices would reassure him of our presence and enhance our ability to comfort him in the days to come when we would finally be able to hold him in our aching, lonely arms.

There's scant little privacy in hospitals—especially children's hospitals. The PICU was organized with six beds per ward, three abreast arranged in two rows, separated by nothing more than a colorfully cartooned curtain designed to brighten the mood and help parents imagine that their critically ill children would one day laugh and play, color and skip like other healthy children.

Nonetheless, as we sang to our Caleb behind these festively decorated curtains, no parent ever complained of a single off-key note. Perhaps the songs of faith gave some measure of solace to other parents as well as to us.

Because we believed so strongly in the physical and psychological benefits of breastfeeding, Kathy had nursed each of our three older children for at least a year after their birth. To keep her milk supply ample, Kathy routinely made use of the hospital nursing rooms to pump her milk into small vials for freezing and storage in hopes of later use.

By the time Caleb was discharged, thirty-two days after his birth, Kathy had stored over one hundred vials of breast milk in various freezers throughout the hospital as well as in the Ronald McDonald House kitchen. It truly was a labor of love, considering the many times each day she endured the inconvenience, discomfort, and occasional agony of pumping the nourishing milk. Her

Though they had successfully ushered me out of the room prior to declaring it a sterile area the previous two days, on that third and final day, I stood my ground and told the head nurse, "Today, I'm staying."

diligence testified to her faithful commitment to our son. Surely Caleb would one day benefit by having his own mother's milk when he was finally able to take food by mouth.

During rounds on Thursday, March 13th, the third day after Caleb's first cardiac surgery, Dr. Hanly, the lead cardiothoracic surgeon, said that our son was the most stable Norwood baby he'd ever seen. I responded by exclaiming, "People all over the world are praying for him."

The renowned surgeon then indicated Caleb's drainage had slowed to the point at which it was safe to close his chest cavity. So, the next morning Dr. Hanly planned to close his chest, which had been open since surgery on Monday. Later that day as Caleb's nurses began to gather their supplies in order to change his dressing, that is, replace Caleb's gauze breastplate with fresh bandages, I elected to remain and watch.

Though they had successfully ushered me out of the room prior to declaring it a sterile area the previous two days, on that third and final day, I stood my ground and told the head nurse, "Today, I'm staying."

The nurse intuitively understood my decision was non-negotiable. As she handed me a sterile gown, cap, and surgical mask, she flatly directed, "Put these on. This is a sterile area."

As the surgeon removed the day-old bandage, I was astounded to observe the translucent Gore-Tex patch covering my son's chest cavity. I could actually see his heart pumping with my own eyes. I could not contain my tears of amazement and joy as I watched that tiny red muscle pump, pump, pumping.

I regained my composure and asked the nurse if it was all right to take a picture. When she resigned that it was okay, I quickly snapped a photo of this most amazing sight. I could scarcely contain my amazement as I exclaimed, "I can actually see my son's heart pumping with my very own eyes." I imagined showing this picture to my son on his sixteenth birthday as I proudly told him, "Son, your whole life the doctors have been telling you your heart is no good. Well, I'm here to tell you I've seen your heart with my very own eyes, and it looked pretty good to me."

Despite the good reports from the doctors, I often felt as though I were an actor who suddenly realized he'd forgotten his lines while standing behind a curtain on a stage awaiting its opening. Other times I found myself panicking with the realization I'd not only forgotten my lines but also the production's plot. Still other times I imagined I'd forgotten where I was and why I was standing behind the curtain in the first place. As I exited the stage, I would eventually comprehend the curtain did not separate me from a mysterious audience; instead, it separated me from an uncertain future.

I found myself longing for the curtain of time to be pulled back or even parted just enough so I could see what would happen. Would my son live to adulthood? Would he live a happy life? How long would he know more trouble and trial than pleasure? Would I be able to help him? I found myself pleading, "Oh, God, would You just pull back the curtain of time so I'll know for certain what my son's future holds?"

But the curtain remained resolutely closed. Nevertheless, I began to understand that during times when God refused to pull back the curtain of time to reveal the future, I had to trust Him while praying and waiting.

While waiting I had two choices: I could worry with anxious fear of the days ahead, or I could occupy the time and enjoy the days at hand. I recognized that all my days were a gift from God. I considered I ought to embrace each day anticipating good, even in the midst of uncertainty, even in the face of great anxiety and grief.

At times, during these early, hazy days of medical commotion—with new sights, unfamiliar sounds, and ominous fears—the life-and-death drama unfolding before me was nearly overwhelming. Nevertheless, in simple childlike faith, even through the haze, I sought to rejoice at each modest victory and marvel at each new discovery, no matter how small.

Despite the celebration of victories, small and great, I struggled with the ever-present foreboding sense that I did not know what the future held. I did not know how long my son would live nor how long he would remain hospitalized. I didn't even know where I would move my family or when the crisis would allow such a move. The uncertainty was dizzying.

Although I often walked about in a haze as though numbly flying on autopilot, I understood I had to keep my thinking lucid. Although sorrow, loneliness, and fear attacked again and again, almost daily, I was determined not to be defeated by them. I would be proactive, making positive and hopeful contributions to my son's complex medical care. I daily reminded myself that as his father, I was the one who possessed ultimate responsibility and concern for his welfare.

After the surgeries and hospitalizations, the medical staff would go on to care for other patients, but I would still be Caleb's father. Nothing could change that. Whatever course his life would take, I was and always would be Caleb's dad.

Corrie ten Boom, the saintly lady who traveled the world declaring the love and forgiveness of God after years spent suffering in a Nazi concentration camp, told the following story from the carefree days of her youth.

Corrie relayed that on a certain occasion as she awaited her father to come tuck her into bed, she became nervous about her father suddenly dying. As he stepped through the door, she burst into tears. "I need you!" she sobbed. "You can't die! You can't!"

Her watchmaker father sat down on the edge of the narrow bed. "Corrie," he began gently, "when you and I go to Amsterdam when do I give you your ticket?"

Young Corrie sniffed a few times, considering this. "Why, just before we get on the train."

"Exactly. And our wise Father in Heaven knows when we're going to need things, too. Don't run out ahead of Him, Corrie. When the time comes that some of us will have to die, you will look into your heart and find the strength you need—just in time."[4]

I determined to likewise take each day one at a time and not run out ahead of God. I would depend on Him to give me strength for whatever the future held. Although I was deeply saddened when I considered the possibility that my son might never see his sixteenth birthday, I had unreserved hope that God would strengthen my resolve to do everything I could to ensure he would.

In light of such uncertainty, I chose not to fret the present nor the future, but instead I determined to embrace the unknown with bright hope, anticipating the day when my son's heart would be whole. Surely that day would come, though perhaps not as I had envisioned, nor precisely as I had longed for.

CHAPTER 16

Sometimes Messages Don't Get Passed

The next day, after watching Dr. Hanly speedily close Caleb's chest, I stayed at his bedside until well after midnight, marveling at how peaceful and nearly normal he was beginning to look. Caleb's normal included a few medical appendages: a single narrow bandage running down the middle of his chest, the bandage covering the surgical incision from the first two surgeries, the several chest tubes drawing fluid out of his thoracic cavity, his temporary pacer wires ("Just a precaution," the doctor had said—sure, I thought), his central line, his intravenous line, his EKG wires, the respirator, his G-tube, his catheter, and his colostomy.

He no longer looked like a science project gone awry. He was my son, and I couldn't wait to hold him. It would be at least another week until that was possible. He would be nearly three weeks old before I would have the pleasure of holding him for the first time. After returning to the Ronald McDonald House at two o'clock in the morning, I sent the following e-mail update to Caleb's many admirers.

Caleb Update: Friday March 15

This morning at 9:00 AM, the surgeon closed little Caleb's chest cavity. Over 12 hours later, he is still quite stable. The next 12 hours will be the most precarious. After that he should begin to make fast progress. We praise God for His abundant and merciful healing power.

Kathy and I had a very good talk with the chief surgeon today, Dr. Hanly. He said Caleb will remain at UCSF Hospital for another two to six weeks. We're voting for closer to two versus six. For those interested, we'll keep you posted.

David

Two days after Caleb's cardiac surgery, my mother and I decided to donate blood to the university blood bank to replace some of the stock used for our son during his surgeries at UCSF. Since I didn't want to have to reply, "Nine days ago," when asked by the blood bank nurse when I last ate, I had a fine steak dinner the evening before donating blood. Now, I realized eating a steak dinner after fasting nine days may not have been the most prudent choice, but it sure tasted good. I was determined that my next meal would be a celebration dinner after Caleb successfully ate by mouth for the first time.

"You had to do some chest compressions? Do you mean to tell me my son coded last night and you administered CPR?" I demanded to know. "Well, yes, it was CPR," the nurse sheepishly replied.

The first two days after closing the chest cavity are always worrisome days for post-Norwood babies. While Caleb experienced his share of cardiac episodes—transient low oxygen levels, excessive blood pressure, and elevated heart rate—his condition continued to stabilize and improve throughout Friday and Saturday. After watching his progress these two critical days, Dr. Hanly announced, "He's going to be a great kid, but first he has a long way to go."

Although I attempted to meet each nurse who cared for Caleb, at times the hectic nursing schedule outmaneuvered me. Times such as these, I called to speak to each nurse before and after shift change.

Sunday morning as we anticipated enjoying a much needed respite at Hosanna Celebration Center, I made my routine call to the nurse's station to check on Caleb. On this particular morning I made the check-in call before I was fully awake or out of bed. The night nurse's report shocked me fully awake.

"Well..." she hesitantly began her report. "Last night Caleb had a couple of episodes...."

"What! What do you mean episodes?" I urgently demanded, sitting up in our bed, suddenly completely alert.

"We...ah...we had to do some chest compressions..."

"You what?" I exclaimed, instantly ready for a fight as my adrenaline and hypersensitive parental instincts shot through the ceiling.

"You had to do some chest compressions? Do you mean to tell me my son coded last night and you administered CPR?" I demanded to know.

"Well, yes, it was CPR," the nurse sheepishly replied.

"Why didn't you call or page us when it happened? I realize I may not be able to do much during the excitement of a code, but

I'd like to have known right away so I could have elected to drive to the hospital to see my son."

To the nurse's silent reply, I indicated we'd be there right away and hung up.

"Let's go," I commanded my wife. "So much for going to worship at Hosanna Celebration Center today."

When we arrived at the hospital, Caleb looked peaceful and contented; nevertheless, we stayed at his bedside the remainder of the day. The nurse offered a weak apology, which I accepted after giving a brief lecture on my policy. I insisted on being immediately informed whenever episodes of any nature—serious or not—occur. She assured me she would pass my request along to the nursing staff as well as the attending physician.

That evening, I sent the following update.

....

Caleb Update: Monday, March 18

Thanks for your love and concern. It's been six days since our little boy underwent his first of three planned open-heart surgeries. His chest cavity was closed after four days. Tomorrow, the surgeons plan to remove his respirator and perhaps one or two of the three tubes in his chest cavity, which have been kept in place to drain fluid away from the heart. So far he is progressing very well.

Yesterday evening Caleb experienced a frightening episode wherein his little heart nearly stopped beating. The rate slowed to a dangerously low level for a short period. Since the nurse was right outside his room, she heard the monitor alarm and immediately called the crash team and physician on duty. After the physician thumped a few chest compressions and administered medication to stimulate his heart, Caleb recovered quickly.

Our primary concern is that the oxygen level to his brain is maintained. Each episode not only tests but also builds our faith. We continue to depend upon God for Caleb's treatment and healing.

Please continue to ask God to keep Caleb's repaired esophagus intact. We expect he will soon take food by mouth. Please also pray he will not get infected with a virus since certain floors of the hospital have been experiencing a minor outbreak of the flu. This can be fatal for a little one with a heart as weak as Caleb's.

We are planning for my return to Okinawa this week if Caleb continues to progress. I'll keep you informed.

Grace and peace, David

Later that day, Kathy and I drove to Travis to arrange for my flight back to Okinawa and shop for supplies at the base commissary (grocery store). We stopped by the Travis hospital to see the neonatologist who'd seen our little boy two weeks ago when he was transferred from the AIREVAC transport incubator to the ambulance. He was very interested in knowing our son's status.

As I explained the details of Caleb's medical treatment, the doctor hung on each word, amazed at Caleb's excellent progress. He was particularly concerned, however, that the university hospital staff failed to inform us of Caleb's cardiac episode that required chest compressions and medication to stabilize his heart. He assured me he'd relay our report to the pediatric cardiologist, Dr. Allgood. After meeting with the neonatologist, we returned to San Francisco and our home away from home, the Ronald McDonald House.

During rounds in the PICU the next morning, a long train of doctors, including the hospital's chief pediatric cardiologist, several attending pediatric cardiologists, the senior fellow pediatric cardiologist, and various other fellows and residents, tenuously made their way over to Kathy and me at Caleb's bedside. The chief pediatric cardiologist, serving as spokesman for this visibly shaken parade of doctors, inquired as to whether we understood exactly what had happened the other evening during Caleb's episode.

"Yes, I understand what happened," I replied in a less than patient manner. "My son coded, which means his heart stopped or slowed to a dangerously low rate requiring chest compressions. Isn't that right?"

"Well, yes, it is," replied the flustered cardiologist as he carefully chose his words. "We just want to be sure you really understood because Dr. Allgood called us rather concerned that you'd not been adequately informed of the situation. Did you speak to her?"

"Well, I'm pleased she called," I curtly replied. "And, no, I did not speak to her, but I did relay to a pediatrician stationed at the Travis hospital that I was less than pleased when I was not immediately informed of the code after it happened. I also relayed this message to the UCSF nurse on duty the following morning and directed her to pass it to the attending physician. If it took an Air Force doctor to get this message through to you, then I'm pleased Dr. Allgood called."

"Yes, well...I'm sorry...this is a big hospital, and sometimes messages don't get passed," apologized the doctor.

CHAPTER 17

The Other Three
Need Me Too!

A s I watched the rather large contingent of doctors parade out
of the PICU, I couldn't help but wonder how less assertive
parents got the attention they needed in large hospital systems
such as this one. As they seek the best medical care available,
parents of seriously or chronically ill children must understand
they truly are the ad hoc primary care manager, the voice, for
their child.

Hence, they need to not only well understand their son or
daughter's maladies but also be willing and able to speak up to
direct and approve of the care provided by the medical staff. This
is especially important when multiple highly specialized doctors
and interdisciplinary staff functioning within a large hospital are
necessary for the child's care.

Sometimes in the midst of such a large operation, the staff can
appear impersonal and detached. While this is certainly not true,
the staff may appear distracted because they are responsible for
providing care to a great number of patients. In addition, the

hospital personnel are people with their own lives and families outside the hospital. They go home after completing their duties at the end of their frequently exhausting, too long shift, needing to give their full attention to their own families.

Conversely, the parents of a child with serious life-threatening medical challenges are never detached. They are always on duty and must be ready to respond 24 hours a day—not entirely unlike serving as a military member on alert, ready to respond to a national crisis at a moment's notice—something with which I had plenty of experience.

I mused about the similarities and stark contrasts between my experience with military duty and parenting a chronically ill child. To prepare for my military alert duties, I attended a four-year military collegiate academy, a yearlong pilot training course, and a four-month aircraft qualification training course involving academic, simulator, and actual aircraft training. Following this five and a half years of training, I finally signed into my first operational unit to receive yet another three months of in-unit study and operational training in the particular mission aircraft I was assigned.

The difference between my military alert duty experience and my parental medical alert duty was readily apparent. I had no training to prepare me to care for my five pound, medically paralyzed, post cardiothoracic surgery patient.

Finally, after nearly six years of generalized and specialized training, I found myself in a semi-underground bunker in Indiana performing alert duty—eating, sleeping, and going about my day in a highly secured facility surrounded by an 18-foot double barbed wire cyclone fence with motion detectors, tightly guarded and patrolled by armed security forces with well-trained police dogs. At all times we were ready at a moment's notice to report to our aircraft to take off and perform our important top secret mission, which we understood was of the utmost importance to national security.

Not only were we highly trained and set apart in a rather sterile environment but also we were required to be well-rested to ensure we could perform our duties effectively. The Air Force went to great pains to protect our time for crew rest before sending us out in those multi-million dollar aircraft. Furthermore, the military had a tightly organized command structure and logistical system to support the crew members and maintenance technicians.

Those in command were tasked with the sacred charge of ensuring the aircrews and ground staff remained properly trained, equipped, and supplied to perform their mission. If anything or anyone threatened to interfere with our ability to perform our mission, it was their job to intervene and mitigate that interference. As a pilot, I and my crew were not alone in preparing for and accomplishing our mission.

The difference between my military alert duty experience and my parental medical alert duty was readily apparent. I had no training to prepare me to care for my five pound, medically paralyzed, post cardiothoracic surgery patient. I had no prior academic or practical exposure to such serious life-threatening medical challenges. I had no commander, organizational structure, or staff to serve me. The overworked hospital staff did their best to keep up with their patient load. They had little time or resources to instruct disoriented parents regarding how to best manage their sick child's medical care.

Because there was no logistics structure in place to keep me well-rested and well-fed, I lacked the stability of the military mission. The Ronald McDonald House was certainly a godsend;

however, I often found myself beyond the point of exhaustion, having spent the majority of each day at my son's bedside. Mental and emotional turmoil can be as tiring as vigorous physical activity, perhaps more so. The stark contrast between my military alert duty and my parenting alert duty was glaringly obvious. How I longed for some semblance of stability during this ad hoc mission.

At the hospital in San Francisco, I often found myself not only feeling disorganized and unsure of what to do next but also alone and lonely. Surrounded by medical staff buzzing here and there, some stopping to briefly inquire about our son or perform his or her part in his care, I nonetheless often felt isolated and unsure how to fulfill my proper role.

Although the sheer immensity of the complex facility sometimes gave the impression that the medical staff was cold and impersonal, this certainly wasn't due to lack of concern. I observed the medical personnel stretched to their limit, trying to keep up with their primary duties. Hence, I gained a keen appreciation for the importance of parents of chronically ill children not only educating themselves but also adamantly building a team with the medical staff attending to their child.

The doctors, nurses, therapists, and other medical personnel are the expert team members hired by the parents to recommend procedures and offer counsel, enabling them to make the best decisions they can for their child's medical care. Although I ruffled the feathers of some, I was becoming much more comfortable and confident in my role as the coordinator of all Caleb's medical care. Therefore, I became my son's ad hoc primary care manager. Furthermore, I observed that most medical providers very much appreciated involved parents.

By the evening of the eighth day following cardiac surgery, Caleb had gained enough strength to begin breathing on his own.

As his level of dependence upon the respirator decreased, the nurses incrementally reduced the concentration of oxygen and number of breaths per minute, which the respirator forced into his lungs, until he was sufficiently over breathing the machine. By the end of the evening, Caleb was weaned from the respirator. At just over two weeks old, the child began to breathe on his own for the first time. While indeed it was a sweet victory, once off the ventilator, Caleb became extremely agitated and began to cry constantly.

We feared his incessant crying would interrupt his breathing, causing his oxygen level to drop dangerously low. Hence, the nurse set up a small mask to blow supplemental oxygen toward his face. Kathy was frustrated because she could not pick up and comfort her small son in that he was kept medically paralyzed to support the healing of not only his esophageal repair but also his recently closed chest cavity.

Finally, his nurse offered him a pacifier. Much to our amazement and pleasure, Caleb immediately started sucking on the pacifier, instantly silencing his cries and bringing calm over his cherubic face. We breathed a silent prayer of thanks to the Prince of Peace for granting peace to our little boy. Kathy was mesmerized at the victory! She declared that seeing Caleb keep the pacifier in his mouth was a most amazing sight. She later reported, "None of our other children ever took a pacifier."

Over the next three days, the nurses incrementally reduced the medicine that had kept Caleb paralyzed for weeks so he could gain control of his gross muscle groups. With each wiggle, Kathy's maternal desire to hold him increased exponentially. Although it was brutal watching his little face cringe with pain as the many medications began to wear off, we could now begin the arduous task of trying to feed him via his mouth.

This would be the next big step. To this point Caleb had been receiving all his nutrition intravenously. With his esophageal problems, learning to eat was likely not going to an easy task. We were hopeful—I was really hopeful—we'd see him commence eating orally prior to my returning to Okinawa the next week.

In that there were not adequate facilities in Okinawa to support our son's medical needs, I would have to return to Okinawa to begin the process of preparing our household for the inevitable move to the States. We reminded ourselves of what Ginny Woodruff, wife of Colonel Robin Woodruff, my spiritual mentor from my days as an AF Academy cadet, had told us. She often said, "Home is where the Air Force sends you." For us this truth was particularly poignant because we were certain of only one thing: we had to leave Okinawa since Caleb was unable to live there.

We spent the next day, Wednesday, March 20th, monitoring Caleb and trying to decide if it was prudent to begin introducing fluids by mouth. There were two troublesome issues. First, two chest X-rays indicated a shadowy spot on his lung, likely indicative of fluid. Second, his EA/TEF repair was very much in question. Caleb needed a barium swallow X-ray study to verify the repair was sufficiently intact to allow oral feeding.

The combination of these two issues required another day of watching and waiting. The doctors warned us that children with EA/TEF often possess little or no instinctive suck inclination. Based on his appreciation for the pacifier, it would seem our Caleb was a glorious exception. We couldn't wait to begin trying to feed him. I told the doctor, "He's ready, Doctor! He's ready to eat by mouth!"

Given my commitment to fast until my son ate by mouth, Kathy suggested, "Perhaps it's you who is truly ready to eat by mouth."

The following day, the doctors scheduled a barium swallow to determine the status of Caleb's esophagus. We needed to be sure the surgical repair was still intact. Kathy's excitement continued to build as Caleb was transferred from the PICU to a moderate care floor. How she longed to hold her son and nurse him. This would happen soon, we hoped—soon and very soon, she prayed.

That evening as we made the routine ten-minute drive back to the Ronald McDonald House, I looked over at Kathy and noticed a single tear gently moistening her cheek. "Why are you crying?" I wanted to know.

She responded with a sudden torrent of tears. Through the choking sobs she earnestly exclaimed with passionate yearning, "I have four children, not just one; the other three need me too!"

Suddenly struck by her maternal heart's cry, I had to pull the car over to the side of the street in that my windshield wipers were powerless to remove the sheets of water suddenly blinding my own vision.

Top: David introduces Sarah, Andrew, and Hannah Joy to their newborn brother, Caleb, in the middle of the night before he is flown via an urgent AIREVAC to California in a desperate attempt to save the small child's life.

Middle: In the C-141 AIREVAC, just eighteen hours after giving birth, Kathy, who is transported in patient status, checks on her newborn son while the flight nurse works to stabilize him for the long flight.

Bottom: David visits Caleb's incubator as the traumatic trip to San Francisco begins.

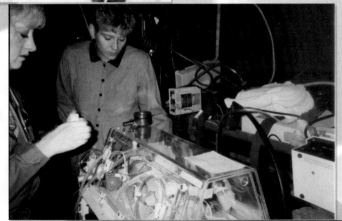

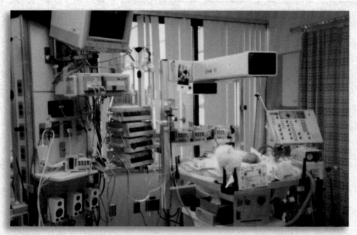

The myriad of medical equipment necessary to keep Caleb alive after leaving the safe and secure environment of his mother's womb was simply mind-boggling.

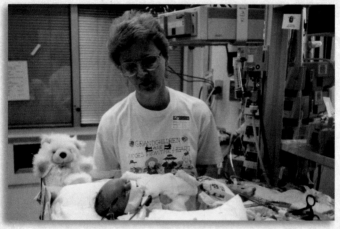

The pity and pain is apparent on Grandma Foster's face as she meets her one-week-old grandson hours after his first of five open-heart surgeries.

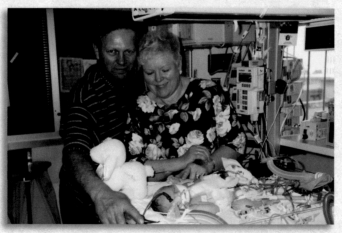

Grandpa and Grandma Marion faithfully flew to California to meet their newest grandson, Caleb, just one week after his birth.

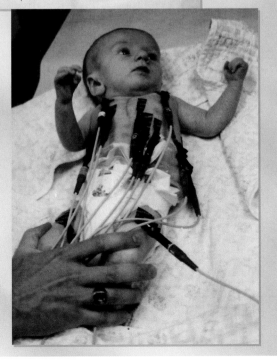

Top: *After his first cardiac surgery, Caleb's chest cavity remained open for ninety-six hours with sterile Gore-Tex stitched over the cavity.*

Middle: *Nearly two weeks after his first open-heart surgery, our little trooper looks out with wide eyes on the world he yearns to meet.*

Bottom: *Wired for EKGs was as commonplace for Caleb as swinging and sliding on a playground is for most children.*

Right: Caleb flaunts his irresistible smile just days following surgery. In that it was opened so often, we fittingly referred to his chest scar as a zipper.

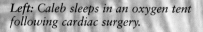

Left: Caleb sleeps in an oxygen tent following cardiac surgery.

Right: Stroller rides up and down the long hallways helped to pass the time during Caleb's lengthy hospitalizations.

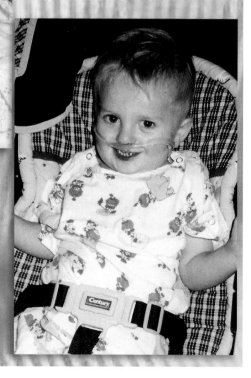

Top: *Big sister, Sarah, holds her little brother.*

Middle: *Andrew bravely holds his little brother despite his incessant crying.*

Bottom: *Little brother crying or not, Hannah Joy smiles while posing with her beloved Caleb.*

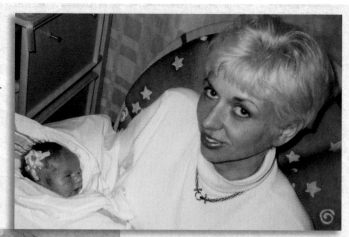

Right: Aunt Kim has the distinct privilege of holding Caleb in the San Francisco hospital soon after he was weaned from the respirator.

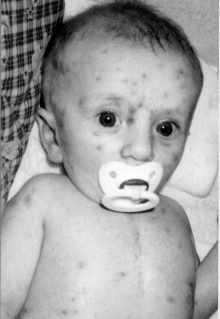

Left: Our best effort to quarantine Caleb from chickenpox failed. Within days of arriving at Grandma Marion's home, the small child broke out with the infamous rash from head to toe.

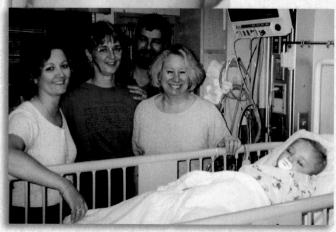

Left: David's sister, Danielle; mother, Joan; and brother and his wife, John and Cindy, were faithful to visit Caleb following each major surgery undertaken in Michigan.

Right: Great Grandma Ennis enjoys holding two-month-old Caleb as he peacefully naps on her lap.

Left: Great Grandpa and Grandma Marion pose for a quick picture with the Ingerson children as Caleb nervously fears he's about to slide off Great Grandma's lap onto the floor!

Right: Have pacifier will travel! Cousin Katie and Caleb are ready to go as they play on the toy truck at Grandpa and Grandma's farm.

Right: Big brother, Andrew, cannot resist touching Caleb.

Left: Caleb's unflappable joy brings great pleasure to all who witness it.

Right: Ten-month-old Caleb smiles brightly as he proudly wears his University of Michigan sweatshirt.

Left: "All aboard! The Caleb Express is headed out!"

Right: Fireman Caleb reports ready for duty!

Below: Caleb smiles smugly as the Ingerson children and Daddy sport their homemade birthday party hats!

Caleb and his siblings pose for his first Christmas portrait.

Uncharacteristic for Caleb, he is in no mood for a picture. Nevertheless, his parents obligingly smile for the visitor's camera as Caleb recovers from yet another open-heart surgery.

Andrew gazes admiringly at his little brother as Caleb and his sisters warm-up to sing Happy Birthday to five-year-old Hannah Joy.

Left: Caleb, his mother, Grandma Donna, and three older siblings tour the famous St. Louis Arch.

Left: Caleb opens Christmas presents with his Aunty Patty.

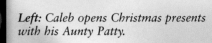

Right: "Ooh! Mommy's famous soft German pretzels taste so good!"

Top: Caleb flashes his characteristically cute smile as he sits atop his favorite cow, the most docile, on his grandparents' farm.

Middle: David is privileged to introduce his young son to Great Grandpa Clayton at his home in Alexandria, Virginia.

Bottom: Caleb tries out his new fishing pole and wonders why he hasn't caught anything yet!

Above: It's a big tractor for such a small boy, but Grandpa Marion encourages Caleb to sit atop it all by himself.

Left: Forever at his Grandpa Marion's side, both Caleb and Grandpa enjoy a catnap before commencing the evening chores.

Right: Grandpa Marion relents as Caleb insists on taking yet another tractor ride on Grandpa's Massey Ferguson.

Kathy gently holds her three-year-old son after his tenth and final surgery.

David, a proud daddy, spends as much time as he can with his beloved son. Little did he know in less than thirty days, his smiling child would be gone.

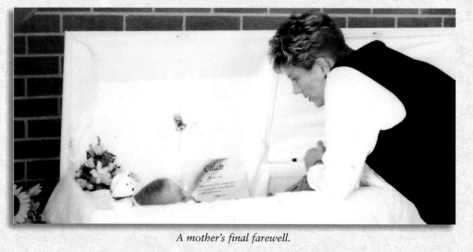

A mother's final farewell.

The Ingerson family takes a break from getting settled into the chaotic Washington DC area at a friend's home just weeks before Caleb's unexpected, sudden death.

Mommy enjoys a bright moment with her son during a family wedding in Michigan, August 2000.

"Little Fighter Man, you've gone on ahead..."

CALEB STEPHEN-ALWIN INGERSON

"I will not die but live..."
Psalm 118:17

Mar. 4, 1997 — Sept. 10, 2000

We released balloons at the end of Caleb's funeral in celebration of his vibrant life.

Caleb Stephen-Alwin Ingerson, with his enduring smile and playful demeanor, inspired many to place childlike faith and trust in their Creator that they would experience the same joyful zest for living as Caleb did each day of his short life.

CHAPTER 18

Daddy's Home!

There is no more pitiful sight than a mother, filled with maternal zeal to hold her children, who is hindered from doing so because suddenly, unexpectedly she is separated by over 6,000 miles of vast ocean for weeks on end. Out of this zeal, Kathy sent her first e-mail message ever to a friend in Okinawa.

....

Caleb Update: Friday, March 22

Hello. Yes, I'm actually replying, me, Kathy. Caleb has been moved to another floor, a good sign, where the care is somewhat less intensive. He is supposed to go to radiology this morning for a barium swallow. The doctors are checking the intactness of his esophagus.

I pray there are no strictures so Caleb will be able to eat orally, soon. If there is a stricture, he will have to go back into surgery. His suck and rooting reflexes are strong. Now that his endotracheal tube is out, he turns his little head and moves his little lips, looking for something to eat, also a very good sign. It is so very difficult not to hold and nurse him.

Love, Kathy

•••

Friday, March 22nd, was a historic day. Having been weaned from the respirator for more than 24 hours, Caleb, at 18 days old, had his first taste; he sucked and swallowed for the first time in his life. As elated as we were to see our son without the respirator, we were all the more excited to see him take fluid by mouth, even if it was only barium and water. Kathy described Caleb's reaction to the barium during the swallow study as "hungrily gobbling it down." We celebrated the day's victory by sending out the following e-mail update.

•••

Caleb Update: Friday, March 22

Today was a day of firsts for Caleb.

1) He ate through his mouth a barium solution, which made his gastrointestinal system visible via X-ray.

2) He ate as his mother held him. It may have only been 20 cc's of barium and water, but that was a whopping four teaspoons, a lot for little Caleb.

3) His mother held him while she tried to get him to nurse. He just slept. He was tuckered out from eating the barium.

4) Caleb was moved from the PICU to moderate care.

That's all for now, David and Kathy

•••

After such an eventful week and such a victorious Friday, Saturday was as satisfying and calming as it was trying and discouraging. We spent the majority of the day sitting in a rocking chair in Caleb's room, taking turns holding him. It was gloriously soothing to rock back and forth and just marvel at the small gift of God we now held in our formerly aching and lonely arms.

We felt as though we'd waited an entire lifetime to gently hold and rock this precious child. A picture taken that day shows us looking more like brand new parents with their first newborn than the experienced parents of four that we were.

The day was likewise trying and discouraging in that while Kathy tried again and again to get Caleb to nurse, he just didn't have the stamina. He tired too quickly; he didn't have the energy to suck longer than the time it took to cause his mother's milk to let down. Despite her maternal frustration, Kathy continued to pump her own milk as she'd done so many times over the past three weeks. Our emotions flip-flopped between satisfaction and discouragement.

Caleb Update: Saturday, March 23

Today was such a discouraging day. It was a classic case of unrealistic expectations. Yesterday, Caleb ate clear water through his mouth. Yea! Then the night nurse was able to feed him a moderate amount of his mother's milk three times. He only vomited the milk the first time; therefore, we expected he'd be able to eat directly from his mother right away, but no. Each time Kathy tried to nurse him, he'd suck just enough to get her milk to let down and then fall asleep. The little guy is just too weak to work hard enough to do the job. Therefore, the nurses are obeying doctors' orders and feeding him his mother's milk through his G-tube.

It is going to be a slow process to get Caleb to eat orally, whether breast or bottle. We're going to have to be patient. One doctor told us to expect to have to continue to use the gastric tube when Caleb is discharged. I guess our expectations were too high. It's a classic catch-22, rather like painting oneself into a corner. If he isn't fed through the G-tube, he won't have the strength to nurse, but when he's fed through the G-tube, he is satisfied and not hungry enough to motivate himself to exert the energy nursing requires. And so it goes....

Caleb actually looks like a normal kid now—if you don't look at the many sutured lines all over his little body as well as ignore the several tubes still running in and out of him, but believe me, there are many fewer now than there were three days ago.

Thanks for the cards, e-mails, care packages, etc.

We feel so loved, David and Kathy

....

As the time neared when Caleb could go home, the stress of needing to know where home was going to be increased. I had spent considerable time researching positions within the Air Force that could not only employ an officer with my pilot qualifications but also ensure a location where I would be able to obtain adequate medical care for Caleb. I also spent much time making phone calls to potential commanders as well as mailing and faxing copies of my resume from a San Francisco Kinko's.

> The well-meaning questioners helped stoke the fires of frustration in that we didn't know where we would be going.

Meanwhile, although Sandy was doing a marvelous job with the older children, she needed to be spelled and the children needed a parent at home to give them a sense of normal life. Likewise, my current job in Okinawa wherein I served as the 18th Operations Group Chief of Air Refueling Tanker Standardization and Evaluation, needed my attention in order for me to conduct a professional hand off of my duties to my hastily named replacement.

No day passed when we didn't field well-meaning yet frustrating questions for which we had no answers: So, where are you going to take your son when he gets discharged from the hospital? Where's home going to be since you can't go back to Japan?

The well-meaning questioners helped stoke the fires of frustration in that we didn't know where we would be going. As the search for the location of our new home narrowed to either the St. Louis area at Scott Air Force Base or the Pentagon near Washington, D.C., we decided I needed to head home to Okinawa to begin preparations to move the family.

I would leave from Travis on a routine AIREVAC flight, which would take two calendar days to return me to Okinawa and would arrive on Friday, the 29th of March, twenty-four days after leaving our other children parentless. I needed to get back to Okinawa to complete and sign the original birth certificate application so Caleb could be enrolled as my military dependent, thus authorizing disbursement of insurance payments.

The importance of this process I would understand much later as the medical bills surpassed $2 million by the time Caleb reached the age of three and a half. I also needed to get back to Okinawa to complete the administrative actions required to finalize my next USAF assignment. My family needed to know where home was going to be.

....

Caleb Update: Saturday, March 23

The doctors say there's nothing more they can or should do for Caleb at this time. He can go home, wherever that will be, as soon as he is eating better, perhaps in a week's time.

Hence, I am planning to leave SF on Tuesday and fly out of Travis early Wednesday morning.

Okinawa family, look for me Friday afternoon,
David

....

As a token of our appreciation for the service they provided our special son, Kathy and I delivered a basket filled with treats to the nurses and staff on the 6th and 7th floors. It was truly a victorious day. We were so thankful as we anticipated Caleb's discharge. It was cause to celebrate.

....

Caleb Update: Monday, March 25

Caleb was so alert today; it was precious. In keeping with the Ingerson children's tradition, his first smile was directed at his father. The nurse, Annette, was a witness; therefore, let there be no disputing this claim to Caleb's first smile. It was directed at his father, at least that's what the nurse told me. I actually missed it, but just barely. I caught the lingering form of a recent smile when I looked in response to the nurse's exclamation, "Look, he's smiling at you."

Although he is still not nursing or eating from a bottle very well, he gets plenty of his mother's thawed milk via his G-tube. Tonight the overzealous nurse poured so much milk into his stomach through the tube that little Caleb's stomach must have been at maximum capacity. He squirmed and complained with such a look of pain on his little face. That was the only time he even grimaced today. The nurses and doctors all continually comment that he is the best appearing baby with the most pleasant disposition they've ever seen of those with this serious heart defect. They all rave about how impressed they are with his progress.

Tomorrow morning Caleb will be transferred back to the top of the hospital, the 15th floor, where he began his stay three weeks ago. He will also have the precautionary pacemaker wires, the last unnatural appendages, removed. After that, he'll be ready to go home as soon as he gains sufficient weight. The nurses continue to ask us where home is. We still don't know how to answer that question. The doctors have all warned us to not take Caleb to Okinawa given the limited medical facilities and personnel available there.

While we would love to take Caleb to Japan to meet our precious Okinawa family, we have ruled it out as impractical and imprudent.

Grace and peace, David and Kathy

. . . .

During the long flight home to Okinawa, with a stop in Hawaii and a stop in mainland Japan, I had plenty of time to think. As exciting as it would be to see my children after a more than three-week separation and as elated as we were that Caleb would be out of the hospital soon, the emotional stress of not knowing where I'd be moving my family or what Caleb's future held continued to weigh me down. One thing was certain. It was time to get back to work. But where?

I spent much of the time in deep contemplation, reading the Bible and passionately writing out my thoughts, hopes, and fears. By the time I completed the return to Okinawa, I had compiled an irresistible sermon, which I preached on Easter Sunday two days after returning home. I approached Pastor Glenn and told him I had to preach on Sunday. Hesitant at first, he readily agreed when he saw how adamant I was.

For my arrival back at Kadena Air Base, Sandy drove the children to the air terminal where they greeted me just before lunch. As I stepped out from the bus, which had transported the passengers into the terminal, the children enthusiastically screamed, "Daddy's home!" as they ran to me and threw their arms around my neck. The reunion was so deeply emotional. Never before, even when returning from my innumerable and much longer military duty separations, had my children clung to my neck as tightly or as long as this time.

When I was finally able to pry their weeping faces from my shoulders, I led them, along with Aunt Sandy, upstairs to the air terminal snack bar to have lunch. The windowed area of the second floor snack bar provided an outstanding viewing area of the runway and flight line. Amazingly, the children seemed to have lost their normal fascination with watching the airplanes take off and land. During the entire meal, they continuously stared at me with wide eyes of anticipation of what I might do or say next, as though they'd not seen me for years.

CHAPTER 19

He's Miracle Baby

A fter lunch we returned to our base home just two miles from the air terminal. As I sat at the dining room table and began to pick through the gargantuan mountain of mail, Sandy reminded me it was 2 PM on Friday afternoon and the 30th day since Caleb's birth would soon arrive. Hence, I needed to drive to the Camp Lester hospital to complete and sign Caleb's birth certificate.

Realizing Sandy was correct, I resigned, "Okay, you're right."

As soon as six-year-old Sarah heard me respond, she urgently pleaded, "No, Daddy, don't go."

"Sarah," I commanded, "I need to go take care of Caleb's birth certificate."

"Well," she sighed, "Caleb is more important than we are anyway."

"Sarah, No!" I vehemently retorted. In response, Sarah immediately began to weep deep heaving sobs. I picked her up in my arms, set her on my lap, and held her as she shook and wept.

"Oh, Sarah, you are all very important," I reassured. A deeply agonizing tug-of-war in my own fragile heart set my mind whirling

131

A deeply agonizing tug-of-war in my own fragile heart set my mind whirling as it occurred to me that I needed to be sure to prove to the other three children how very special they were to us...

as it occurred to me that I needed to be sure to prove to the other three children how very special they were to us, especially in light of the extra attention their little brother was receiving. It's too easy to be excited about the needy child and forget the important emotional needs of the other children.

I determined to ensure the children wouldn't feel neglected again, although I rightly sensed it would be easier to conceive than to accomplish. I could scarcely shake the apprehensive feeling that swept over me as I tightly held my firstborn daughter in my arms. Nonetheless, I could not have fully appreciated how challenging it would be in the coming years to offer sufficient emotional support to the siblings of such a chronically ill child.

After nearly a month in California tending to my child who had undergone three major surgeries, I had finally returned to Okinawa. Twenty-six days after we'd left the island in such a frantic hurry, I was finally home. Aunt Sandy hadn't missed a beat. Although the children were elated to see me, they were excited about Aunt Sandy returning each morning to stay with them while I went back to work.

Finally, a week after my return, my mother arrived on the island to assist with the care of the three older children. My mother, who loves to travel, had flown to Okinawa each of the three prior years to visit us on the small tropical island that was home to the Ingerson clan. Although she'd not planned to visit us a fourth time, after spending several days with us in San Francisco, she firmly decided to dig into her savings and buy a fourth airline ticket to Okinawa to help with the children until we could move back to the States. After over a month of caring for the older children round-the-clock, Aunt Sandy was relieved of her surrogate mothering duties.

Meanwhile, back in San Francisco, Kathy was settling in to care for Caleb alone in the big city until Aunty Patty joined her from Hawaii.

. . . .

Caleb Update: Tuesday, March 26

It was hard letting David go today, but it had to be done. The kids need to see at least one parent. I cried all the way back to the Ronald McDonald House from Travis. My support left me. Now I have to totally depend on God while living in this big city by myself. Caleb is doing okay. He needs to start gaining weight instead of losing it. He has lost one and one-half pounds. That is a lot for a little one. He looks so scrawny. Please pray.

Love, Kathy

. . . .

Then there was another setback. A pesky shadow on Caleb's daily chest X-ray again raised its ugly head the day after I left San Francisco. Consequently, Caleb was not transferred back to the 15th floor as scheduled. Kathy sent the following update.

. . . .

Caleb Update: Thursday, March 28

Caleb is not allowed to eat orally at this time per doctor's orders. Civilians give orders too. This is due to the fact that he has a spot, according to today's chest X-ray, on his right lung. It appears to be fluid. Just in case, he's being treated for pneumonia. His orders to be transferred from the 7th floor moderate care unit to the 15th floor ICN in advance of and preparation for discharge have been cancelled.

Otherwise, Caleb is doing fairly well. He has lost one and one-half pounds and continues to lose. He looks so scrawny. He needs to start gaining weight. He is fed around the clock via his gastric tube. No more oral feeding until his lung clears up. The lung on yesterday's X-ray looked a little better, but it's still too dangerous for him to eat orally.

Thanks for praying. Love, Kathy

Caleb's continued need to gain weight was unnerving. Nonetheless, the next several days were ones of continued progress. The next day his chest X-ray appeared clear, so the doctors were comfortable allowing Kathy to again attempt to nurse her son. Success! Although Kathy happily reported that she'd successfully nursed Caleb in a message e-mailed to our friends around the world, she also communicated her agony upon hearing of how the other children missed her. It deeply saddened this mother of four to learn of how affected the older children were by the emotional uncertainty of our family's disrupted life and future.

Caleb Update: Friday, March 29

Caleb had a good day. Consequently, so did Mom. Caleb's X-ray was clear. That means no fluid in his lungs. Praise God. Oral feedings have resumed. He nursed for three minutes and took half a bottle. This amount is a huge improvement. Three days ago he wasn't interested in sucking at all.

Caleb still needs to gain weight. He has to regain what he has lost before we can be discharged.

Thanks for praying. Love, Kathy

P.S. David arrived safely in Okinawa. The kids were so excited. He told me Hannah Joy cried for Mommy when he put her to bed. Sarah made an off-the-cuff comment that Caleb is more important than her and her siblings. She then sat in her daddy's lap and cried for five minutes. This is the hardest part for me. I just want my family back together. I don't care where, just back together.

....

In the meantime, Aunty Patty arrived from Hawaii. She had volunteered to come to San Francisco to offer moral support and help Kathy care for Caleb. As Caleb began his gradual weight gain, Kathy planned his discharge. She had arranged for a commercial flight to Detroit with supplemental oxygen for Caleb, at the UCSF cardiologist's recommendation. Because the supplemental oxygen was unavailable for the first several days after Caleb was discharged, Kathy and Aunty Patty would have to keep Caleb at the Ronald McDonald House in San Francisco. Although staying in the Ronald McDonald House with a patient was strictly against their policy, the staff willingly agreed to make an exception in Kathy's case since she had nowhere else to go.

Back in Okinawa, on Easter Sunday I climbed the stage and stood behind the podium to address the church. As I scanned the quiet audience, I well remembered that evening, just a month ago, when so many of these faces faithfully filled the hospital chapel with not only their presence but also their prayers as they bravely petitioned God for the life of my son.

I began by humbly declaring the victory of my son's life. "As you are well aware, I've just returned from spending over three weeks in California attending to my newborn son. This is the son whom the doctors said would likely not live beyond a few days. This is the son for whom the doctors recommended we provide compassionate care and watch die within those very few days. But, I'm here this morning to proclaim to you that as of today, my son is twenty-seven days old!"

The church erupted with applause and exuberant shouts of joy. The spontaneous roar from this congregation of 300 was nearly deafening. They were celebrating the victory they'd fought for us so valiantly in prayer. I continued by describing a most encouraging moment Kathy had witnessed just the day before. During evening rounds, Kathy overheard the scoffing doctor giving report to a huddled group of his peers.

This doctor was the one who'd warned us that if we elected to follow through with intervention versus simply letting Caleb die, that is, employing non-intervention, we'd better be prepared for a difficult road, which might include caring for a child who very well may spend his whole life in and out of hospitals, even suffering serious neurological effects.

Kathy overheard this very doctor excitedly exclaim, "This is Caleb; He's Miracle Baby because we're all so shocked at how well he's doing!" The congregation again roared in vigorous celebration. It seemed the applause would never end.

CHAPTER 20

Don't Forget the Mop and Broom

The next week at work, it should have been all systems go. Although I was ready to expedite my family's move to the States, I was at a loss to know what to do. Moving is difficult in and of itself, especially when moving to or from an overseas location, but the added time constraint and not knowing where we were moving made it all the more difficult and frustrating.

With such uncertainty, we planned to send Kathy and the children ahead to stay temporarily with her parents in Michigan while I remained behind in Okinawa to finalize our next move and complete some open projects at work. Not knowing how long they would stay in Michigan made it difficult to know how settled they'd need to become.

Kathy's mother, Grandma Donna, volunteered to take care of Caleb after he was discharged from the hospital as Kathy planned to travel back to Okinawa to help move the household. During this time, Caleb and Grandma Donna would begin a precious bonding relationship that would weather many storms of medical treatments, surgeries, and hospitalizations.

Similarly, Kathy's father would develop a great love for our little boy. In the coming months and years, Grandpa Gerald would eventually develop a practice of taking this special grandson for many tractor rides on his Massey Ferguson. All Caleb had to do was mention the word "tractor" and off they'd go on another ride—Grandpa was a pushover.

Meanwhile, back in California Caleb was discharged from the hospital, and Kathy and Patty faced the challenge of caring for him without the capable aid, and more importantly, moral support of the experienced nursing staff. Despite the demonstration Caleb's nurse had performed, Kathy, even as a trained nurse, felt severely over-whelmed the first time she had to change Caleb's colostomy bag all by herself. "It looked so easy when the nurses did it," she exclaimed. However, that was not Kathy's experience as the watery contents of the bag spilled out all over her Ronald McDonald House bed.

The first night was terrifying in that Caleb cried incessantly as though in constant pain. The following day, Patty wondered if the problem wasn't simply that Caleb had been uncomfortable as he was so scrawny and had very little body fat with which to cushion his tiny frame. Perhaps, Caleb was simply in pain as he slept on the hard surface of his small cradle, which the Ronald McDonald House staff had provided. Therefore, the second night Kathy padded the cradle, creating a much softer sleeping area. Much to their relief, the child slept soundly, without a peep, all night long.

Both were aghast at how pitiful the scrawny Caleb appeared.

Finally came the long awaited flight to Michigan. Kathy had previously arranged for dry ice in which she packed the many vials of frozen breast milk. She was quite a sight walking through the San Francisco airport hauling a small refugee-thin baby in an infant carrier, a cooler full of frozen breast milk on dry ice, a large green therapeutic oxygen bottle, and her own luggage.

Flying cross country with a heart failure baby was a horrific experience. Caleb was sorely uncomfortable and pitifully cried the entire four hour flight. Kathy had an impossible time keeping the oxygen nasal cannula on his face. Consequently, she simply held the cannula near his nose and mouth, desperately hoping it would help keep his oxygen saturation at a safe level. The passenger sharing the row with Caleb and her was so visibly perturbed; he surely must have wished there had been an empty seat available anywhere else in the plane so he could have moved away from the pathetic newborn screams.

Nonetheless, Kathy and Caleb somehow survived the flight. Kathy's mother was waiting at the gate with a friend. Both were aghast at how pitiful the scrawny Caleb appeared. So frightening was his delicate appearance, the ladies later admitted they were terrified something awful might happen while Kathy left to gather her luggage from the baggage carousel.

It took Kathy two weeks to get our little boy settled in Michigan. She taught her mother how to care for the child, met several doctors at the University of Michigan, and developed a good rapport with Dr. Rosenthal, the chief pediatric cardiologist, as well as two general surgeons and a pediatrician. Saturday morning, during the first of the two weeks she spent in Michigan, Kathy called me in Okinawa with an urgent message. With obvious concern she weakly muttered, "We need to do something! Caleb's penis is swelled up like a melon."

After I got over my weak in the knees reaction, I asked, "Ahh.... Kathy, what can we do?" It was the only response I could muster.

We settled on a plan wherein Kathy would take Caleb to see Dr. Rosenthal to get his opinion as to what needed to be done. Dr. Rosenthal referred her to a general pediatric surgeon and recommended we inquire about the prudence of circumcision. The surgeon readily agreed that performing the age-old procedure would likely reduce his incidence of infection. Thus we made plans to perform the procedure after we all returned to the States in three weeks. Even a simple procedure such as this was not straightforward for Caleb. With his precarious heart condition, Caleb would need to be put under a general anesthesia.

One night as Kathy's mother was preparing Caleb for bed, she noticed his G-tube had somehow come out of its hole. As an experienced nurse she was not particularly alarmed. She calmly called out, "Kathy, I need your help putting Caleb's G-tube back in."

"What?" my confident wife replied. "How did it come out?"

"Oh, I don't know," her mother matter-of-factly shot back. "Let's just stick it back in. I'm sure it'll be no problem at all."

Unfortunately, this was not as easily done as these two self-assured women assumed. As Kathy attempted to gently slip the pliable tube back into its hole, she shrieked, "The hole has closed up. I can't push the tube back in."

"GERALD!" Kathy's mother cried. "Come quickly, we need a man's help here."

Within moments, Kathy's businesslike dairy farming father appeared, still wearing his smelly milking overalls. "Let's take him down to the kitchen where the lighting is better," Gerald directed.

After placing the calmly compliant Caleb on the kitchen counter under the bright fluorescent lighting, these three confident, no-nonsense adults again attempted to insert the pesky tube back inside the abdomen of their heart patient. After three futile attempts to jab the G-tube back into place, Kathy was desperate. "I can't get the tube back in place," she lamented. "The hole has really closed tightly. What can we do now?"

"Oh, just thrust it back in there," her mother retorted.

"You can do it, Kath," her father encouraged.

Her father carefully stretched the child taunt as on a medieval rack and held Caleb down and still. Initially, the scrawny child with bright pink scars crisscrossing his small chest and abdomen in all directions began to wriggle and squirm against the unyieldingly hard surface of the kitchen counter. However, he suddenly calmed as though he sensed security from the ever tightening hold of his grandpa's powerful arms and calloused hands.

Finally, with one last quick and aggressive jab, Kathy succeeded in forcing the pliable tube back through its hole into Caleb's abdomen. Remarkably, the small child neither flinched nor made a sound. All cheered in victory. As his grandpa relaxed his vice-like hold on the child, Caleb just looked around in mild disinterest as if to say, "What's all the fuss about?"

After two weeks in Michigan, Kathy commenced her long journey back to Okinawa. Still on patient status, she flew back to Okinawa via the USAF MEDEVAC system. This flight transportation system required a complex multi-stop circuitous routing via various U.S. Air Force bases in the States and in the Pacific area before arriving in Japan. Hence, the arduous trip required three days of flying, stopping to change planes, and flying again.

Although she was exceedingly tired upon arrival on Okinawa, Kathy hit the ground running. After spending some much needed time with our older children, Kathy busied herself organizing our household for the immediate move to the States. During nine hectic days of organizing and packing, several generous friends gave of their time to help us prepare our household for the rushed move.

One friend, Mila, and her two boys were especially helpful. With neither specific request nor invitation, she and her two teenage sons surprised us by showing up at our front door with mop and broom in hand. They were ready to do anything necessary to help us clean and prepare our home to pass the military housing inspection. Words cannot adequately express the encouragement she and her boys were during this intense time of crisis.

We learned a valuable lesson from Mila and her sons. In contrast to the common offer, "If there's anything I can do, give me a call," Mila just showed up. From her example we learned that when a friend is facing seemingly insurmountable challenges, asking that friend to "give me a call," though well-intended, feels flippant and insincere. Although the offer of assistance is certainly sincere, the reality is most won't call.

The reasons most won't call are varied. They are oftentimes numb and incapable of effectively planning what needs to be accomplished. Their absolute lack of energy prevents them from so much as asking for help. Furthermore, the sheer helplessness felt by those coping with a critically or chronically ill child is overwhelming and disorienting.

If a person truly wants to help, she should consider Mila's example and just show up at the friend in need's home and declare her intention to help with simple household chores or other obvious common needs. Mila demonstrated her genuine concern and love by not only appearing at our front door to help pack and organize several days before our packers and movers arrived but also by returning the next several days to help keep watch of the packers.

What an expression of loyalty and love Mila and her children were. We would all do well to follow her example. Don't invite the friend in distress to call; just show up—and don't forget the mop and broom.

CHAPTER 21

You'd Better Fly!

Kathy and the children made tearful good-byes to our many friends on our island home of Okinawa and then, along with my mother, flew straight to Michigan. Finally, my next duty assignment confirmed. I would report for duty at the USAF Air Mobility Command Headquarters located at Scott Air Force Base in Illinois.

One week later I departed Okinawa and proceeded directly to Scott AFB in order to sign in at my new unit. I immediately signed back out for house hunting to secure a place for our family to live for the next three years. Kathy joined me in Illinois.

The realtor we hired was surprised to learn we had allotted only two days to locate and purchase a house. After looking at twenty-eight houses in two days, we settled on the first one we saw on the first day. During dinner out, we fielded numerous phone calls from our realtor as she negotiated with the seller's realtor. After several hours of faxing offers and counter offers back and forth, we finally settled on an agreeable price and signed the purchase agreement.

We'd learned while in San Francisco to celebrate each and every victory, no matter how small.

Contrary to what our realtor thought possible, we accomplished our goal in just two days—just in time to return to Michigan for Caleb's circumcision. The procedure was successful with no adverse side effects—another victory to be celebrated. We'd learned while in San Francisco to celebrate each and every victory, no matter how small.

The next several months kept us busy with all the normal tasks and responsibilities involved with moving within the military community, including some related to returning from four years overseas. First we needed to acquire adequate transportation since the vehicles we owned while in Japan had steering wheels on the opposite side as U.S. cars. This proved to be no problem. We visited just one local dealership and promptly purchased two adequate used cars for less than most people spend on their annual family vacation.

It seemed we were on autopilot, just going through the motions. All the while our minds, whether we verbalized it or not, were mentally preoccupied with anticipating Caleb's next open-heart surgery, which would need to take place sometime between July and September.

In addition to purchasing a house and two vehicles, I was occupied training for my new position and getting acclimated to my new responsibilities at my new base of assignment. The stress of our family separation was compounded by the challenge of trying to close the purchase of our new home in minimum time. Our goal was to take possession of the house and refinish certain rooms by applying fresh paint and new carpet before moving the children to Illinois. Kathy flew to Illinois to join me for the property closing and a week of arduous house preparation. Once we finished, we drove to Michigan to retrieve our children and return to our new home in Illinois.

The next month was relatively calm for the older children as they played and became acquainted with their new neighborhood. But for Kathy and me, it was intense. We had barely a month to decide if there was an adequate surgical facility nearby St. Louis where our son could get the next needed step of the Norwood cardiac treatment plan.

The senior attending pediatric cardiologist at the UCSF referred us to Dr. Strauss, a renowned pediatric cardiologist at Washington University Hospital in St. Louis. Dr. Strauss graciously agreed to accept Caleb as a patient and coordinate closely with our new pediatric cardiothoracic surgeon and cardiologists, whether they would be in Michigan or St. Louis. The community of doctors at this level of subspecialty is sufficiently small that all the doctors were familiar with each other and comfortable working together.

I set about calling the surgical units in the two pediatric hospitals in St. Louis, arranging to meet and interview the surgeons. Of these two hospitals, one had no pediatric cardiothoracic surgical capability. At the other facility, when Kathy and I met the surgical team face-to-face, I asked how many HLHS babies they'd treated. When they indicated it had been less than ten, I quickly queried, "How've they fared?"

"Oh, they all died," they readily admitted.

"Okay then, well, thank you for your time," I muttered as my wife and I quickly left their office and drove home to Illinois.

During the forty-five minute drive home, I turned to my wife and stated the obvious, "Well, Dear, at least now we know that driving back to Michigan for Caleb's next open-heart surgery is our only option."

Her impassive response told me she had expected this all along.

After many weeks of attending to our critical, chronically ill son, I had a difficult time returning to a normal routine. Fortunately, the older children easily adapted and helped their parents settle into some semblance of normal. Nevertheless, at night after putting our older children to bed, I found myself wondering what I, the father of a chronically ill child was supposed to be doing. Weren't there any well-defined duties?

Many evenings, in my quiet desperation to know what to do to help speed along the process of bringing Caleb to full health, I found myself asking: What do I do now? I felt agonizingly lost after such a hectic three months. It seemed as though all I could do now was provide daily care for my son, wait for his next surgery, and hope for a successful outcome. The days were stressful and the nights were sleepless.

Less than a month before Caleb's next open-heart surgery, our three older children began to show signs of chickenpox. Hoping to keep Caleb from infection in his weakened condition, Kathy immediately made arrangements to transport Caleb to her mother's care in Michigan. Grandma Donna drove four hours south while Kathy hastily packed a bag with all Caleb's supplies and drove north to meet her mother halfway.

Kathy passed the child into her mother's care, intending to quarantine him from the virus. Obviously, as nurses, both Kathy and her mother should have known it was certainly already too late. But in her desperation to keep Caleb's surgical schedule on track, Kathy hoped against hope that maybe, just maybe, her delicate son had somehow not yet been infected.

As Grandma Donna settled Caleb into the farmhouse, her mother, Caleb's 86-year-old Great Grandma Ennis, who had lived with Kathy's parents for over fourteen years, was beginning to show signs that her weakened heart was failing. Although she'd been diagnosed with congestive heart failure more than three years previously, she nonetheless lived a high quality of life, serving as an integral part of the household on the farm.

Within a couple of days of getting Caleb settled, Donna noticed her mother's breathing was sounding increasingly labored. As Great Grandma Ennis painstakingly walked from her bedroom to the living room, she appeared quite pale and out of breath.

"Mom, are you okay?" Donna inquired.

"Uh, oh, uh, I'm...I'm okay," Great Grandma Ennis sputtered.

"Okay, Mom, just have a seat and take it easy," Donna nervously intoned.

The next morning as Grandma Donna was emptying Caleb's colostomy bag, she noticed a couple small red spots on his abdomen. "Oh, now this child has chickenpox too!" she blurted.

As soon as she finished attending to Caleb's colostomy bag, she called Kathy to consider what course of action she'd need to take. "Kathy, I'm particularly concerned about this virus causing a problem for my mother. Older people are particularly susceptible to shingles," Donna opined.

Kathy tried to reassure her mother. "Okay, Mom, I'm sure Great Grandma Ennis will be fine. Just try to keep Caleb away from her. Meanwhile, I'll call Dr. Rosenthal to get his opinion."

It was humorous that once again these two experienced nurses had allowed their maternal instincts to supersede their knowledge of how this virus works. If Caleb's chickenpox infection was to adversely affect his great grandmother, it was already too late.

The pediatric cardiologist and the surgeon were both in agreement that the most prudent course of action would be to delay the surgery until the chickenpox had completely run its course so as not to present an infection potential at the hospital. We readily agreed in that it was really the only viable option.

Grandma Donna juggled caring for our son with his congenital heart disease, other medical challenges, and chickenpox infected body while caring for her mother who was now in the terminal stages of congestive heart failure. Kathy remained in Illinois tending to our older children, now covered from head to toe with the infamous itchy rash. She lamented that she could not be in Michigan to help her mother.

As Donna began to notice her mother's breathing becoming increasingly labored and slow, she prepared herself for the worst-case scenario.

Over the course of the next several days, Great Grandma Ennis's condition deteriorated. Donna successfully kept her mother comfortable while she also cared for our little fighter and his itchy skin blisters. Just weeks before her 87th birthday, Great Grandma Ennis, with a look of calm tranquility, breathed her last breath and departed this world for one far better. Kathy's mother had been able to keep her promise. Great Grandma Ennis died peacefully at home, in her own bed.

Undeterred and running on adrenaline, Grandma Donna continued to care for our little Caleb as she finalized her mother's funeral and burial arrangements. After the chickenpox ran its course in our three older children, Kathy and the children traveled to Michigan, arriving just in time to attend Great Grandma Ennis's funeral.

Within two weeks, evidence of Caleb's chickenpox infection likewise disappeared. Therefore, at six months of age, Caleb underwent the hemi-Fontan, Norwood stage two, surgery under the knife of Dr. Ed Bove, the renowned pediatric cardiothoracic surgeon at the University of Michigan Mott Children's Hospital.

Although the surgery was successful, Caleb's hospital stay extended for over two months due to many post-surgical complications. One of those complications was a significant increase in gastric reflux—better known as acid indigestion. Gastric reflux results from stomach contents leaking backwards from the stomach into the esophagus causing painful irritation. This is a common and often severe problem for children with EA/TEF.

The small child was constantly retching after being fed. It was pitiful to watch and positively agonizing to hear. Whenever he experienced a serious bout of reflux, he would wretch as though trying to vomit. His heart rate would slow and his blood oxygen saturations dip precariously low. This problem needed a solution. I sent the following e-mail update to our many concerned friends and family.

....

Caleb Update: Wed, 17 Sep

Caleb took a turn for the better yesterday, but he is still in a very precarious condition. His current health concerns are too complicated to explain in-depth, but here is a synopsis:

1) Heart: lacks proper function (weak pumping) and has leaking tricuspid valve

2) Esophagus: refluxing, hence very irritated by stomach acid

3) Breathing: Experiencing severe apnea (i.e. he alternately breaths with very shallow breaths followed by deep gasps)

4) Thoracic lymph system duct was damaged during surgery and is leaking fluid into chest cavity

5) Nerve running through chest next to thoracic lymph duct possibly damaged during surgery, resulting in breathing problems.

Tomorrow he'll undergo more tests/studies to determine appropriate courses of action.

David

....

We requested a consultation with a general pediatric surgeon to try to determine if there was a course of action that would help alleviate our son's ongoing problem with reflux. The surgeon readily agreed that a Thal fundoplication, commonly referred to as a wraparound procedure, would likely reduce Caleb's incidence of reflux, thus helping his cardiac function and overall health. The cardiologist and cardiac surgeon, however, did not feel it was prudent to proceed with the wraparound surgery given Caleb's precarious heart condition at that time.

The wrap entailed taking part of the tissue of the upper part of the stomach and wrapping it around the lower esophageal sphincter to help cinch it up, thereby decreasing his esophageal reflux. We were torn between Caleb avoiding more surgery at this time and the possibility of reducing the awful reflux if it could be surgically treated.

During the long hospitalization, my wife kept a constant vigil at our small six-month-old's bedside. Five times my wife called, asking me to return to Michigan. My Air Force boss graciously allowed me to take time off from work each of those five times. Two of the five times I drove. Three times I flew.

A friend asked me, given the high price of airline tickets, why I sometimes flew instead of each time driving the eight hours. I replied that I chose my mode of transportation based on the seriousness of the call from my wife. I can still hear her nervous voice the second time she called and portentously declared, "Caleb isn't doing very well. If you want to see your son again, you'd better come now—and you'd better fly."

To this day, remembrance of these words still stirs fear inside me and sends a shiver down my spine that is as difficult to describe as it is to shake off.

CHAPTER 22

An Absurd Scene

Finally, after nearly two months of agonizing hospitalization, Caleb's post-operative complications began to subside. Specifically, the drainage from Caleb's chest reduced to an acceptable level. Therefore, after a second consultation with general surgery, cardiology, and his cardiothoracic surgeon, we decided he was sufficiently strong to tolerate a sixth surgery, the Thal fundoplication, or wraparound, to cinch his lower esophageal sphincter in order to reduce his maddening gastric reflux.

Furthermore, we expected many of Caleb's chronic challenges, particularly his lowered heart rate and oxygen levels, would be improved by reducing his incidence of reflux. Therefore, the general surgeon performed the wraparound the very next day. The doctor emerged from the OR after just two hours declaring success. Within another two weeks, by mid-October, Caleb was finally strong enough to be discharged after a full seventy day hospitalization.

During these tumultuous seventy days, I returned to work at our base in Illinois, while my mother, who had recently retired from teaching high school, volunteered to come stay with us and

"Get up, Sarah. It's time to go to school."

The surprised six-year-old innocently replied, "But Grandma, I went yesterday!"

care for the older children. Since we'd enrolled Sarah in the local school's first grade, one of my mother's primary tasks was walking Sarah the short, one block distance to school.

Since Kathy had homeschooled Sarah for kindergarten, the young girl was not at all familiar with the public school system. Nevertheless, on the first day of class, she dutifully got up, dressed, and walked to school at her grandmother's direction. The second day, my mother again woke Sarah and directed, "Get up, Sarah. It's time to go to school."

The surprised six-year-old innocently replied, "But Grandma, I went yesterday!"

As my mother's stay stretched seven times longer than antici-pated, she simply hunkered down and determined to be there for us as long as necessary. Many friends from our church as well as dear friends who lived nearby in St. Louis reached out to us and offered to help while my mother held down the fort in Illinois.

Meanwhile, in Michigan, Kathy daily struggled with discour-agement as Caleb's long recovery flip-flopped from marginally positive to abject defeat. Kathy's daily and often despondent messages sent from Caleb's bedside evoked a strong sense of desperation in me. What could a father do when his six-month-old son and wife were over five hundred miles away?

During these days, I often felt numb, impotent, frightened, and helpless. I knew I had to act, but I felt so lost and far away. My other three small children sorely needed a parent, but my mind was always with my chronically ill baby and his mother. It was often difficult to even hug my other children who were seven, five and three.

I felt so disconnected and lost. Nonetheless, despite my sluggish stupor, I sprang into action each time my wife called and requested I come join her at our son's bedside. My autopilot sense of duty kicked in each time. Focusing on accomplishing my duties was the only genuine respite from my mind-numbing fear.

One weekend when I flew to Michigan, we arranged for Kathy to fly home to Illinois to see our other children. Our St. Louis friends offered to meet Kathy at the zoo so our children and theirs could enjoy the zoo together. Messages such as the one that follows meant so much during this exhausting time.

RE: Caleb Update: Thurs, 18 Sep

Kathy,

We are still waiting and praying for some good news about Caleb. You must be exhausted. I wish we were there just to be able to see you and give you some encouragement in the flesh. We're doing what we can to hold your arms up like they did for Moses. Don't give up. God is still in control, no matter what the outcome. We have some good friends there in Ann Arbor who I'm sure would do anything they could to help you if you need a place to take a shower or a nap. Let me know if you want me to contact them.

Maybe we'll see you this weekend at the zoo, but please only come if you want to and have the energy. If you just want to spend the weekend at home with the kids, we understand. There is no pressure at all to go with us...I'll check with Joan at the end of the week.

Well, I'll let you go for now, Carol

Many friends sent us expressions of love and support. We marveled as friends held up our arms in prayer as Moses' aides did when Israel battled their enemies.

. . . .

Holding up your arms: Thurs, 18 Sep

Dear Kathy,

I sit here at the keyboard and wonder what I can say to truly be of help to you. I know that when you are so close to a situation, it can be overwhelming when you look at all of the circumstances. It is in times like these that praying in faith and calling those things that are not as though they are, are the hardest things to do. I believe God gave us the best example of this when Aaron and the other Hebrew held up Moses' arms when he was too tired to do so.

So I guess the best thing I can say to you is that many are holding up your arms in prayer. And the best thing of all is that the battle is not ours, but it's the Lord's. We have all committed Caleb into His hands and now it is up to Him. Not to say that we will quit praying, but now I believe it is time to praise Him for the answer that is on its way.

With much love, Jennifer

. . . .

We cherished each and every message and note of encouragement. The sentiments relayed by Jennifer, a new friend in Illinois, gave us just enough hope to stave off utter discouragement. The emotionally bolstering impact of such messages of love and support were inestimably important. I did my best to reply to each person in appreciation for their support.

....

Caleb Update: Fri, 19 Sep

He genuinely seems better. He's eating again. The doctors are aggressively trying to get the upper lobe of his right lung to clear.

Tomorrow will be a big test day. He'll have an upper gastrointestinal X-ray, a 12-hour breathing study, and a diaphragm function X-ray.

Kathy is ecstatic to be able to spend two days with the three older children and Grandma at home in Illinois while I'm here in Michigan for the weekend with Caleb. She'll return on Saturday evening and then I'll go back to work in Illinois.

David

....

RE: Caleb Update: Sat, 20 Sep

Dear David and Kathy,

My prayers and thoughts are with all of you every minute of each day. You all have the strength of an ox. I wish I could be there with you during all this. I worry about the two of you also.

I Love You All, Danielle/Aunt Danielle

....

Caleb Update: Much Better Today: Sun, 21 Sep

Today Caleb was nearly back to his cheerful old (old?) self. He smiled and laughed quite a bit. Yesterday's echocardiogram showed good heart function, for Caleb: less tricuspid regurgitation, no plural effusion, that is no fluid around his lungs, but still a collapsed upper lobe of the right lung.

He is eating well but still on continuous feeding. We hope to wean him off the continuous feeds soon.

I'm enjoying my second night in the hospital. Caleb finally fell asleep at 12:28 AM. Just now a two-year-old moved into the bed next to Caleb. She is very loud...crying...unhappy...keeps saying, "I want to go home!" I'm hoping Caleb will not be awakened by her incessant crying...so far so good.

David

Finally, after seventy days, Caleb was strong enough to go home. All total, I had spent thirty days away from work, including days traveling. Hence, in just one hospitalization, I had exhausted all 30 days allotted annually to military members to attend to serious medical issues for their dependents. If I needed more time off to attend to my son during the current calendar year, I would need general officer approval. I hoped it wouldn't come to that.

On a pleasant late fall afternoon, shortly after our return from Michigan, Kathy and I sat on our back patio, enjoying a few moments of quiet while watching our children play. We surprised ourselves as we suddenly and unexpectedly recounted the harrowing and absurdly challenging events we'd endured since Caleb's birth.

"David, do you realize what we've just been through?" Kathy inquired as she began to rattle off the events of the last six months: "the shock of Caleb's unknown and numerous birth defects, his first surgery just hours after birth, the excruciating flight to the States and separation from our other kids, the month-long California hospitalization with two more major surgeries, the grueling flight to Michigan, the stress of finding a new USAF officer position as well as our sudden move from Japan to Illinois, the month-long stay and fourth surgery in Michigan, and the hasty purchase of a house and two vehicles. Oh…and don't forget the untimely chickenpox followed by my grandmother's unexpected death, Caleb's second open-heart surgery, and the agonizing 70-day hospitalization followed by a sixth surgery."

"Well…uh…let's see if we can make the next six months a bit calmer," I thoughtfully replied.

Several months after the infamous seventy day hospitalization and just after his first birthday, we took Caleb to see a general pediatric surgeon at the Washington University Children's Hospital in St. Louis. Having been referred to this doctor by our son's local cardiologist, we sought help to repair Caleb's imperforate anus and urinary rectal fistula.

The young, energetic surgeon readily agreed to perform this, our son's seventh surgery, commonly known as the pull-through. This surgery, which resulted in constructing a neo anus or new man-made anal opening, was successful; unfortunately, Caleb's heart was deemed too weak to justify a subsequent operation to close his colostomy. Therefore his loop colostomy continued as his primary means of waste disposal.

I wondered why we'd risked anesthesia for the pull-through if we weren't able to close off the colostomy. I alternated between fighting dark, depressing thoughts and brightly anticipating the future. Deeply depressing was the possibility that I'd unnecessarily pushed our son too hard for the pull-through surgery. Yet, on the other hand, with a positive attitude I anticipated the victorious day when we could finally close off Caleb's colostomy and attempt to put his neo anus into operation.

Over the next spring, Caleb was plagued by various illnesses as well as a subsequent hospitalization caused by dehydration as a result of a severe rotavirus infection. One Friday evening, little more than one week after the pull-through, Kathy became concerned about what she considered excessive bleeding from the repair site.

Consequently, she called the phone number the surgeon had given her for emergency after-hours concerns. The senior fellow on duty suggested she bring Caleb into the emergency room for evaluation by his staff. She proceeded to comply with his suggestion, only to later regret her decision.

Upon arrival at the ER, Kathy was amazed to observe so many young patients awaiting treatment but not surprised when she soon learned of the near epidemic of rotavirus in the St. Louis area. The ER visit ended with the surgery fellow having advised her that although the neo anus site may not have looked satisfactory, it was healing normally. During the drive home, Kathy experienced a deep sense of foreboding as she realized our son had likely been unnecessarily exposed to this virus. Her worst fears were realized when less than ten days later we had to admit Caleb to the hospital with severe dehydration due to excessive vomiting and diarrhea related to the rotavirus.

For the next three weeks, Caleb rode quite a hydration roller coaster. Kathy stayed home while I spent night after night in the hospital sleeping on a four-foot long vinyl sofa next to the hospital crib. I awoke frequently each night, drenched in my own uncomfortable sweat. Since I had exhausted my available time off from work, we decided I would remain on duty and accomplish my work tasks from Caleb's hospital room while Kathy stayed home with the other children. After all, we expected Caleb to remain in the hospital for only a couple of days. Little did we know the hospitalization would stretch into three weeks.

I continued performing my official duties from Caleb's hospital room. My responsibilities at that time included managing and facilitating direction of the airlift supporting President Clinton's extensive month-long trip throughout Africa. What a sight I was juggling the hospital room phone, my cumbersome official business mobile phone, and three large 3-ring binders that contained details of dozens of the airlift missions supporting the president's travel.

Despite their inquisitive or disapproving glances, the staff was quite accommodating when I explained my responsibilities in support of the president. I continued to work because it was easier to accomplish the duties myself rather than take the time to train someone else to replace me. In addition, I did not want to ask my boss just yet to request of the general for more than the maximum allowed 30 days excused from duty to accompany a dependent for medical support. I thought it too early in the year to make such an extreme request. I would save that for a later date, hoping it would not become necessary.

All the while, I simultaneously attempted to tend to my severely dehydrated son. Some of the many nurses failed to hide their stark disapproval of a flight suit uniform-clad father constantly talking on all available phones, referencing his big books while attempting to supervise and contribute to his son's care.

Others simply shook their heads in disbelief as they observed the absurd scene.

CHAPTER 23

Caleb Won the Lottery!

As Caleb neared eighteen months of age, his echocardiograms began to show severe leakage of the tricuspid valve. His local cardiologist, Dr. Arnie Strauss, in coordination with Dr. Amnon Rosenthal, Caleb's Michigan cardiologist, and Dr. Ed Bove, his cardiothoracic surgeon, recommended we proceed with the Fontan procedure as soon as possible. I readily agreed; hence, Caleb was scheduled for the surgery at 18 months of age, somewhat sooner than the norm.

The objectives of this, Caleb's eighth operation, were not only to complete the third stage of the Norwood but also to cinch down the tricuspid valve, thereby decreasing its leakage. These repairs would decrease his heart's work load, thus mitigating further dangerous enlargement. However, after opening Caleb's chest, a surprised Dr. Bove gravely observed Caleb's severely enlarged heart. Therefore, the surgeon determined he could only repair the leaky tricuspid valve. Anything else was just too risky. We were devastated.

Although this recovery was not as prolonged as Caleb's previous recovery from cardiac surgery, it was nearly as topsy-turvy. There were times when we weren't sure he was going to make it. Through

I did not want to disappoint my wife or other faithful friends who seemed to assume I had such great faith. I did not. I was miserable.

it all, we tried to trust God. I found it increasingly easier to say than do.

I did not want to disappoint my wife or other faithful friends who seemed to assume I had such great faith. I did not. I was miserable.

Often I found myself wondering why our son was so afflicted when I had sought to live such a dedicated life of service. Intellectually, I understood it was foolish to assume any correlation between my faithfulness and life's circumstances. However, my mind was traumatized by this agonizing question; my only escape from being consumed was to refuse to insist on making sense of it.

I tried to force myself to stop entertaining the nagging why question. In great desperation, I found myself replacing contemplation with action. If only I could stay busy, presumably helping my son survive, perhaps I would not have to entertain my fearful doubts and nagging questions. I had the notion that if I refused to give thought to my doubts and fears as well as refused to entertain the questions of why, the pain would somehow be lessened. In reality, ignoring the gnawing questions was merely a temporary defense mechanism that only deadened the pain for a limited time. It did not remove the nagging questions.

Despite my introspective darkness, there were times of rejoicing. For the most part, between hospitalizations Caleb was a very happy child despite his complex medical problems that necessitated the administration of numerous daily medicines and procedures. Four times each day we had to draw up his medications. We administered the nine or more medicines he took daily by either inserting them directly into his stomach via his G-tube or by allowing him to take them from a syringe into his mouth. By and large he was very compliant and often declared, "I take it myself. In my mouth."

His features were smallish and his blue eyes penetrating. With his small pointed nose and squeaky voice, he was adorably cute. Due to the significant energy required to crawl, heart-failure babies, like our son, seldom do so but go straight to walking, albeit later than otherwise normal heart-healthy toddlers.

However, amidst the pandemonium of our active household and with his restless fighter spirit, Caleb refused to sit idle while his three older siblings raced around him. Consequently, at approximately eighteen months of age, Caleb began to implement a curious and adorably cute scoot maneuver to get around the house. Seated on his bottom while leaning on his right arm, he virtually pivoted and bounced from bum to right hand. He got to the point where he scooted remarkably quickly, leaning to the right, literally bouncing off his right hand and bottom as he motored along.

On Caleb's second birthday, we took him to see his local cardiologist who remarked, "He is doing fabulously well." Two days later, we celebrated Caleb's second birthday with over a hundred people attending the biggest birthday party we'd ever hosted. We had so much to celebrate.

More than a month before Caleb's birthday, we asked the children what type of theme they'd like for their brother's birthday party. They excitedly exclaimed, "We want a costume birthday party, Mommy!" We helped the children create their own costumes from two trunks of dress-up clothes. Wearing his father's pilot helmet and his Grandpa Foster's parachute jump suit, Andrew dressed as an astronaut. Sarah and Hannah Joy dressed up as a nurse and ballerina while Kathy dressed Caleb as a pilot in a flight suit, which had been made in Korea for his older brother several years before.

For more than two weeks, the children helped their father create two handmade papier-mâché piñatas, one shaped like a kitten and one like a bunny. During the birthday bash we discovered that their construction was a bit robust since it took all the children in attendance more than three strikes each at the tough-skinned piñatas to break them apart. Once an aggressive thirteen-year-old succeeded in breaking open the reinforced piñatas, the children scrambled for the candy and treasures that finally spilled out.

Just before his birthday, Caleb began to walk. This was the best present. As nine-year-old Sarah hoisted and held up her little brother by his hands, Caleb teetered on his own feet while she gently coaxed him to try to take a step. Finally, in response to her coaching, he did in fact take his first step, then his second, and a third. Within minutes, he was suddenly waddling all around the room with a beaming look of victory and grand accomplishment. Not only did Caleb begin to walk, but he also began to talk. And he talked and talked and talked and talked and talked.

Months later, on a Wednesday evening as we relaxed after dinner in the home of our friends Rich and Mary, our conversation was abruptly interrupted by their son Chris. He suddenly came running inside and exclaimed, "Caleb fell into the cactus patch and I can't pull him out!"

Rich and I rushed out to see Caleb wallowing in the cactus garden, desperately trying to stand up and walk out. I immediately stepped in, picked up my small son, and rushed him into the kitchen where Mary and Kathy began to remove the bothersome cactus spines. As I held Caleb, we were amazed to see hundreds of small transparent barbs imbedded in the small child's fingers.

Caleb was surprisingly calm until he felt the pain the sharp spines caused as his mother painstakingly pulled them out. As Caleb's patience wore thin, I tightened my grip to keep him still. In that I had to go to work later that night at the 24 hour Command Center at the base, I had already changed into my flight suit. Unbeknownst to me, the prickly barbs had already imbedded themselves into the body and sleeves of my flight suit, like a seamstress's pincushion.

As my overnight shift at the command center wore on, the sharp needles worked their way all around my flight suit, causing me no small discomfort. Occasionally I'd experience a sudden, sharp jab that elicited an involuntary, "Ouch!"

No amount of squirming in my chair eliminated the discomfort. What a sight I must have been as I wiggled and squirmed in my seat, seeking relief as the needles mysteriously jabbed me in sensitive areas of my body all night long.

That same year, in mid-spring, I was at work when the phone rang. I already had one client on hold on one of the four lines of my office phone system while I dealt with another headquarters customer face-to-face. I was juggling large-scale airlift requests made by NASA as well as requests from a couple other government agencies. My job was to facilitate the priority assessment system and allocation of limited USAF airlift resources.

It seemed everyone's airlift request was the highest priority. In reality, after researching the situations, it oftentimes turned out that what a certain individual saw as the highest priority was really not a sufficiently high enough priority to warrant reprioritizing limited USAF airlift resources. When I made the person requesting the airlift aware of such a determination—often at the eleventh hour, just in time for their mission to be canceled—what sometimes resulted were passionate, heated telephonic and occasional tense face-to-face conversations. Such was the case with the headquarters customer standing in front of me. He was not going to be easily dissuaded from continuing to press for his request to be supported.

Meanwhile, the customer on hold was in line to be told his boss was going to be disappointed because his airlift request could not be supported as well. He would learn this just two days before his several hundred ground troops needed to be transported from one location to another. They were scheduled to participate in an important large-scale military exercise involving several various National Guard and active duty U.S. military organizations, set to converge on a central location to simulate a regional military conflict.

With an active phone call on my telephone headset and two computers on my corner desk, I stood engaged with a customer who was passionately venting his frustration due to my inability to support his airlift request. In the middle of all of this, my wife called.

Another office mate took the call, put her on hold, and calmly announced, "Major, your wife on line three."

For the thirteen years I'd been an Air Force officer, my wife well understood and complied with the unwritten rule of my household: do not call your husband at work unless you have an urgent matter. I understood that as a military officer, taking personal phone calls while on duty was not only a poor example to younger troops and peers but it also detracted from accomplishment of my duties. Our days at the headquarters were long enough already. It made no sense to allow personal interferences to extend the workday by distracting me from tackling the tasks at hand.

Therefore, when I picked up my wife's call on line three, it was with a curt, "Yes, Dear, I have a customer on hold and one in front of me. Do you have something urgent?"

Her measured response ignored my question as she calmly uttered, "Dr. Strauss called."

Suddenly the room and my entire world seemed to wildly spin and an unexpected rage erupted from somewhere deep inside my gut. The information my wife was about to relay to me was to change and affect my life for the rest of my days. Kathy had received a call from Dr. Strauss. He relayed to her the contents of a letter from Dr. Bove, our son's cardiothoracic surgeon. Bove's letter included a copy of a letter to him from the assistant director of the University of Michigan blood bank.

Somehow, as soon as Kathy said, "Dr. Strauss called," I knew what she was going to say. I knew she was going to tell me that our son was infected with HIV. I do not know how I knew it, but just as it happened the moment after Caleb was born when I sensed an irresistible urge to roll him over and inspect his backside, I somehow innately knew our son was infected with the dreaded Human Immunosuppressant Virus.

My reaction to the call was violent. I loudly shouted, "No, No, God, No!"

In response to my angry shout, my wife wryly quipped, "If only that were true."

During my furious tirade, I struck the steel corner of my desktop with my fists. Not until the next day did I realize I had so vigorously pounded the steel desktop that not only had I bent it but also I had bruised the sides of my hands. They were sore and ached for days.

As illogical as it seemed, given the allegedly negligible HIV infection rate due to blood transfusion, I had frequently been ill at ease about my son so often needing whole blood during surgery. In fact, the chance of being infected with HIV from a single blood transfusion was about as low as the odds of winning the lottery with a single purchased ticket. Although the risk of infection was indeed low, unfortunately in this case, my paranoia was warranted.

As a friend ironically noted, "Caleb won the lottery!"

During the next several emotionally draining days as we pursued HIV testing for our son, I struggled to suppress the anger that had been simmering since that dreadful phone call. Finally, on Wednesday, April 14th, just one day after receiving final confirmation that indeed Caleb was HIV-positive, I lost my composure and angrily shouted at a fellow officer at the office. The resulting embarrassment was more than I could stand. The person toward whom I acted unprofessionally refused to back down and surprisingly raised himself up to engage in a near physical confrontation. The tense moment demanded diffusing.

Hence, at the command of our superior officer, we settled the matter in his office. Later that evening he took it upon himself to visit me at my home. With deep shame, I acknowledged to him that never before in all my years on active duty had I lost my composure on the job. I was so absolutely outraged since I'd learned my son had been infected with HIV due to a contaminated blood transfusion; I could scarcely control my raging anger.

"It's so unfair," I bemoaned. "Why should my son suffer at the hand of an immoral person who donated his blood, surely aware of his HIV at-risk behavior?" I told my boss it felt like my son had been raped.

CHAPTER 24

An Answer to Her Prayer

We learned that the donor, from whom Caleb had received a unit of blood during his second open-heart surgery, tested HIV-positive during a subsequent donation nine months later. Our son's pediatric cardiologist, Dr. Strauss, advised us to have Caleb tested merely as a precaution. He attempted to allay our fears by explaining that HIV transmission by donated blood is exceedingly rare, nearly unheard of in countries such as ours where the blood supply is tested for HIV antibodies.

He referred us to the specialized division of the pediatric infectious disease department at Washington University Hospital. The specialized division focused solely on HIV-positive children. Although traveling fifty minutes into the city simply to have our son's blood drawn seemed unnecessary given the numerous clinics much closer to us that could have drawn the blood and sent it to the specialized clinic, I agreed to make the drive.

Just one day after drawing Caleb's blood, Dr. Storch, the department chief directed his administrator to phone us and request my wife and I come to his office to discuss the test results.

During the call I pressed the administrator, inquiring why Dr. Storch wanted to see us face-to-face.

"We live over 40 miles away," I emphatically declared. "There's no reason for us to drive all that distance to meet with Dr. Storch unless the test was positive. Was it positive?" I demanded to know.

Apparently not knowing how to reply, she murmured something about standard protocol in a decidedly unconvincing fashion.

In response to her elusive answer, I further replied, "Okay, fine. I understand our son is indeed HIV-positive and you therefore want to officially advise us of that face-to-face. Well, since we already know he's positive, what more needs to be discussed today?"

The administrator, taken aback, began her measured response, "Well...ah...I think Dr. Storch wants to meet with you regardless of the test results...so, if you can please come right over, he'll be waiting for you."

"Yes, we'll make the fifty minute drive back to his office as a professional gesture, but please advise him that we'll need time to think through all the options before commencing any particular medical course of action."

"Of course, he'll expect that. Fine. We'll see you in fifty minutes."

As soon as I hung up the phone, I told Kathy that we were going back to Dr. Storch's office. More than a little perturbed, hope now completely deflated, she resigned herself to go along and see what they had to tell us. Before loading the car and driving back to the specialized clinic, I sent an urgent message to our mass e-mail list, requesting they pray for our son given his new HIV-positive status.

> The doctor and his startled staff looked at us as though we'd lost our minds.

Upon arrival at the clinic, the receptionist whisked us into a large conference room with a surprising number of individuals seated around the outsized table. Dr. Storch began by making too-polite introductions as we sat anxiously awaiting the inevitable and unwelcome announcement. My mind raced, expecting that the longer it took the doctor to complete his introductions and welcome, the less the chance the news was good.

Once Dr. Storch finally got beyond all the obligatory niceties, he gravely acknowledged our son was indeed HIV-positive. After making his anticlimactic pronouncement, Dr. Storch paused longer than necessary. Apparently the doctor assumed we would need time for the unwelcomed news to sink in.

After a much shorter pause than he'd anticipated, I spoke up and in my most businesslike voice declared, "Fine. Now that we have official confirmation of what we've known for the past two days, let's get down to business. What's the next step?"

With that, Dr. Storch began his careful discussion of our medial options. His dour countenance failed to hide his lack of pleasure at having to introduce yet another set of parents to his all-too-familiar world of juvenile HIV. Upon completion of the discussion, Dr. Storch advised us that it was important to understand we should be very careful not to advise anyone else of our son's HIV-positive status. He suggested that until we'd had adequate time to think it through carefully, we should not tell anyone, not even immediate family members. The doctor gingerly warned us, "Now, it takes time for this to sink in..."

"Doctor," I interrupted, "my son was born with major heart disease, a tracheoesophageal atresia and fistula, an imperforate anus and fistula, and has had eight major surgeries. I'm still coming to grips with his many major medical maladies. This is just another issue to deal with."

We laughed out loud at the doctor's ridiculous recommendation. The doctor and his startled staff looked at us as though we'd lost our minds. They were speechless. Kathy broke the ice by informing them of one of the likely differences between us and other HIV patients and their families.

"Oh, it's already too late to warn us not to tell anyone about his HIV-positive status, Doctor. We've already told several hundred individuals via e-mail, and they've likely forwarded the message on to hundreds more, perhaps thousands."

The look of shock on their faces was classic. Apparently, we were the first parents of a young patient who were not ashamed or afraid of the possible public rejection related to the stigma of HIV. Our perspective was that in the community of faith, in which we lived and moved, support would surely be maximized if our friends and family were aware of the struggles we faced.

As a result of the preliminary testing, we determined Caleb's immune system was moderately affected or "destroyed," as Kathy exclaimed. As my rage changed to confusion, I journaled my angst.

....

Wednesday, 12 May: Over a month ago, we received word that Caleb was transfused with a unit of blood from a donor who tested HIV-positive subsequent to that donation. How could this happen? So many people are incredulous. What am I? Am I incredulous? Am I angry? One thing is certain. I am confused. I am not prepared and am unwilling to immediately commence administering high-powered HIV medications to my son. I understand high-powered drugs such as these, rushed through the approval process due to the public outcry and fear of HIV, have numerous side effects, the likes of which are only now beginning to be understood—especially among children, and particularly among children with heart disease.

Telling our older children of Caleb's HIV infection was more tricky than I'd envisioned. We had intentionally not yet informed them since we knew it would require significant explaining. Nevertheless, children have an innate way of acquiring information before their parents intend. This was vividly illustrated for me as we put our children into bed the evening after learning Caleb was indeed HIV-positive.

As I was putting Andrew into bed, I began the discussion by asking him if he understood we had been taking Caleb for special, new medical tests.

To that query, the innocent six-year-old nonchalantly announced, "Oh, yes, Daddy. Caleb has HIV and he's going to die."

Wow! How was I supposed to take that? Andrew really took my breath away with his immediate matter-of-fact response. Since Andrew slept on the top of the boys' bunk bed and Caleb on the bottom bed, I quickly stole a look at Caleb, who didn't seem to have heard or understood the comment from his brother.

"Andrew, where did you get this information?" I wanted to know.

"We've heard you and Mommy talking about it," he innocently replied.

I guess we'll need to be more discreet in the future, I silently noted. "Andrew, you know your brother has many complex medical challenges that threaten his very life. Now, he just has one more, and we're going to do everything we can to help him overcome it and live. In fact, with God's and the doctors' help, we believe he is going to live a long, happy life. We just need to take extra care of him. Do you understand this?"

"Yes, Daddy," Andrew contentedly replied. Then he suddenly grew sullen and inquired, "Daddy, am I going to die too?"

"Why, no, Andrew. We hope and believe not any time soon. Why do you ask?"

"Well, if Caleb is going to die and you can't see his virus, I just thought I was going to die too."

"Oh, son, we're going to do everything we can for your brother who has some very difficult challenges because of some problems inside him, including this new virus, but there's nothing inside you that's a problem. We believe you are both going to live a long, happy life. But, I'm glad you told me about your concern. I want you to always be able to tell me about what you're thinking so I can help you." With that, Andrew turned, lay down, closed his eyes, and fell fast asleep.

"Oh, God," I prayed, "help me to help my children, especially when I don't know about or understand their thoughts and fears. And likewise, Lord, please help me be honest with You about my own dark thoughts and menacing fears."

I was learning that unfounded fears, if unspoken, grow in intensity and have a capacity to be paralyzing. They need to be verbalized to be defeated with logic, truth, and faith.

As soon as I got over my initial shock and began to come to terms with our son's newest medical challenge, I began reading all I could about not only the disease but also the controversial treatments. As a result of my reading and ponderings, I concluded that I would agree to traditional, albeit, very recently developed treatments; however, if we were to entrust our son's care to the doctors, I wanted to consult with the best in the field.

We requested to transport our son to the National Institutes of Health (NIH) in Bethesda, Maryland, just north of our nation's capital. The infectious disease department of Washington University was pleased to support our request.

We arranged for transportation through our base flight surgeon on an Air Force C-9 AIREVAC flight out of Scott to Andrews Air Force Base, from where we picked up a rental car. Dr. Strauss had prescribed oxygen for my son for in-flight use. Our documented goal was to keep his blood oxygen saturation at 70%. The average person with normal cardiac function can expect their saturations to be no lower than approximately 97%. The poor in-flight nurse was horrified when he observed my son's oxygen level at 73%. I tried unsuccessfully to encourage him that 73% was not a bad figure for our boy. The look of horror on the flight nurse's face was as laughable as pitiful.

The next several days spent at the NIH were days of victory as well as defeat. Our objective was to secure for our son the best specialists with the greatest sense of advancing HIV combat technology and treatments. The NIH objective was to treat and study certain HIV patients to help develop the latest anti-HIV treatments to ensure an eventual cure.

Specialist after specialist examined Caleb, putting him through a battery of tests from psychological to cardiac. The child development specialist was particularly amazed and intrigued by Caleb's keen fine motor skills and mental attentiveness. Our son became a star in the eyes of the NIH staff. Given his complex medical conditions, the staff recounted their amazement at how well he was doing all-around. I sent the following message the first night.

....

Caleb Update: Thurs, May 13

Since Caleb's arrival here at the NIH, he has amazed the medical staff. Many commented that they expected him to be sicker. The staff of the NIH, the foremost HIV experienced clinic in the country, has noted they are really shaken by Caleb's case. In other words, Caleb is one of a very few cases of HIV infection via blood transfusion they have become aware of since testing was implemented in 1985.

Along with winning the heart of each medical person we've met here today, Caleb amazed the neuropsychological examiners by demonstrating that his cognitive and fine motor development are on par with normal two-year-olds. Despite the danger of the HIV taking up residence in his brain and spinal cord, it would seem the child has suffered no ill effects yet. Thank God.

Caleb further amazed the pediatric cardiology staff when he slept through the one hour echocardiogram examination of his heart. The chief of the oncology/HIV centers told us he was shocked when he met Caleb. From listening to his staff discuss Caleb's case, he expected a child on life support, not the vibrant Caleb he met. We told him it was God who was responsible and deserved the credit, thanks, and praise for how well Caleb was doing.

Grace to you, David

....

The greatest event of the day was when we had the distinct privilege of explaining the life changing message of the Gospel to a fellow parent, a mother of five whose fourth child had a rare and very troubling medical syndrome aptly dubbed gigantism. At the age of two, her child already weighed over 200 pounds. It was downright comical observing our 20 pound two-year-old playing in the toy area next to her 200+ pound two-year-old son. Our primary concern was to ensure he didn't accidentally sit on Caleb while they played next to each other.

As we spoke with this mother, she explained that just the previous day she felt herself at the end of her rope. In desperation, she pleaded with God to send someone to help her understand what she was missing as well as help her deal with her son's tragic medical ordeal. She wept great tears of joy as we led her in prayer to accept the grace of God by acknowledging and placing her faith in Jesus Christ. That very day, Linda got an answer to her prayer.

CHAPTER 25

We Hurt Alone

As we lifted our heads after praying with Linda, the formerly distraught mother, with obvious relief in her voice, commented, "This is the best day of my life. I feel like I'm finally truly alive and filled with hope for the future, no matter what may lie ahead for my son. I am confident. I can finally face whatever may come." In amazement and awe, we thanked God for our encounter with Linda and her son.

After a week of evaluation and consultation with the various NIH doctors and specialists, we returned home. Although it was an encouraging week in that virtually every doctor who saw Caleb was amazed at how well he was doing despite his complex medical history, they ultimately declined accepting him as a patient due to his complex medical challenges—particularly his heart condition. Nonetheless, they validated the proposed treatment plan recommended by the infectious disease department at Washington University, St. Louis Children's Hospital.

Although Caleb appeared to be doing remarkably well, his immune system, in just two weeks, had already begun to show signs of weakening. Dr. Storch advised us that Caleb would become increasingly vulnerable to life-threatening opportunistic infections if the HIV attack was not soon thwarted. Therefore, we put Caleb on a regimen of three high-powered anti-HIV medications, called antiretrovirals. We asked our friends and family to pray with us for Caleb that he would suffer none of the troublesome side effects for which these medications were infamous.

I began to post some of my daily journaling at a website so friends could log in and follow our son's progress.

Caleb Update: Wed, Jun 23

As of today, Caleb has now been on antiretroviral medications for 30 days. The first two weeks were rather rough. Due to the significant increase in the volume of fluid medications he's now getting, he has struggled with frequent episodes of reflux accompanied by occasional vomiting. The refluxing is hard on this little boy, not to mention on his parents. It is always worse during the night when we'd like to be sleeping. It's agonizing to hear the little child retching as the gastric juices back up into his esophagus. The sound is frightening. Kathy has been laboring nightly with Caleb for over two years without complaint.

Caleb's next needed open-heart surgery, formerly scheduled for June 17, has been delayed until his immune system shows a positive response to the antiretroviral medications. Our specific objective is to improve Caleb's CD4 white blood cell count to above 500 cell/mm3. His last count was 256, a dangerously low level, making him vulnerable for opportunistic infections. Normal is 1,500 to 2,000.

A dear friend, Jennifer, spent an entire night with Kathy and Caleb, learning how to take care of Caleb's many medical needs. She had graciously volunteered to care for him while we vacationed at Pere Marquette, a state park north of Alton, Illinois. These days were a much needed time of refreshing.

Parents of chronically ill children need to take time away from the burden of caring for their ill child. Often parents will succumb to the ill-conceived notion that any time away is somehow disloyal. This is not so. Parents need to get away and recharge their batteries. But more importantly, the other children need uninterrupted time with their weary parents. This we set out to do as we hiked and played with our older children around Pere Marquette.

While relaxing at the state park, I read Elizabeth Glaser's book, *In the Absence of Angels,* which chronicled her courageous battle with HIV. She and her two children were infected with HIV by a blood transfusion she received after delivering her first child in 1981. Both she and her first child have since died of AIDS. My son and many others have Elizabeth Glaser to thank for her success in generating attention for private and public funding of pediatric AIDS research. Until just before her daughter died in 1988, there was no FDA approved pediatric HIV medicine. Today there are over a dozen, certainly largely in part because she forced the issue and raised millions of dollars for research through the Pediatric AIDS Foundation of Santa Monica, California.

Caleb continued to grow and develop remarkably well during the early summer despite the added challenge of adapting to the antiretroviral medications. He began to routinely repeat everything he heard his parents say as well as began to construct his own original two, three, four, and even five word sentences. That was fantastic progress for a child with such a difficult start.

> "If you don't use gloves, you may jeopardize the opportunity for your other children to have a father while growing up."

Despite the good news of Caleb's progress, despite the good sense we had to get away and vacation with our older children, and despite our daily diligence to provide the best care for each of our children, Kathy and I were struggling. My journal tells the story.

Sunday, 4 July: The past several months have been very trying. Kathy and I have fought like never before. I've been so restless, very frustrated, and often angry for seemingly no reason.

We had no manual to teach us how to avoid such frustration. We had no example to encourage us to have realistic expectations. We didn't know what expectations we ought to have. I reflected that it took an additional three to four hours per day to adequately care for Caleb. We had to draw up his medicines. He took very specific doses of more than eighteen different medicines, six times per day. Each had to be carefully measured and drawn into various syringes. We had to carefully measure the special nutritional formula we pumped into his stomach or by G-tube each night. His colostomy bag required frequent cleaning, repair, and replacement.

Each time we handled his colostomy or other body fluids, we were advised to use medical gloves to protect us from the potential danger of HIV. We emptied box after box of latex medical gloves. As illogical as it was, I struggled with the feelings of disloyalty to my son as I initially considered donning the gloves to care for him. I settled the matter in my deeply conflicted mind by resolutely declaring, "I won't wear gloves to care for my own son."

An insightful friend, aware of my angst over this issue, gently admonished me by saying, "If you don't use gloves, you may jeopardize the opportunity for your other children to have a father while growing up." Thus, with my friend's helpful rebuke, I realized my other children were depending on me as much as Caleb. They were depending on me to remain healthy and alive. Therefore, I put on the gloves.

On a certain Saturday when Kathy was away working her weekend job as a home health care nurse, Caleb suffered four colostomy blowouts all in one morning. As I laid him on the dresser that doubled as a changing table, I observed we'd run out of latex gloves. To make matters worse, I had an open hangnail on one of my fingers, making me potentially vulnerable to the menacing danger of HIV infection.

"This is not a good day, and I am not entirely pleased." I declared to no one in particular.

I once estimated I spent ten to fifteen hours per week making telephonic medical arrangements. I coordinated with doctors, established medical referrals, followed up with medical insurance issues, and ordered Caleb's exorbitantly expensive and rare medications as well as latex gloves, colostomy supplies, and enteral feeding supplies. There were several mountains of paperwork. I filled five 3-inch 3-ring binders as well as two file cabinets with his medical and insurance paperwork. He had medical appointment after appointment. We had his blood drawn frequently to monitor his immune system status. He had to see the gastroenterologist, the cardiologist, the infectious disease specialist, and his own primary pediatrician at the base. I weekly or more frequently ordered and picked up his medications.

Despite the exhausting extra attention and care Caleb required, on more than a few occasions when awakened to the pitiful and discouraging sound of the two-year-old retching in the middle of the night, I'd get out of my own comfortable bed to go tend to him. Notwithstanding my extreme fatigue, upon laying Caleb back into his bed, I'd find myself plagued by a compelling restlessness that held me in a sleepless fit. I'd go into my study and would find myself alternating between fierce anger and longing for relief from my lonely agony as well as from my son's many sufferings.

In the excruciating quiet of those wee hours, I felt so alone. In a house with a wife and four children, my only weapon to distract me from the extreme loneliness was a seething rage, which I desperately tried to keep stuffed under the surface of my heart. I considered that my son had been so wronged by being infected with HIV through an infected unit of blood. I was enraged that a death sentence had been pronounced over our beloved Caleb by a donor who should have presumed he was giving life when he donated his blood, if not for his at-risk behavior.

After taking the high-powered antiretroviral medications for just six weeks, Caleb's viral load (amount of viruses per ml of blood) decreased from 28,000 in mid-April to less than 400 by mid-July. This was good news in that for all intents and purposes a blood test showing less than a 400 viral load meant the ongoing effect of the HIV virus on Caleb's immune system may have been effectively neutralized. We were thankful that although his immune system was still severely compromised, we could now expect it to begin rebounding. Nevertheless, we couldn't help but wonder what effect these high-powered anti-HIV medicines would have on his restructured heart.

Dr. Strauss in St. Louis, after consulting with Dr. Bove in Michigan, called in mid-August to relay his latest evaluation of Caleb's heart. His assessment was not good news. He was not inclined to advise we proceed with attempting the Fontan, the third vitally needed heart surgery, which had been unsuccessfully attempted one year prior. His recommendation was based on two issues. First, he felt Caleb's heart, aside from his HIV-positive status, was too weak to warrant risking the surgery. Second, given the weakness of his heart, the surgery might not actually improve his circulation, in other words, likely accomplish nothing beneficial.

We were devastated. The most disconcerting aspect of this news was that because Caleb was HIV-positive, a heart transplant was no longer an option. The normal protocol for a heart transplant patient is to suppress the body's immune response through medication, thereby decreasing the body's tendency to reject the new foreign heart. In Caleb's case, our medical objective was to enhance his already compromised immune system. A heart transplant would put us at cross-purposes, thereby increasing the likelihood that Caleb's body would reject a new heart. Therefore, for Caleb, a heart transplant was out of the question.

Caleb's options were now limited to miraculous healing, a medical advance sufficient to allow heart transplantation for HIV-positive patients, or a breakthrough in cardiothoracic surgical therapy for children with Hypoplastic Left Heart Syndrome. The somber news of our now limited options was sobering. We silently wept alone, unable to even embrace each other. Neither Kathy nor I had the strength to face the other. We hurt alone—isolated in our own personal dungeons of despair.

The topsy-turvy news flip-flopped from dire to decent. One month later, in September, Caleb's infectious disease specialist notified us of the latest blood test results. Caleb's immune system had begun to rebound, albeit very gradually. His CD4 count was now up to 395 from a low of 256. Though there was still a long way to go to get to 1,500. His count had been slowly climbing since commencing the antiretroviral medications. His viral load was now down to 41, down from just under 400 the previous month, and down from an initial high of 28,980.

CHAPTER 26

With Renewed Hope

About that time I began to feel chills as I prepared for bed one night. The next morning I awoke to the vivid discomfort of a scratchy throat and mild headache. I was greatly concerned about the potential of introducing germs into our household with an HIV-positive son whose compromised immune system made him precariously vulnerable to infection. Therefore, I phoned the flight surgeon's office at the base clinic and requested their first available appointment.

Later that day at the clinic, as the medical technician took my vital signs, I shocked her with my reply to her standard queries about my reason for coming into the office. I calmly advised, "Due to my two-year-old son's HIV-positive status and resulting compromised immune system, I want to do everything I can to avoid introducing contamination, be it viral or bacterial, into my home in order to help protect him from the danger of opportunistic infection."

"Ah…ah, yes…s, Sir," the terrified tech nervously stammered. She quickly completed her checklist and rushed me to the first available examination room.

After once again getting through the strained introductions and explaining my reason for seeking medical attention, the flight surgeon compliantly prescribed as many symptom-easing medications as I knew existed. The doctor's fingers seemed to fly across his computer as he keyed in numerous prescriptions, such as Tylenol, Motrin, and Robitussin. Finally satisfied he'd prescribed all that he could think of to combat my various viral symptoms, he also added a prescription for a general antibiotic—just in case I was to also unexpectedly suffer a bacterial infection.

The young lieutenant colonel excitedly declared, "Let's get you a surgical mask to wear around your son whenever you feel any symptoms coming on."

"Sure. Thanks, Doctor," I flatly replied as I unenthusiastically stood to leave his office.

"Wait a minute," the energetic physician beckoned. I dutifully returned to my seat as he vigorously motioned with his hands as though holding a basketball in front of him. He enthusiastically declared, "If you can just hold onto your son for five more years, as rapidly as medical technology is advancing, I'm sure within that time there'll be a cure for his heart disease and HIV infection."

I could muster no response other than to thank him with a weak nod of acknowledgement for his enthusiasm and positive anticipation of development of a cure in time to save my son. In my mind I thought him foolishly optimistic. But in my heart, I wanted to believe his optimism. I yearned to embrace the possibility, but in the drudgery of this difficult and dismal day, it was impossible for me to grasp. Nevertheless, I would remember and speak of his words again and again over the coming years.

"There'll be a lot of his blood around the operating room, you know!"

Later that day I smiled as I recalled the doctor's enthusiasm and imagined myself cleverly replying, "Okay, Doctor. I'm holding him. Now what do I do?"

In the meantime, I called Dr. Bove in Michigan to discuss our son's case. I gave him a status update of Caleb's latest encouraging HIV numbers and made a strong case for proceeding with the Fontan. I argued that we needed to give our son every fighting chance to live to adulthood, even as we were counting on a medical breakthrough to help bring ultimate healing treatment.

Although the surgeon seemed willing to be convinced, he declared, "No one's ever operated on an HIV-positive cardiac patient before. There'll be a lot of his blood around the operating room, you know!"

"I don't care about that," I retorted. "If my son needs this procedure and is strong enough to handle the rigors of anesthesia, then we need to proceed. After all, it was in your facility—using blood your hospital blood bank purchased from the American Red Cross—where my son was infected with HIV in the first place."

After receiving the latest information from Caleb's most recent cardiac study, Dr. Bove agreed to perform the surgery. We scheduled the procedure for November 2nd, which would give Caleb's immune system more opportunity to continue to strengthen.

By the end of October, Caleb's immune system showed signs of rebounding. His CD4 count of 428 was up from 395 the previous month. This was a good trend, good enough to encourage the cardiologist to agree with the surgeon in recommending going forward with the next open-heart surgery. However, in the less-than-good news department, Caleb's viral load had crept back up to 543 from an exceptional low of 41. While this number was not a great concern, it was cause to monitor him more closely. More closely monitoring Caleb meant more blood draws.

For me, the parent with the duty of taking the child to the phlebotomist, this news was certainly not good. Although our clever son was only two and a half years old, he knew full well where we were going when it was time to go have his blood drawn. He was reasonably cheerful whenever I put him into his car seat. He was a cheery companion as we walked into the hospital or clinic, but once he began to recognize the stark white walls of the laboratory, he began to try to writhe out of my arms or let loose of my hand. Sooner or later, I'd have to pick him up and carry him the rest of the way into the inner sanctum of the blood lab as he squirmed, wriggled, and protested, "I want to go home. I want to go home."

Although it hurt, as his father, to have to wrestle him to the phlebotomist's chair, I would usually challenge the technician and try to divert attention from my squirming son by joking, "He's tough. He'll take it with a dirty needle."

Remarkably, once the technician began her procedure by tying the rubber-hosed tourniquet around Caleb's arm and searching for his many-times poked veins, he suddenly sat motionless with barely a whimper. It was as though he resigned himself and seemed to understand from experience that if he relaxed, it would be over sooner and hurt less—what a remarkable child.

On Halloween of that year, we packed up the car and made the trip from our home in southern Illinois, just east of St. Louis, to the University of Michigan Children's Hospital for the third time. Caleb was scheduled for an evaluatory cardiac catheterization on Monday, November 1st, with open-heart surgery tentatively scheduled for the next day. If the catheterization didn't reveal any unexpected problem area, we would proceed with the final heart reconstruction surgery.

We nervously hoped the catheterization would reveal that Caleb's heart condition warranted the inherent risk this surgery afforded. The objective of this final surgery, known as the Fontan, was to attempt, for the second time, to complete the rerouting of Caleb's circulation, thereby reducing the overall workload on his weak heart. A dear friend from Illinois had set up a website for us to post updates on Caleb's medical status. The next day, after the catheterization, I posted the following update.

Caleb Update: Mon, Nov 1

Today was a long but productive day. We had a good consultation with both Caleb's cardiologist and cardiothoracic surgeons. The indications from his cardiac catheterization show we are clear to go ahead with the second attempt at the Fontan tomorrow. We are hopeful we'll experience none of the frightening complications we've faced in the past, even though there are many risks involved with this procedure. Thanks to all for your love and prayers. David

I advised the medical staff that I would not authorize any blood or blood products be administered to my son except from a specific directed donor approved in advance. Approximately one week before surgery, a Michigan cousin donated a unit of whole blood for Caleb's exclusive use during or following cardiothoracic surgery. He made his donation at a blood bank in Ann Arbor, Michigan. The staff then transported the unit of blood to a testing laboratory in Detroit.

The day of Caleb's surgery, just before they placed him on heart-lung bypass, I called the OR to confirm the directed donor unit of blood had arrived. I was shocked when the OR personnel answered, "What directed donor blood?"

In my outrage, I immediately called the surgical coordinator and demanded she stop progress on my son's opening until we could ascertain the status of this unit of blood. She advised me that we only had about forty-five minutes before it would become too risky to delay further, given the weakness of Caleb's heart.

Within minutes, the blood bank determined that unfortunately, the unit of blood had not yet been transferred from the Detroit laboratory. Immediately I called the surgical coordinator and insisted she get personally involved in resolving this dilemma. Several long minutes later she called me back to confirm the blood was en route to the OR in a taxi. I therefore told her to authorize the procedure to commence.

The surgery was a smashing success. Consequently, I e-mailed our large following of supporters.

Caleb Update: Fri, Nov 5

Thanks to all those who are praying for our little fighter. Caleb came through surgery on Tuesday with flying colors. We experienced a few bumps in the beginning as the directed donated blood was nowhere to be found. We thought we were going to have to make a choice between proceeding with the surgery without the blood or rescheduling, but the blood was found in Detroit, an hour away, and sent immediately via taxi. The blood arrived just in time as Caleb came off heart-lung bypass. He was immediately transfused with this unit of whole blood.

Caleb's numbers looked good right after surgery. That is, the pressure in his heart was good. The next day, his atrial pressure was a little high as his heart was adjusting to the new blood routing, the Fontan circuit. He also had to have another chest tube put in to allow air around the left lung to escape and to enhance fluid drainage. He was extubated Wednesday morning; hence, we were able to restart his HIV medications Wednesday evening after being off just 96 hours.

There is a delicate balance between maintaining his heart care and HIV treatment. We are also hoping that Caleb has little drainage from his chest cavity via his chest tubes. Some children remain in the hospital for up to a month waiting for the drainage to subside following this procedure. Persistent drainage will put dangerous stress on Caleb's tenuous immune system.

This precious young child seemed to thrive in the midst of such medical misery. Caleb amazed us with his bright, unflappable smile, which he sported within an amazingly short period of time after the nurses extubated him, even when still groggy from the strong medications. His endearing, cheerful nature rewarded the many family and friends who came to visit. My brother, John, and his wife, Cindy, made it a point to arrange their schedules to make the two-plus hour drive to come visit our son whenever he was hospitalized in Michigan. We were immensely encouraged by their thoughtful gesture.

On Thursday, Caleb was transferred from the Intensive Care Unit to a standard private room. He continued to make marvelous progress. Meanwhile, I enjoyed the opportunity to greet and briefly speak with a nine-year-old Bosnian cardiac surgery patient. Samaritan's Purse, a Christian relief ministry headed by Franklin Graham, transported the young child and sponsored his medical care. Sofet's fast recovery from surgery amazed all observers. He was released from the hospital that afternoon. He smiled nearly as widely at my American accent while speaking my limited Bosnian as he did when the doctors told him he could go home.

During this hospitalization we embraced many opportunities to encourage and pray with other families who were dealing with desperate situations. All but the most hardened of parents appreciated the smallest gesture of concern. One couple, parents of a three-day-old son born with numerous congenital defects, including missing feet and hands, wept mixed tears of sadness, anxiety, and joy as we spoke together at the Ronald MacDonald House until the wee hours of the morning.

At one poignant moment, the father held his wife's hands and declared that armed with renewed faith and courage after hearing our story, they could marshal on for their newborn son one more day. With renewed hope, they would not give up.

CHAPTER 27

A Successful Surgery

On Sunday evening, we nearly pulled one of Caleb's remaining drainage tubes completely out of his chest. The evening on-call doctor came, pulled the tube the rest of the way out, and stitched the wound closed. The doctor commented that the day staff would likely have removed the chest tubes earlier except they could not believe Caleb had only drained 14.5 ounces of fluid versus the normal two to three times that amount.

The next day Caleb was weaned from supplemental oxygen and his pacer wires removed. After he received a discharge echocardiogram, Bove's surgical nurse practitioner, Louise, told me Caleb's tricuspid valve was not leaking at all. Great news. This valve's leakage had been quite troublesome in the past. She also took the opportunity to remind me that Caleb's heart function was not normal. "Not normal," she explained, "for anyone, Hypoplastic Left Heart Syndrome (HLHS) or not." She further explained that Caleb's abnormal heart function amazed the doctors in that this child's uniquely poor heart function was apparently sufficient for him. Once again, we gave God glory and

> *Once again, we gave God glory and thanks for a child whose heart continued to amaze us all, particularly the doctors.*

thanks for a child whose heart continued to amaze us all, particularly the doctors.

More good news followed the next day. We had enrolled Caleb in a study designed to help surgeons understand how to better perform the required surgical procedures for future HLHS patients. The focus of the study was the heart's electrical system. Consequently, the day after surgery our pediatric cardiologist, Dr. Rosenthal, conducted further testing on Caleb's heart in the catheterization laboratory. Dr. Rosenthal was unable to send Caleb's heart into an arrhythmic condition when he pulsed it with a mild electric charge. This good news indicated Caleb was likely not in danger of experiencing an electrical arrhythmia—a danger to which HLHS patients were often prone.

Caleb Update: Tues, Nov 9

Thanks again to all who are praying for our little fighter. Amazingly, he was released from the hospital yesterday. Now we are watching him at Kathy's parents' farmhouse to be sure he is strong enough to endure the 500 mile drive home to O'Fallon, Illinois.

People often asked what we were learning in the midst of such trying times. Most importantly, we were learning that life is a gift from God. We came to understand we ought to cherish and appreciate it more than we had before. Our lives are very fragile and temporary. As James wrote, our lives are but "a vapor that appears for a little time and then vanishes away."[5] While we and so many others were appropriately exerting so much time and energy trying to help our son extend his life, we ought not to have forgotten that in the grand scheme of things, whether 70, 80, or even more years—life is short.

Therefore, it's all the more important to be mindful of things spiritual and eternal. For all are destined to die and then face the judgment. Thank God we needn't face that judgment alone. Christ Jesus came into the world to die to pay the penalty for our sins. God did this because He loves us. Jesus said to God, His Father, one day in prayer, "Now this is eternal life: that they know you, the only true God."[6] Knowing God is the key not only to life eternal but also to life abundant.

By late November we were generally pleased with Caleb's progress since his most recent surgery; however, his blood oxygen saturation (sats) continued to hover around 65%. A person with a normal heart has sat levels in the 95 to 100% range. With his new reconfigured blood flow, Caleb's sats should have been reaching the 80 to 85% range. In that Caleb had been demonstrating a general lack of energy and mild irritability, we decided to take him to see his St. Louis cardiologist for another echocardiogram. "Kathy, this must be Caleb's 100th echo!" I chided.

After the echocardiogram, we discussed with Dr. Strauss the possibility that Caleb's heart and circulatory system was having a difficult time adjusting to the new routing of his blood. We suspected the fenestration, an important release opening that the surgeon placed in Caleb's right atrial baffle during his November 2nd surgery, could be allowing more blood than expected to shunt into his atrium from the inferior or superior vena cava.

This errant shunting could mean some of the blood was not traversing to his lungs for oxygenation prior to being pumped back to the body—hence, his excessively low oxygen sats. Therefore, we decided if his oxygen saturation didn't improve within two weeks, we'd need to place him on oxygen while sleeping at night—wouldn't that be fun. Caleb was not fond of having the all too familiar oxygen cannula in his nose.

Often during errand running, it was a relief to Kathy and a pleasure for me to take Caleb with me. One particular day he accompanied me to the base hospital pharmacy to pick up his digoxin. As we stood in line, an elderly gentleman in front of us noticed my cute two-year-old standing next to me and turned around to say hello.

"Well, hello, young Fella. How are you? I see you've been eating a sucker. It was a grape sucker wasn't it? Was it good?"

In a decidedly less than patient tone, I replied, "No, Sir, he hasn't had a sucker. That's just his lip's natural color."

With incredulity, the white-haired gentleman intoned, "Well, of course he's had a grape sucker; his lips are purple."

"No! He hasn't had a sucker. So if you must know, that purple color is normal for him. He has a heart condition and we're in line to pick up digoxin, one of his heart medications."

The look of terror on the kindly gentleman's face was telling. He promptly turned away and likely marveled that it could be possible for a small, cute child like Caleb to have a heart condition. He probably understood heart conditions were only for old folks. If I'd been trying to get the old timer to buzz off, I succeeded. Unfortunately, the episode demonstrated that in my frustration, I became too easily impatient with people who had no particular reason to understand about my son. The man in line was simply trying to be friendly to a cute little boy.

As I later reflected on that incident, it served as a reminder that I needed to maintain my own health—mental, emotional, and physical—as I strove to help promote my son's health. In the stress of the normal business of life, I'd found it more difficult to set apart time for exercise at the gym. Likewise, I realized I'd often demonstrated impatience with my wife and other children—yet another sign I needed to take stock of my own state. I realized the poorer my own physical condition became, the easier it was to be irritable. Thinking back on that afternoon at the pharmacy, I firmly decided if nothing else, I would recommit myself to working out at the gym at least three times per week to help maintain my physical and emotional well being.

By mid-December, Caleb's HIV viral load was satisfactorily undetectable. This good news indicated that although we'd taken him off the antiretroviral medications from 72 hours before until 24 hours after his most recent open-heart surgery, there seemed to have been no ill effect. Be that as it may, the previous six weeks had been very challenging. The child had been quite uncomfortable. We suspected it was due to his increased hypoxia as his oxygen saturation continued to hover around 65%.

Caleb pitifully complained, "My eyes hurt...I'm tired."

Despite how pathetic he sounded, I was becoming increasingly weary of hearing him exclaim that he was tired. We knew we would have to do something. We just didn't know what.

In mid-February, we took Caleb to see another specialist, a gastroenterologist. In response to his query as to why we were there to see him, I responded, "We don't yet have your name punched on our dance card."

While he seemed only mildly entertained at my attempt at humor, he was gracious and offered us some insight we'd not learned from anyone else. He was convinced our son needed more calories. Consequently, we increased Caleb's daily caloric intake by increasing the amount and rate at which we pumped formula into his stomach at night. We also planned to conduct certain GI tests to help us try to rule out whether or not the repair from one of his past surgeries, his Thal fundoplication, may have come undone. We were concerned. Although Caleb had grown an inch taller and was nearly three feet tall by then, he had not gained any weight in over six months.

While in St. Louis at the children's hospital, we stopped in at Caleb's cardiologist to have his oxygen saturation checked. As we suspected, based on increased energy levels, his oxygen saturation was up from 65 to 70%. This was very good progress in that, medically speaking, Caleb's oxygen level had gone from bad to slightly less bad. We elected to think of it as having gone from not-so-good to a little better than not-so-good. We certainly saw a notable difference in his energy level with no more complaints about his eyes hurting.

On February 14th we paused to acknowledge the first annual National CHD (Child Heart Disease) Awareness Day. We sent a message to all Caleb's admirers, reminding them that heart defects are the most common birth defect and the number one killer of babies. If even minor heart defects are included in the statistic, it's estimated one in one hundred babies are born with heart defects. Obviously, the risk of a life-threatening heart defect such as Caleb's is much less prevalent; however, it is still a greater problem than most people realize. Increased awareness is certainly an appropriate goal.

Our own awareness of CHD was numbing. Caleb's improved oxygen saturation did not last long. By the end of March we were becoming desperate to determine the cause of the problem. During a subsequent echocardiogram at Dr. Strauss' office, we finally located the culprit.

Caleb Update: Sat, Mar 31

Caleb has been quite blue since his last heart surgery. Today we found out why. It seems he has a vein attached to his heart that is spilling blood to the wrong side of the heart. Consequently, this blood is not being oxygenated. Instead, it's getting pumped directly back to his body through his liver, bypassing his lungs. Surgery is required to rectify this erroneous circulation. We need to remove this errant vein as soon as possible. We expect the operation to be scheduled for the second week of May.

Regarding Caleb's HIV infection, his latest CD4 count is 230, down from a high of 495—not good. Nonetheless, with such a weak immune system, we thank God because the precious child has not suffered any AIDS-related opportunistic infections. Join us in praying he'll remain free of all infections.

As we anxiously awaited confirmation of the date for Caleb's next cardiac surgery, I departed for Savannah, Georgia, for training to fly the Gulfstream. I would be flying national and world leaders in this corporate aircraft from Andrews Air Force Base, Maryland.

In the middle of my training, Kathy called to inform me we had a date set for Caleb's fifth open-heart surgery, May 11th. Although it would not be easy, I would try to time our family's move to Washington, D.C., and my training so as to allow me to be present for our son's next operation.

The day of the surgery came, and much to our surprise, went remarkably well. The surgeon was elated he did not have to cut on Caleb's heart muscle. The troublesome hepatic vein, as Dr. Bove referred to it, was easily visible as soon as he opened our son's chest. Therefore, he simply ligated the errant vein and sewed up our precious son. Contrary to the frightening expectations of which the medical staff warned us, the surgical procedure was not only successful but much simpler than anticipated. We were as pleased as can be.

CHAPTER 28

We Laughed
Until We Cried

Because the surgeon was able to accomplish his objective without placing Caleb on heart-lung bypass, our son was taken off the respirator within four hours of surgery—yet another remarkable victory. The doctors were as absolutely amazed as we were. They'd never seen anything like it. We all were in awe. In celebration, immediately upon arriving at Grandpa's farm, my exuberant son climbed aboard the immense Massey Ferguson with his Papa Marion and took a tractor ride out to the corn fields. What a day of celebration it was. We then focused our attention on our upcoming move to the Washington, D.C. area.

Our families once again rose to the occasion and greatly helped us with the move. Carefully orchestrating our son's most recent cardiac surgery, moving our household, and beginning a new job is no small logistical undertaking. In early June, both Kathy and I traveled ahead of our children to sign in at Andrews AFB, our home for the next four years. We arrived early to secure the much in demand on-base housing so as to be nearby the base hospital, just in case Caleb required immediate medical care.

Two weeks later, Kathy's mother and mine drove the children to our new home. Their help in getting our family settled was inestimably valuable. Our biggest challenge was keeping Caleb out of the poison ivy, which I had found while building a tool shed in our backyard. Highly susceptible to poison ivy, I discovered too late that the area behind our base house was teeming with it.

One night, as my wife lay awake due to my incessant scratching of my terribly agonizing head-to-toe rash, she dryly asked, "So, Dear, I'm not sure I understand the reason for which you insisted on designing and building from scratch a ten by ten windowed tool shed, complete with a multicolor paint scheme and asphalt shingling during such a stressful time. Couldn't we just have purchased a prefab and paid to have it delivered and set up in our backyard?"

Obviously, my wife failed to comprehend her husband's claim that accomplishing such a project had great masculine therapeutic benefits.

In July, the children were invited to join some friends and attend Vacation Bible School (VBS) at a local church. Due to the exhausting duties of getting Caleb settled with his new doctors, encouraging her husband in his new job, and getting her home set up and organized, Kathy happily accepted the invitation from one of her best friends, Carleen, and sent the children with her.

To ensure Caleb made his way to the two- and three-year-old class, Carleen walked him to the teacher and nonchalantly advised her to be sure to use gloves if she had to handle his body fluids.

Overhearing the conversation, a suddenly distraught fellow parent demanded, "Why? He isn't HIV-positive is he?"

"Well, we aren't supposed to tell, but yes, he is," Carleen candidly replied.

The nearly hysterical parent emphatically declared, "Either he goes, or we go! I don't want an HIV-positive three-year-old in the same class with my child."

At that, Carleen realized the situation had gotten out of control, so she appealed to the children's pastor who calmly inquired, "Is he a genuine risk to the other children in the class?"

"No, he isn't," Carleen explained.

"Okay then, even if it means we lose the child whose mother is so distraught over this situation, Caleb may carry on and join the class."

After the initial commotion, the VBS teacher led the children out to the parking lot to jump in an inflated Moon Bounce. For some unknown reason, she decided to send the entire class into the Moon Bounce while Caleb was directed to wait his turn—outside the structure. He would play alone in the inflatable structure. He was only allowed inside after the other children had all finished their bouncing and exited the play area.

I never found out if he actually jumped alone or just stood still, peering through the clear vinyl window, wondering what to do all alone in the big bouncing play area. My heart broke with sorrow for my son when I learned of what had transpired. I couldn't avoid imagining the scene—my small son standing with a forlorn look in his eyes, all alone, gazing through the Moon Bounce window, not understanding whether or how to jump.

As difficult as it was getting acclimated to a new home, new job, new doctors, new pharmacy, new medical insurance provider, and new non-durable medical equipment supplier, we gradually settled into the hubbub of the Washington, D.C. area, known for its infamously congested Capital Beltway traffic.

Meanwhile, Caleb seemed to be having the best time of his life.

My administrative tasks included making the arrangements for unfamiliar and non-formulary medicine. This meant appealing to the base hospital commander, a one-star general, to ask for his approval to stock certain unusual and expensive drugs in the base pharmacy just for our son.

I also had to make arrangements for all the specialists needed to follow and treat my son. He needed not only a new pediatric cardiologist but also a new pediatric infectious disease doctor, a new general pediatrician, a new pediatric gastroenterologist, a new pediatric immunologist, a new pediatric audiologist, a new pediatric ENT, and a new pediatric optometrist. I spent hours too numerous to track making the various arrangements and appointments.

Meanwhile, Caleb seemed to be having the best time of his life. His blood oxygen saturation level, averaging 85%, was as high as it had ever been. He was growing. He was now about three and a half feet tall. He walked with a particularly peculiar stride. He leaned slightly to the right and swung his right arm rather vigorously while his left arm stayed relatively stationary at his side. He also often glanced up at others around him, and as soon as his mischievous look caught the eyes of his observers, he rapidly jerked his head and diverted his gaze away, presumably so as not to be caught checking on those around him. His slightly smug, crooked smile was irresistibly cute. His golden hair didn't entirely masquerade the notably flat spot on the back of his head, which had resulted from laying in one particular position for three weeks during the medically induced paralysis just after he was born.

At the dinner table, our family tradition is to read and discuss a short passage from the Bible or a devotional book after our meal. Each family member gets his or her opportunity to read from time to time.

Caleb often insisted on taking his turn. He would scramble to the nearby shelf to retrieve the illustrated children's Bible with its stiff cardboard-like pages, open it to a random story, and proceed to mouth the words he must have imagined the book contained. With his precious little head down, peering intently into the book in front of him, we would hear him annunciate, "Shwoeee shwoeee shwoeee... Shwoeee shwoeee shwoeee..."

If he sensed he was being interrupted or not listened to intently, he would pause his reading, look up, put his finger to his lips, and clearly declare, "Shush, I'm reading."

Approximately three cycles of Caleb's reading was all the older children could tolerate before one of them inevitably retorted, "Dad, Mom, can we have someone else read now? That is, someone who actually knows how to read."

At bedtime while administering his evening meds, if I impatiently began to open his G-tube, Caleb would often shake his head and declare, "No! I do it myself. In my mouth, not my tube." He would then take the medicine-filled syringe from me, squirt its contents into his mouth, and swallow. At other times for some unknown reason, perhaps just to prove who really was in charge, he would adamantly declare, "Put it in my tube!"

After our nightly medicine routine, Caleb would insist I read him a book, then another book, and yet another book until I was so tired that I just wanted him to lie down and go to sleep. I distinctly remember one night when he defiantly declared, "I need to read another book!"

"No, you don't need to read another book," I corrected. "You need to go to bed."

"I need to read another book!" he adamantly replied.

To this I responded by immediately putting him into his bed and declaring, "No. You don't need to read another book. You need to go to sleep."

Despite the challenges, that summer was pleasant. Caleb's cheerful, mischievous, fun-loving personality and calm demeanor shone as never before. He seemed as genuinely content and happy as any normal three-year-old. His speech development seemed right on par with that of the older Ingerson children. His defiant tendency was very mild and normal.

Caleb was a happy child despite his awareness of his tube and his bag. On more than one occasion, he came to his mother with a forlorn look while making a gentle, "Ah, ah ah," sound. When he knew he had her attention, he declared, "My bag! My bag! It's leaking!"

That was his way of telling us the colostomy bag's seal was compromised and its contents leaking—meaning the bag needed urgent attention. He simply didn't appreciate the mess. He wanted to keep clean and neat.

With a playground immediately across the street from our base house, the children and I enjoyed many pleasant afternoons swinging, climbing the various monkey bar play structures, and barreling down the three slides: two straight and one curvy, the children's favorite. Beyond a shadow of a doubt, the high-speed merry-go-round was their favorite attraction. Our primary objective, when Daddy served as the motor to drive the high-speed rotations, was to ensure all riders were securely positioned before the RPM's reached their highest speeds.

Daddy would inevitably get dizzy while the bright blue, yellow, and red painted pie pieces of the merry-go-round blurred into a hazy rainbow of orange, green, and mostly purple—the same color as Daddy's face while recovering from his huffing, puffing, and running next to the merry-go-round, pushing it to his maximum RPM.

One fine sunny afternoon while exploring the playground, Caleb slid down the curvy slide and lost his balance halfway down. He bumped his face on the edge of the slide, resulting in a minor nosebleed with some blood smearing on the support pole. Knowing his blood to be a hazard, I understood it was my duty to clean it off the play structure in order to protect any other child who might play there. Therefore, after dutifully instructing my older children to play safely and nicely, I walked Caleb home to his mother who'd care for his bloody nose.

As we departed the play area, Caleb declared, "I need to go swing."

While walking the short distance back home, I assured Caleb, "Yes, we'll go back to swing in a few minutes."

Kathy attended to Caleb's bloody nose while I prepared a solution of ten parts water and one part chlorine bleach to clean my son's HIV-contaminated blood from the play structure. Although we previously had the playground all to ourselves, upon our return, we observed another parent and child using the playground equipment.

The other parent, a mother, noticed me cleaning off the slide and asked, "What happened? What are you cleaning off? Is that blood?"

"Yes," I replied, "we noticed the blood on the structure and decided we'd better clean it off—you never know if a child who may have bled on the playground equipment might be infected with a communicable disease—HIV or something like that. We need to protect our children."

"Wow. Oh, yes. You're right. Thank you for doing that," the incredulous and appreciative mother declared, completely ignorant that the blood belonged to my child who was indeed HIV-positive.

Later that evening, Kathy and I enjoyed a hearty laugh as I relayed the scene to her. We laughed until we cried as we considered the reaction of this mother had she understood the blood on the slide to have belonged to our HIV-positive son. We imagined her appreciation and incredulity would have been replaced by shock and disapproval. Many times when the stress of caring for a chronically ill child feels overwhelming, a good laugh is as therapeutic as any medicine.

CHAPTER 29

A Day We Would
Never Forget

Caregivers for chronically ill patients often struggle with mixed and challenging emotions. Our awareness of the numerous and precarious medical challenges our son faced induced much mental anxiety as we considered what the future might hold for him. Nevertheless, I was particularly keen to do all I could to help ensure no other child was infected with HIV due to a simple blood transfusion.

As a result of seeking out others who were doing what they could to help stem the dangers of transfusing HIV-infected blood, I came across NAVTA, the National Association of Victims of Transfusion Acquired AIDS. I joined their membership and subsequently had been invited to join their board of directors and serve as Secretary.

One Sunday evening, after depositing the children in bed and preparing for bed ourselves, I began to discuss with Kathy the NAVTA planned activities that would include our son participating in various media opportunities in support of the fight against blood transfused AIDS.

Kathy suddenly slapped me hard across the face...

My wife forthrightly declared, "No! I do not want my son to become some poster child for transfusion-acquired AIDS."

Suddenly, seething with rage because my wife would dare defy my word, I immediately responded by getting right up in Kathy's face.

From two inches in front of her face, nose to nose, I adamantly retorted, "But we need to use him to help our cause while he's still young and cute." I vigorously pronounced, "I am the man in this house and I have decided that this is what we're going to do."

In response, Kathy suddenly slapped me hard across the face while adamantly retorting, "No! I can't stand to have our son paraded around and see his face on newspaper and magazine covers. He is a child. I want him to enjoy his childhood."

She slumped onto our bed and continued crying into her hands while I stood dumbfounded and insulted, having just been slapped by my wife of fourteen years. With an offended male ego and a powerful adrenaline rush, I calmly but angrily advised my wife in no uncertain terms: "My wife does not slap her husband in my house."

I was so angry. Never before in our years of marriage or years of courtship had either of us assaulted the other. I had never laid a hand on my wife. I was so incensed; I refused to allow her to so offend me. Therefore, after regaining some semblance of control, I adamantly advised Kathy that if she was going to lose control and slap her husband, it was a certainty she needed immediate mental health intervention.

Therefore, at that very instant I would call the base hospital in order to coordinate her admission to the mental ward until we could isolate and treat the cause of her violent and offensive behavior. Still incredulous that my wife had actually slapped me, with one hand I gently massaged the offended cheek and with the other hand I reached for our telephone and dialed 911.

"Okay, go ahead and have me admitted," Kathy challenged. "We'll see just how well you'll do caring for all four of our children while contending with all the extra attention and care Caleb requires. Oh, and don't forget about your Air Force job, Major."

Meanwhile, the 911 operator answered and mechanically deadpanned, "911, what is your emergency?"

"My name is Major David Ingerson and my wife has just physically accosted me and is therefore in need of immediate psychological intervention."

"Ah...what is your location, Sir?" came the obviously startled reply from the 911 attendant.

"We're at 1459A Fairway Drive, Andrews Air Force Base, Maryland."

"Alright, Sir, let me make sure I understand. Your wife is violent and you believe is in need of immediate intervention—did you say psychological intervention?"

"Yes, psychological intervention." I declared.

"Ah, okay, Sir, give me a moment..." As the 911 attendant's voice trailed off, my attention turned to my wife, now sobbing nearly uncontrollably. "Alright then, if I can't get you admitted tonight, you can just leave. No wife of mine assaults her husband in my home."

"Okay," Kathy resolutely replied, "then I'm going to check into an expensive hotel with a Jacuzzi tub and enjoy the evening away." With that, she suddenly disengaged from our spat, picked up her pillow from our bed, and marched downstairs to sleep on the couch declaring, "I'm not here. If you need help during the night, you'll have to call the mental ward since I'm not here to help you."

Frustrated at the confounding situation, I terminated the 911 call. Still fuming, I slunk down onto our bed and braced myself for the long, lonely night.

Sometime after midnight I was awakened by a soft beeping. I groggily shook off my slumber, got out of bed, and stumbled toward the beeping noise. It was coming from Caleb's room. As I approached the door, the beeping got so loud I was surprised all the other children had not been likewise awakened. The noise was emanating from Caleb's enteral feed pump. I tried pushing all the various knobs, controls, buttons, and switches on the device, but to no avail. I could not get it to stop beeping. I noticed a red LED message that kept continually flashing: OBSTRUCTION PLEASE CLEAR OBSTRUCTION.

I had no idea what could possibly be obstructed. The pump appeared so simple. A long tube extended from a plastic pouch, which hung from an IV pole and contained high-calorie formula. The feed pump simply regulated the rate at which the formula was pumped into Caleb's G-tube. What could possibly be obstructed?

After several frustrating minutes fiddling with the device, I realized I would be unable to stop the incessant beeping without finding and clearing whatever was obstructed. Finally, I decided to go get Kathy's help since she surely would know what to do. I marched down the stairs to the living room where she was sleeping.

I stood in front of our couch and strongly cleared my throat, "Ah, ahguhm, Kathy," I began. "Kathy, I need your help. Caleb's pump is beeping and says it's obstructed. I can't seem to find and clear the obstruction. I need your help, now."

"No, I'm not here," she challenged. "I'm in a mental ward—remember?"

"Okay. I'm sorry for my anger," I replied without a hint of remorse. "I just could not believe you slapped me and I cannot tolerate such behavior in my house."

"Yes, I'm sorry for losing control," she offered in a very businesslike fashion. "But you deserved it. You were right up in my face, challenging me with this HIV business when you understood my position."

"Okay," I suddenly began sobbing. "I'm sorry too. I don't want our son's childhood ruined either, but think of the 10,000 hemophiliacs who've already lost their lives due to HIV-contaminated blood."

"I'm sorry, but I just can't handle it now." Kathy bellowed.

"Okay, alright," I resigned. "We'll keep our son out of it for now." Regaining my composure, I continued, "Can't you hear that beeping?"

"Oh, yes," she starkly teased. "I have heard it for well over an hour. I wondered how long it would take you to hear it and get up."

"Can you please come upstairs and help me take care of it?" I asked.

As it turned out, the obstruction was in Caleb's actual G-tube. It required replacement. Fortunately for me, Kathy had plenty of experience changing Caleb's G-tube since that first traumatic time it accidentally fell out when they were in Michigan at her parents' home. By this time changing the clogged G-tube had become routine for Kathy, but for me, it was frightening.

After the new G-tube was securely in place, we restarted Caleb's feed pump and went to bed. Although we lay down on the same bed, we both stared straight up into the darkness and briefly discussed the night's happenings. We agreed we really did need each other, and it was a mistake to lash out at each other, insisting on our own way. We were in this thing together. We'd need to support each other and be sensitive to each other's feelings, beliefs, and positions on the various issues at hand.

I would need to respect Kathy's refusal to agree to include our young son in the fight against transfusion-acquired AIDS at this time, and Kathy would need to understand just how important it was to me to do what I could to try to help other parents avoid such agonizing pain.

Most importantly, we again realized the primary job we had as parents was not to tend to our children's every need; rather, it was to love and support each other so we could be strong for our children when they needed us. As much as we had always respected each other, our mutual admiration grew that day. Through the testing of our resolve, we determined to keep our relationship unbendingly strong.

Days later, Kathy apologized and declared she would never slap her husband again. She confided that she was actually scared of my anger that night and fearful I might just find a way to have her committed. She was so very hurt that I had actually wanted her removed from our home.

In response to her apology, I likewise apologized for being so insensitive and pushy. I promised to strive to be more gentle. I also agreed to never again try to have Kathy admitted to a mental institution. Kathy appreciated my apology and commitment to keep her around.

By the end of the summer, we had narrowed our church search to three choices. One was the very church from which Caleb was nearly rebuffed during VBS. The others were actually closer to the base and more convenient. After visiting all three, I decided to speak to the pastor of the farthest one about the VBS incident. Hence, I called the church office and requested a meeting with the senior pastor. Pastor Mark graciously received me and satisfied all my concerns.

He actually declared, "If we didn't welcome an innocent child such as yours into our midst, we might as well put a sign over the door which reads, Ichabod, and close the place down."

Pleased with his response, Kathy and I decided Cornerstone would be our home church during our assignment at Andrews.

The next Sunday the church was hosting its annual fall picnic at Whitemarsh Park in Bowie, Maryland. After the service our family of six loaded our van and followed the line of vehicles to the park, anticipating a relaxing time while getting acquainted with folks and participating in the various picnic activities.

Whitemarsh Park is a somewhat secluded park with several baseball and soccer fields, a picnic area with picnic tables, and a large adjoining playground with swings, slides, and monkey bars. There are several large capacity pavilions and plenty of grassy parking. It's a comfortably relaxing location, nestled in the middle of the city with a long winding wooded entrance, which gives the distinct impression of being miles from a metropolitan area.

The crystal clear sky sported only a few puffy white clouds visible here and there through the magnificent deciduous shade tree canopy. It seemed the entire wooded park was lush and green, smiling and relaxing. There was life all around. Children were running and playing, jumping and laughing.

Managing the many details of moving our family every three or four years from one Air Force assignment to another can be very stressful. Deciding upon a church family, getting acquainted with the membership, and building meaningful relationships were among the most important of the various moving tasks. Building friendships during this move was particularly challenging in light of our young son's many medical needs.

We had made it our family goal to settle with a new church home within the first six weeks of arriving at each new permanent change of duty location. This move was different. Due to juggling the many complex medical matters pertaining to settling Caleb, it took us twice as long to firmly settle on a church home. Consequently, we were more determined than ever to energetically get to know and make friends with as many as we could. That determination made this beautiful day a doubly special day of celebration. It was our very first Sunday settled in our new church home. It was the day of the annual fall picnic. It was September 10th—a day we would never forget!

CHAPTER 30

He's Not Responding!

After Caleb and I observed several games of kickball and soccer, we walked around the deep green grassy playing fields back to the shady tree-covered picnic and playground area where Kathy was eagerly chatting with various new friends. We arrived at the playground area just in time to observe the children's pastor gathering the children and leading them in a short worship and silly song sing-along. Several of our children, including Caleb, eagerly hustled up to the makeshift stage under a large picnic pavilion and joined the revelers in the serious as well as silly sing-along.

Watching the children, especially Caleb, mimic the pastor's hand motions while they sang was precious. Little Caleb was mouthing each song and following each motion to the best of his ability. He was as cute as any three-year-old, particularly so because he was small of stature for his age but having mental and motor skills on par with his age group. He therefore appeared advanced beyond his age. I silently reflected on my satisfaction that our family of six was whole, complete, and utterly relaxed in our new home just three months after moving to the bustling Washington, D.C. area.

Following a fine meal of the usual picnic fare, most of the children dashed back to the swings, slides, or monkey bars. Twice, Caleb climbed up one of the tall metal slides but hesitated at the top and decided against sliding down the threateningly tall structure. Both times I readily cooperated with his retreat and rescued him. I encouraged my son by acknowledging, "Young man, you are very brave for such a special small boy to climb way up to the top of the slide."

A short time later, Caleb and I shuffled through the wood chips covering the playground area over to where his mother was visiting and getting acquainted with some ladies. The conversation was relaxed and comfortable but nonetheless energetic. The temperature and weather were as pleasant and perfect as could be for an early September day in Maryland. The few cumulus clouds seemed content to remain high and white with no hint of gray storm destructive potential.

Although it was warm in the sun, there was plenty of natural shade surrounding the wooded playground area. My wife stood next to a wooden park bench near several bright green bushes and one very tall pine tree with all the lower branches carefully trimmed far above our heads, creating a generous shaded canopy. She was listening to others while sharing about our family.

As a military family, we understood the importance of being forthright in getting acquainted early on in a new home and church. It's important to be intentional to get to know people in order to reduce the time required to develop close, meaningful friendships.

Having announced our engagement more than a year before graduating from the Air Force Academy, one day Kathy, my wife-to-be, lamented her concerns about marrying an Air Force lieutenant to her mentor, Miss Ginny. Kathy was greatly concerned that due to moving every few years she'd lose her friends. The kindly wife of retired Colonel Robin Woodruff replied that she too had faced the very same dilemma.

Miss Ginny explained that the remedy to the very real fear of losing friends every few years was to consider not that you're plagued with losing friends but that you're blessed with gaining new ones every few years. This positive and upbeat take on the situation not only put Kathy's mind at ease but also helped her understand that in order to successfully gain those new friends every few years, she'd need to be forthright and positive about meeting people.

We would have been pleased for the picnic to last for hours in this very comfortable setting. As I listened to Kathy describing a past family life experience, Caleb suddenly declared that he needed to go swing. I replied he should be patient and I would take him to go swing momentarily.

Again, he defiantly demanded, "I need to go swing!"

"Okay, Fella, just a minute—hey…"

I was holding my son in my arms in front of me with both hands squarely under his bottom when suddenly, immediately after his second demand to go swing, he abruptly jerked his head back toward my knees and rigidly remained. Although not at all prone to temper tantrums, I suspected this posturing was nothing more than a defiant tantrum in which my young son was emphasizing his insistence to go swing. I fully expected he'd bounce back up and again demand to go swing, but strangely, his head remained rigidly down at my knees without bouncing back.

"Kathy,
DO something!"

I therefore put my right arm under the middle of his back and raised him back to me, exclaiming, "Hey, Fella, what're you doing?"

I saw that his face was suddenly ashen gray and his eyes were already glazed and half closed. In a flash, I intuitively knew he was gone, but in the harried incredulity of the moment, I refused to acknowledge it.

My mind racing, my mouth automatically formed a silent scream, "Son, where are you? Come back." Instantly, I sensed he was miles, years, an eternity away from me. I felt his heavy, lifeless, stiff frame in my arms, but I could not reach him.

Kathy was standing close enough to observe the strange phenomenon. She appeared frozen—unable to move.

In a flash, without thinking, I shouted, "Kathy, DO something!" She simply looked at our suddenly stiff son in my arms and weakly asked, "Shall we do CPR?"

Our eyes met for a millisecond. I saw resignation and years of agony and empty longing I would later come to understand was a mother's deep longing to hold her son during his dying breaths. Nevertheless, as a man of action, I unthinkingly and immediately shouted, "Yes. Do CPR." Despite Kathy's desire to hold her son, she led me to place his stiffly limp body on the ground.

Several surrounding us immediately took charge. Before I knew it, two individuals were administering CPR. One was a sixteen-year-old girl, who'd just been trained in CPR at school, while the other was an adult part-time volunteer EMT, well-trained and practiced in CPR. Despite their best efforts, the child failed to respond favorably to their compressions and breaths. Within ten minutes, an ambulance arrived with two slow-moving EMTs who took over the CPR and began the transport operation to a local urgent care facility.

As I stood back watching and praying—silent screams erupting in my head—I felt as though I was floating above the surreal scene before me. Although I was right in the middle of the situation, I could neither feel the grass beneath my feet nor see clearly which way to look. I shook myself out of my stupor and observed one of the two EMTs very nonchalantly calling his dispatcher on his portable radio. In his unhurried state, he seemed oblivious to the commotion around him.

I interrupted his routine radio call and asked him with sudden and urgent passion, "Aren't you going to transport him to a hospital? Why aren't you hurrying more?"

Obviously not understanding and seeming unconcerned about my relationship to the patient, he simply replied by distractedly looking at his empty clipboard and deadpanning, "Sir, we're taught not to run or appear to be in a hurry; it tends to upset the patient and family and make them think the situation is urgent."

"Listen to me," I began to shout, "this child is my son and it is urgent."

"Alright, step aside please," he calmly intoned as he methodically turned to walk toward the center of activity.

At this point, I understood I couldn't handle the behavior of the EMTs and resigned myself to get my car so my wife and I could follow the ambulance to the urgent care facility. By the time I had maneuvered our car to a spot just behind the ambulance, Caleb had been loaded. My wife then stumbled to our waiting vehicle and climbed in without a word. She sat stoically staring straight ahead, neither blinking nor moving.

Finally, the ambulance began its slow motion drive out of the park. The half-mile winding access road through the wooded recreation area seemed many times longer than it really was.

"When will we ever leave this interminable park?" I wondered out loud. My stony wife neither moved her head nor acknowledged my angst and frustration. She merely continued silently staring straight ahead.

During our drive to the urgent care clinic, I asked my wife if she knew who was taking care of our other children. "They're fine," she immovably began. "Carleen took them."

I had to stop suddenly as a traffic signal in front of us unexpectedly turned red. The ambulance carrying my son, with neither flashers nor siren activated, successfully made its way through the stoplight before the light turned red. I was stuck. I was frozen at the red light, unable to follow directly behind the ambulance, not understanding why the EMTs weren't in more of a hurry.

The sky above, still brightly blue, seemed disconnected from my crazed mind. I expected dark storm clouds with flashing lightning and thunderous crashing sounds, but none appeared. The bright blue seemed to defy the horrendous moment. My mind and heart raged with confusion and shock while my wife sullenly stared straight ahead. No tear moistened her eyes as she stared. No emotion showed on her face. I was alone in my agony and confusion. Where was I? I needed to take charge. I needed to act. My son needed me!

"Oh no," I exclaimed. "I don't know where we're going. Do you?"

"Yes, I think I know where the urgent care clinic is located," my wife quietly and mechanically reassured me. After the light changed to green, I followed her directions and soon located the clinic.

At the clinic, our son's body was already lying on a white table with about eight medical personnel standing around the table, strangely still, seemingly doing nothing. As we watched the non-commotion, in incredulity I motioned to the man who appeared to be in charge, instructing him to go ahead with his checklist but to be advised our son's cardiac physiology was unique in that he was a hypoplastic left heart patient with a unique Fontan-like repair.

Reality swept over me like an immense crashing wave as I observed—unbelievably—that none of the personnel moved. No one stretched a hand or instrument toward the small, still child. The numerous medical personnel all stood surrounding the gurney as though they were calmly gazing at a strange mannequin in a museum.

With our abrupt arrival, all eyes were on me as the lead doctor inquired, "Sir, do you want us to attempt to resuscitate?"

I tried to demand but barely squeaked a weak, "Yes." Somehow, I already knew the resuscitation attempt was nothing more than an academic procedure. Too much time had passed without oxygen to our son's brain.

After three meager attempts to resuscitate, the doctor resolutely but anticlimactically pronounced, "He's not responding."

CHAPTER 31

To Love Him Still

I started to sink. The room began to spin—it went dark. I fell to my knees and silently screamed, demanding that this was not happening. I couldn't face the reality. We had worked so hard. We had prayed so hard. So many people had faithfully lifted our son to God in prayer. He couldn't be dead. It was too cruel. He needed to live. It made no sense. In my fog, I suddenly saw my wife with a stoic, blank look on her face. I shook off my stupor as the clinic staff left the room and allowed us a few minutes with our son.

I knew but refused to believe my son was dead. He was dead, but I wanted to be dead. He was dead, but I felt dead. He was dead, but I could not comprehend. It made no sense. How could he be dead? How could he be gone so quickly? He was dead. The room spun. I couldn't see. I felt a cold, dry, deadly choking. I felt so alone. But I was not alone. My wife was in the room, but her mind seemed so far away. It was as though she was as far away as my son. I could reach neither of them.

I did not know what to do. I had not practiced nor read of what to do during the immediate moments after your son dies. I did not have a checklist. I was hardly aware my wife was there with me. It was unbelievable, impossible. Not knowing what else to do, I shook off my confusion and grogginess then summarily launched into action. I became meticulously focused. I immediately began to take charge and sought to make arrangements for an autopsy. I arranged for my son's body to be transported to the pathology department at the AFIP (Armed Forces Institute of Pathology) at Walter Reed Army Medical Center in Bethesda, Maryland.

The clinic personnel seemed surprised at my sudden energy and meticulous instructions. I made numerous inquiries into the logistical issues surrounding the transport of his body and his autopsy. The system seemed too sluggish and unresponsive for me. No one seemed to understand a father taking charge. They all seemed inclined to expect the situation to take care of itself without the intervention of the newly bereaved father.

When finally satisfied I'd done all I needed to do, we left the clinic with the knowledge that our son's body would be transported to Walter Reed at Bethesda at some point the next day. We stopped to pick up our other three children, dreading their anticipated reactions. The sun had not yet set as we arrived at the Lucas' townhouse.

Kathy and I walked into the front entryway and immediately encountered all the children sitting quietly in the living room, awaiting our arrival and announcement. We sat down on a stool too small for both of us, facing a long, dingy, brown-covered couch on which sat all the Lucas children and ours—seven children under the age of twelve.

Knowing that something serious had happened to their friend and brother, the children all sat attentively looking at Kathy and me, eagerly awaiting our expected announcement. As we sat down, I could scarcely control my emotion as I looked into the young, vibrant, eager eyes of the children. I could not think of what to say that would be age-appropriate. As I mused, I suddenly heard myself say, "Children, Caleb is dead."

"Boo hoo!" Carleen's youngest daughter, five-year-old Aly, shrieked and immediately wept loud sobs with her head buried in her hands. As a look of shock and bewilderment spread across the other children's silent faces, Aly lifted her head, wiped her tears, and innocently but eagerly inquired, "So, when's Caleb coming home?"

We marveled that only a five-year-old could instinctively understand the appropriate time to involuntarily cry and yet have no understanding of what had actually occurred.

We braced ourselves and attempted to explain that Caleb would not ever be coming back because he had gone to heaven. At this, the seven children began weakly crying and attempting to make sense of the unexpected, strange news. It was as though they instinctively knew it was not normal, not natural for a three-year-old child to die. It smacked against the natural good order of how things worked. Although in their juvenile minds the children were ill-prepared to comprehend death, they nonetheless seemed to well understand it was not supposed to happen this way. Death was for old folks—not three-year-olds.

It was more than I could bear. I stood up and walked out of the room with no emotion, no thoughts—only darkness and a strong foggy sense of foreboding. I felt like I was walking in sand and hardly going anywhere. The children remained on the couch, crying and trying to understand. Kathy tended to her children. Carleen attempted to comfort Kathy. I was lost in swirling confusion.

This was not supposed to be happening. We'd spent the majority of the past three and a half years striving to help this child heal, striving to get all the best medical care and support available for our child. We'd prayed. We'd asked and had hundreds, perhaps thousands of faithful friends pray. But still he died. He was dead. I felt dead.

Upon returning home, to avoid the agonizing pain of accepting and dealing with our son's death, we set about making all the necessary arrangements for the funeral and memorial services. My first task was to pen the following words to our website watchers who frequently checked our site for updates of Caleb's medical progress.

A message from the Ingerson Family: Mon, Sep 10

Thank you very much for the love and support you've offered our son during his three and a half years. As our lives have been enriched by having this special child in our family, so our lives have been enriched by your faithful friendship and love.

Today, after a lovely time of worship and preaching with our new church family, we enjoyed a church-wide picnic. Our new local church home is Cornerstone Assembly of God, a church that took a difficult stand for our son in that they chose to invite us to enjoy full fellowship in the face of a family who threatened to leave the church if they allowed our HIV-positive son to remain in the three-year-old VBS class.

During the picnic, the Cornerstone worship team led us in several songs as the children were invited to come stand and lead us in worship at the front. As soon as Caleb noticed his sisters had gone to so do, he insisted on accompanying them to the front. Precious in my mind's eye will be the memory of seeing him standing with the other children in heavenly worship less than an hour before he left this earth for his heavenly home.

A short time later, after Caleb finished playing on the swings and slides, I was holding him in my arms when suddenly he reared back until his head fell at my knees. While lifting him back up, I asked, "What are you doing, Fella?" When I saw his eyes, only incredulity kept me from immediately realizing he was dead. We suspect he experienced something like a sudden electrical arrhythmia that caused his heart to go into immediate cardiac arrest.

Kathy and two others nearby began to administer CPR, to no avail.

Despite attempted cardiac resuscitation by the hospital staff at a local urgent care clinic, Caleb never regained cardiac function. It's bittersweet to know he died of heart failure in my arms and was immediately translated into the Savior's arms, the arms of the Savior whose heart burst for him on the cross.

To all we say, "Rejoice in the Lord; and again I say rejoice."

You may be interested in reading the kind words below, poignantly phrased by the pastor of our former church, Metro East Christian Fellowship.

Grace to you in Jesus, David

....

Re: Caleb Ingerson: Sun, Sep 10

"Precious in the sight of the Lord is the death of His saints." Caleb, the fighter, has finished his final battle. Early this afternoon at his new home church just outside Washington, D.C., Caleb Ingerson bravely faced the final enemy.

He suffered what was apparently a massive heart attack just after lunchtime. His body went limp and his ferocious heart just stopped beating. There are scant details, but he was rushed to the hospital as many of us here prayed for his brain not to be injured from oxygen deprivation.

We rejoice in the sure hope that this young warrior left this world of difficulty and entered into the sweet shalom and fellowship of the Lord. It was Caleb of old who silenced the unbelieving Israelites when he said, "We should go up and take possession of the land, for we can certainly do it." Young Caleb has now gone up and taken possession of the land the Lord Jesus has prepared for him.

We sensitively grieve with Kathy and David and the children—although not as those who have no hope. We also rejoice that Caleb faces no more doctors and hospitals, shots and shunts, purple lips and GI tubes. No longer does this precious child struggle against the congenital complications he so courageously contended with, nor will he need to face the grim future that the Virus would have brought him.

No more fighting for the fighter—no more tears or sorrow or pain or death; only the beautiful release of going home to the One who loves him even more than his family or myriad masses of admirers. Now he knows more than any of us who remain, and in his now-perfect mind and heart, he celebrates the joy of the Lord for eternity.

Our hearts and our love go out to you, David and Kathy, Sarah, Andrew, and Hannah Joy. You all served this child of God faithfully. He never lacked love, care, and spiritual covering. May the Lord bless and keep you.

Pastor Rich, for all the flock, your friends at MECF

The public saw my words of faith and victory, but inside, my mind was clouded by fear and doubt while my heart was terrorized by anxiety and a menacing sense of foreboding.

236

The public saw my words of faith and victory, but inside, my mind was clouded by fear and doubt while my heart was terrorized by anxiety and a menacing sense of foreboding. I emptied my honest agony into my journal later that night after all had gone to bed but me.

Late Sun, 10 Sep: My son Caleb died in my arms this afternoon. I did not want him to die. I am not pleased. Oh, God, I will miss him so much. Oh, God, I had such high hopes for him. Oh, God, I was such a poor parent. I loved myself more than I loved him. Oh, God, please forgive me. I feel so very ashamed. I enjoyed fighting for him. Oh, God, I am so sorry. I wanted to love him. I want to love him still.

CHAPTER 32

A Measure of Hope

The next day, on autopilot, I began to discuss various arrangements with Kathy and my squadron leadership. We decided to have Caleb's body embalmed after the autopsy so we could have it transported across state lines from Maryland to our hometown in Michigan. He would be buried in a grave purchased years before and graciously donated to us by my stepfather's family.

The next week I was extremely busy making arrangements for the funeral. We arranged for transport of the body from the AFIP lab where the autopsy was conducted. This would be done through a local funeral home whose staff contacted a funeral home in our hometown. Our mothers, both living in Clinton, Michigan, met the local funeral home director to facilitate the arrangements. Later, when I met with him face-to-face to make payment for his services, I learned that the price for the burial and various associated services was half the regular price when the deceased is a young child.

"What's the reason for the reduced rate?" I inquired.

"We like to sleep at night," came the straightforward, expressionless reply from the funeral director.

"Oh, God, don't You see? This is not normal. This is not the normal order of things. This is not the way it's supposed to happen.

Suddenly, a haunting discussion unfolded. "Oh, God, don't You see? This is not normal. This is not the normal order of things. This is not the way it's supposed to happen. Everyone intuitively knows this. Even funeral directors, whose very livelihood comes from providing funeral and burial services, understand that it's not supposed to happen this way. But, God, You are the only one who has control. You are the only one who could have made a true difference. The doctors could not save my son. My wife could not save my son. Those who administered CPR could not save my son. Only You could have saved my son. But, You did not! Oh, God, this is not the way it's supposed to be."

At that time I reflected on a discussion I'd had just five months previous with my close friend and pastor from Okinawa. I reread from my journal the haunting words that had come not only from my faithful friend but also from a flight surgeon.

. . . .

Thu, 13 Apr: Bro' Glenn and I spent a protracted time together discussing a whole host of things. At one point I described a flight surgeon's intense words. He enthusiastically pronounced that if I could just hold onto Caleb for five more years, he was certain that within these same number of years they'd find a cure for his heart disease and HIV infection. To that, Bro' Glenn gravely exhorted that I'd better hold onto him while I had the opportunity. He uttered those words with such finality—I was stirred by their menacing tone.

. . . .

When I reread that excerpt from my journal, I felt a distinct chill. Fear and doubt enveloped my mind. Had I not done all I could to hold onto him as the flight surgeon had admonished? Had I not sufficiently held onto Caleb while I had the opportunity as my faithful friend had encouraged? Were the extra hours devoted to his care, day after day, insufficient? Were all the doctor and hospital referrals not enough? Did I not hold him enough? Did I not read to him enough? Did I fail to protect him when he was infected with HIV? Did I fail to hold onto him?

I remembered other difficult times less than two weeks before Caleb's untimely death. I was increasingly interested in lobbying Congress to pass legislation to improve blood safety. I had teamed up with the NAVTA. I had written numerous letters to all the congressmen I could. I had received scant replies. Kathy was not particularly supportive of my efforts. She did not see the reason for my involvement in promoting blood safety. She could not see how it could be helpful to our children—to our son. I reflected on a journal entry just less than two weeks before Caleb's death.

Mon, 28 Aug: This was a very challenging weekend. Kathy and I fought over blood issues. Although it was very difficult, we overcame and kissed and made up.

According to the journal entry, although we'd fought, we'd kissed and made up. But, now, we weren't fighting. Now, we weren't kissing. Now, we were both independently striving to accomplish whatever goals we thought important. We discussed various logistical and administrative issues that needed coordination and planning, but we behaved as though we'd put our own relationship on hold. It seemed we had neither time for each other nor inclination to nurture each other. We were both deserted islands, stuck in our own oceans of isolation. Kathy tended to the children while I tended to the matters pertaining to funeral arrangements: autopsy, embalming, body transport, and memorial ceremonies.

In our short time in the Washington, D.C. area, we had already garnered a large circle of friends. A dear USAF chaplain and friend came to our base home and asked if we would like the base chapel to host a memorial service before we departed the Washington area to bury our son's body in our hometown in Michigan. Although I hesitated, when I considered all our many friends in the Washington area and the many others we'd known previously who'd moved to the area, we decided it prudent to have such a service.

Although the ceremony was hastily arranged, it was very well attended and very well received. Fellow squadron mates as well as friends from all around the Washington, D.C. area attended. My Aunt Sue Ruth from New Jersey and her husband, Uncle Joe, drove the two hundred miles to attend the ceremony. The Messianic Jewish USAF physician, who had been very impressed with Caleb, attended and offered the Kaddish, a traditional Jewish funeral prayer in Hebrew, much to our delight. I put together a video overview of Caleb's short life set to vibrant, up-beat music.

One of the many friends from past assignments in attendance was a dear friend from our church in Okinawa, Irvin. After the service, Irvin relayed to me a story his wife, Terry, had shared with him. As Terry was driving the day after receiving word of Caleb's death, she lamented in prayer that Caleb should not have died.

In response to her ponderings, she understood God impressed a picture on her mind. In her mind's eye she saw a number of chronically ill children on life support systems, all connected to various leads, probes, tubes, and machines. The children were slowly slipping to the grave. In stark contrast she saw our precious little Caleb, the fighter, fully aware, fully alert, eagerly running and playing, climbing tall slides, and sitting while bouncing in his father's arms with not a single sign of medical malady. Then, dramatically, in a flash, he was transported from his earthly father's arms to his Heavenly Father's arms. Caleb, as his name implies, went boldly and victoriously, not fearfully or timidly to his heavenly reward.

For the first time since my son died, I began to see a glimmer of light. I began to suspect that perhaps God could be glorified through my son's life and death. There would be many dark days ahead, but now I had a visual image I could relate to and recall again and again as the dark days repeatedly tried to sap the life from my heart.

Sentiments of love and encouragement poured in from around the world through e-mail and post. We read each word of each note. These words served as salve to our tattered souls. Later, even years later, these same words of affection and support brought comfort of inestimable value, granting solace we could not have anticipated. I've learned that whenever someone has lost a loved one to death, particularly deaths we tend to perceive as untimely, words of comfort need not be grand or greatly insightful—they just need to be communicated.

Significantly, an endearing Bosnian family we'd befriended during our years in Illinois sent the first flowers, commemorating Caleb's life. One day, not long after we'd become acquainted, the patriarch, Nesib, pulled up his shirt to display his scars, the result of torture suffered during 317 days in a Serbian concentration camp. In response I pulled up my son's shirt to display his surgical scars. I was amazed how Caleb's scared chest endeared Nesib and his entire family to our precious child. We were likewise amazed and humbled at the love and concern those first flowers demonstrated.

One need not be pithy or clever to send meaningful words of comfort. Those that are meaningful are those that are sent. A simple expression of, "I'm sorry for your loss," can mean more to a troubled soul in their hour of darkness than the grandest symphony of complex unsaid condolences. Here is a sample of some of the sweetest music to our tattered hearts expressed the day after Caleb's sudden death.

Re: Caleb Ingerson: Sun, Sep 10

Your entire family remains in our thoughts and prayers. God's peace be with you.

Larry

Re: Caleb: Sun, Sep 10

Cindy called all the intercessory prayer folks and they are praying for your family...I will continue to keep in touch.

Andy

Re: Caleb Ingerson: Mon, Sep 11

All our love and prayers are with you at this time of Caleb's going to see Jesus face-to-face. I know that we are just new friends and that the Cornerstone family may just seem like many faces, but we want you to know that we are family together. I believe that in many ways, God will allow this body to rally around your family at this time and for years to come. When one of us is grieving, we all grieve.

We thank God for the chance to know Caleb; even if just for a brief time. I too will long remember the scene of Caleb along with you all praising the Lord with everything in him. We are here to help in any way possible, without limitations.

I will call you about 9:30 this morning just to talk.

Sarah, Andrew, and Hannah Joy, we are praying for you especially. You are all very special kids with a great love for Jesus. We love you all.

Together in Jesus, Pastor Mark

....

Re: Caleb's last update: Mon, Sep 11

We got the call yesterday afternoon and went to our knees in prayer. The children were precious and prayed for Caleb to get better. Later last night, we heard about Caleb going to be with his Heavenly Father. Josh and Nikki cried and prayed that you all would not miss him so much.

Our hearts are sad and go out to you at this time. We also glory in that God chose to leave Caleb long enough to touch the lives of many. God worked through you and Kathy, and your faith and love for God was and is evident.

We love you, Rich, Mary, & kids

....

Re: Caleb's last update: Mon, Sep 11

You asked about an appropriate memorial and what would happen at a Jewish funeral.

I would suggest a tree planted in the villages or fields around the city of Hebron in Israel. These were given to Caleb, son of

Jephunneh, for his possession when the city of Hebron (Kiriath-arba) was given from the Tribe of Judah to the Kohathites (the priests and children of Aaron) as a city of refuge for the manslayer.

Only the prayers would be different in the funeral if a Jewish funeral—same L-rd. The Kaddish comes to mind (interesting in that the word death is not to be found in this prayer in remembrance of the dead). Of course, a relatively plain coffin that will disintegrate is the norm...

Schuyler

....

Re: Caleb Ingerson: Mon, Sep 11

I am truly sorry for the loss of your child, Caleb. I will pray that God will wrap you in His arms during this time...I have visited Caleb's website and I always thought he was such a cute little boy. Please know we are here for you during this time.

Katie [pdheart], Mom to Harmony, truncus repaired Sep 25, 98

....

Note: The above message is from a mother in the pdheart group. The pdheart and HLHS listserv were groups of parents of children with congenital heart defects who participated in group e-mail forums. We drew strength, comfort and information from these e-mails. Whenever a child died whose parents had been active on the forums, a degree of corporate grieving ensued.

....

Beloved Caleb: Mon, Sep 11

It is with much sorrow that I write to you this message. Please know our hearts ache with you in the loss of our precious Caleb. After speaking with David on the phone, I want to encourage you about Caleb testifying of the love of our Savior. He did that every day of his life.

He taught me that I could love a child not born of my womb as though he were. He taught me and my family unconditional love from such a pure heart that you knew it could only be born of God. When he worshiped, it was with such sincerity and purity as well as such mature faith that he challenged me to do the same.

Some of the most spiritual times of my life were spent with Caleb or praying for Caleb. He will always be one of the greatest testimonies of God's majesty and love...I will ever know. So rest assured my dear friends; Caleb's testimony speaks loud and clear and will for as long as any of us, privileged to have known him, live on earth.

It is so like you to be concerned with others while your loss is so great. What a testimony you all are—from the children thinking about Kory to you thinking about your Bosnian friends. Please know that we are praying for you and that I will be on the first plane to you if you want me to come.

Please keep us updated on funeral arrangements. Kory and I would be honored to come to Michigan for the funeral.

With much love, Jennifer

....

Re: Caleb Ingerson: Mon, Sep 11

I am so sorry to hear about the loss of dear little Caleb. He fought such a difficult battle, and now finally he rests with all our little CHD angels. God bless him and you and your family.

Much love and sympathy, Bev [pdheart]

....

Re: Caleb Ingerson: Mon, Sep 11

We've been apart for a long time now. I've read your messages. But in reading the below message, I can't hold back my emotions. I have seen these past years how strong you've been. You are a great inspiration for me. I've been low, but how can I compare to the loss of a child without saying, "Is anyone listening? God are You there?"

My entire family's prayers are with you always, John

Re: Caleb's last update: Mon, Sep 11

I was so sorry to receive the news about Caleb. I can only begin to imagine the pain of losing a child and no condolences that I offer can relieve that pain. We at Project ARK were privileged to know Caleb and the two of you. Caleb was an incredibly sweet boy, who found his way into the hearts of all of our staff. We all think about him and talk about him more often than you would imagine.

Your devotion to him was also extremely inspiring to all of us. I am glad that you had the chance to be with him at the end. Please know that our hearts are with you.

Dr. Greg, for myself and the entire Project ARK staff

Re: Caleb's last update: Mon, Sep 11

I was driving to the store this morning, and I asked myself why I was feeling so depressed, and of course the reason was the death of Caleb…we all care…I think the best thing we can do is continue to spread the word for CHD awareness. More awareness means more funding for research. That's our hope for the future. Only that can help save our children and future children.

Bev [pdheart]

....

Re: Caleb Ingerson: Mon, Sep 11

As I read your letter, I am so filled with sorrow for you. I can't begin to realize your pain; and yet we rejoice with you for where Caleb is today. What a wonderful inspiration Caleb was to my family and to all who had the privilege of knowing him. What a little joy our God created. How masterful was His touch in that creation, in all of our lives. What a precious little boy he was.

Thank you for sharing him with us. His beautiful smile will be forever in our hearts and minds. What a testament of God's love your family is to all of us. He is our God, our Creator, and our Father. And when it is time for us to take residence in the place that He has prepared for us, we will be all together, all of us who love the Lord, a heavenly family together in His presence.

With all of our love, In Jesus Name, Bob, Colleen, and Shana

....

Re: Caleb Ingerson: Mon, Sep 11

I am so truly sorry for your loss. I am rejoicing that Jesus can now hold your son in His arms. I just can't stop crying. I am sorry.

Heart hugs, Kathy [pdheart]

....

Re: Caleb Ingerson: Mon, Sep 11

I read your post this morning and have been praying for God's grace upon your family all day. I really don't know what to say. I cannot—and don't want to—imagine what you are going through right now, but know that God is with you and deeply loves you. I pray that He will sustain you through your grief and that your family would look to Him alone to be your source of strength. Please let Caleb's brother and sisters know that I am lifting them up as well.

I remember when my Caleb was born five years ago and we found out that he had CHD. While we drove the long stretch of interstate to find out if he was going to make it or not, God reminded me that Caleb did make it to the Promised Land. He trusted God and got his reward. Praise the Lord that I had that promise to carry me through, and for your Caleb—he is definitely in The Promised Land.

God bless and keep you, Kim in Texas [pdheart], mom to: Bryan 10, hh, Kyle 9, hh, Grace 2, hh, and Caleb 5, TGA, ASD, VSD, PS, arterial switch 3-22-95

. . . .

Re: Prayer cover: Mon, Sep 11

I want to come to the memorial service at MECF. Please let me know when it is. I'm so sad and simultaneously happy for you/Caleb. I don't like it when funerals bring people together, but this one is already different. You are such a special family and he is such a special little guy.

Love to you all, Larry

. . . .

Re: Caleb Ingerson Services: Tue, Sep 12

I am so sorry to hear about the loss of Caleb. He was blessed to have you as parents. After reading the wonderful messages you posted on the HLHS listserv from time to time, I know his life was filled with love and joy. I mourn with you.

I have not spoken to Ivor recently, but I was his advisor and again, your support helped him get his Bachelor's degree...

Take care, Monica [HLHS listserv], Mom to Angela 5 , HLHS and Nicholas 8, HH

Re: Caleb's Memorial Services and Funeral: Tue, Sep 12

Last night before going to bed, I told Preshus Joy about Caleb. She was totally taken by surprise and was speechless for a few moments. Then her first words were, "But, Dad, I just prayed for him and his..." I then interrupted her and gently told her that the Lord Jesus has taken Caleb home to Heaven to completely heal him and take him away from all the pain and difficulty that he was going through here on earth.

We, as a family continue to uphold you in our prayers.

Love In Christ Jesus, Pastor Wally

Re: Caleb Ingerson: Tue, Sep 12

I am so very sorry to hear of your loss. I know no words that can take away your pain, but please know that I am praying for strength for your family in this time of loss...

Hugs, Sandy [pdheart], mom to Jordan 6 hh; Kieran 3 "complex heart" 10 defects too many to list; and wife to Kent, my rock

Re: Caleb's Memorial Services and Funeral: Tue, Sep 12

Please know that my heart breaks and rejoices with you. It is such a bittersweet thing to lose a child, but such a great thing to give them up to the Lord. I can only imagine what you and your family are going through at this time...

Claire [pdheart]

Re: Caleb's last update: Tue, Sep 12

I'm so sorry for your loss. Wish I could offer you a shoulder or hand instead of just mere words at this time.

Children's Heart Foundation based in Chicago is doing wonderful research.

Take care, Diane [pdheart], mom to Elizabeth 2, Madison 4, Alexandra 5 DORV Pulmonary atresia w/VSD, Disc. LPA, Pulmonary branch stenoses, MAPCA's; Alberta, Canada

Re: Caleb's last update: Tue, Sep 12

I will lift you and your dear family and Caleb up to the Lord in prayer as you embark upon this different journey. "For everything there is a season and to everything there is a reason."

Your Friend in Christ, Claire, [pdheart] mom to Gabriel HLHS

Re: Caleb's Memorial Services and Funeral: Tue, Sep 12

May our God of peace and strength be with you at this time. Kathy, I shared with Sara at Bethany Place and she wants to attend the memorial service. She was also broken and touched by the news. I will continue to lift your entire family up in prayer and will see you in a week. I love you with the love of the Lord. God be with you.

Your Bro In Christ, Gordon A

Re: Caleb's last update: Tue, Sep 12

I can't begin to tell you how incredibly saddened I am to hear of Caleb's passing. Any words I find seem so trite and empty. I cannot imagine the loss you all must feel. So many times today I thought about what a single action or moment would be like without one of my children in my life, and it brought me to tears. Please know that our thoughts and prayers are with you, David, Kathy and Caleb's siblings, as you attempt to get through this. What a special little boy he was.

Much love, Darcy

Re: Caleb Ingerson: Tue, Sep 12

I love you both. I am praying that your faith will deepen even more through this ordeal. Let God be your strength right now.

God bless you and your family, Marge and Ed

Re: Caleb's Memorial Services and Funeral: Tue, Sep 12

We were very surprised and saddened to hear about Caleb's death. Sue and I are planning on coming to the memorial service at the Base tomorrow. We intend on arriving at the visitor's center about 11:30 AM...We will see you then.

Joe

Re: Caleb's last update: Tue, Sep 12

We, too, have a great faith that your son is basking in the presence of our Lord Jesus Christ. I have often admired your godly advice on pdheart list and the encouragement you gave to so many others. Our family is praying for yours as you mourn, not as the world mourns, but nonetheless, the pain must be exquisite. May our God comfort and give you peace as you deal with the days ahead.

In His love, Jayne and Gerard [pdheart]

Re: Caleb's Memorial Services and Funeral: Wed, Sep 13

I will be traveling in the States the 25th of September through the 14th of October. I will make contact with you during that time. Thanks for the call. Much prayer and love comes from Okinawa.

Your Brother, Glenn

Re: Global Grief: Wed, Sep 13

Our global waiting room is grieving for the families who have lost their angels and for the impact this terrifying news has on families of children who are in need of surgery or who just had surgery and are still unwell.

To all the families involved, you have my deepest sympathy. Losing our children is the greatest fear we as parents have—our precious angels no longer in our arms. Others further down this path of CHD know of the grief. We can give hope and strong shoulders to lean on.

In sympathy, Punya, [pdheart] foster mum of Jesse 10 PA/IVS, ASD, TS hypoplastic RV, congenital toxoplasmosis resulting in mild CP, atypical ADHD, global language dysfunction, epilepsy, perceptual difficulties, otherwise active, able and aware; Fremantle, Western Australia

. . . .

RE: Caleb: Wed, Sep 13

...chosen son born under less than ideal circumstances. Moved others with just his presence. Suffered in life while giving us hope and inspiration. Finally, leaving us with memories that will stay forever...like Jesus. He was courageous and brave throughout his struggles of surgeries. Taken on the biggest and most menacing illness currently known, HIV. Kind of like David and Goliath? He has taught us much. He came to us as a blessing in disguise.

Ken

. . . .

Indeed, as one friend wrote, the pain was exquisite. Not only was it oftentimes exquisite but also it was terrifyingly unrelenting—as though it would gnaw through my very marrow. Nonetheless, these messages from faithful friends and family brought us a measure of hope in the midst of hopelessness. Their power to soothe and console extended from the agonizing days, into the numbing months, and through the healing years.

CHAPTER 33

A Thing of Beauty

No sooner had we considered traveling to Michigan for the funeral then I firmly decided I would bring the keynote message.

My wife gently asked me, "Are you sure you want to do this?"

"My son died in my arms. I will bring a message of hope and challenge to those who attend the funeral. My decision is non-negotiable."

The trip across the Midwestern States from Washington, D.C. to Michigan was a harried blur. Because our minds were so preoccupied with logistical details, we had little time for grieving. We spent the better part of two days greeting well-wishers at the traditional viewing. We were initially shocked to see how very tall our beloved Caleb's body appeared, stretched out in his white cardboard casket. I was also rather amazed at how fine a cardboard casket could be made to appear. I'm sure no one else was aware that it was constructed with nothing other than painted corrugated paper, cardboard. In that money was tight and also because we had no life insurance on our son, we purchased the cheapest casket available.

My wife gently asked me, "Are you sure you want to do this?"

"My son died in my arms. I will bring a message of hope..."

I had directed the Walter Reed AFIP personnel to store my son's heart and brain in order to support further medical study. I hoped this would one day aid in developing not just palliative but healing treatments for congenital heart disease and HIV. I chuckled when I considered that surely no one at the viewing or funeral had any idea there was no longer a heart or brain inside the tent of our son's body.

Upon arrival at the funeral home, six-years-old Hannah Joy marched straight up to the casket and coaxed her brother to get up. "Come on, Caleb, let's go and play," she cajoled him. When she saw that he was unresponsive to her pleading, she went to her mother and asked, "Mommy, is that Caleb over there?"

To the innocent child, Kathy tenderly replied, "No, Dear, Caleb is not there; he's in Heaven."

"But Mommy, he looks like Caleb," Hannah argued.

"I know he looks like Caleb, Honey, but that's just a tent he lived in while here on earth."

"Hmmm...Mommy," the innocent child asked, "since he looks like Caleb, can we still call him Caleb?"

"Yes, Sweetheart, you may call him Caleb." What other response could her mother have given?

Effervescent Hannah Joy bounced back to the casket and again cajoled Caleb to come out and play. When he didn't immediately respond, she proceeded to again grab his crossed hands and pull. Surprisingly he still didn't get up, but when in frustration she let go of his hand, it literally sprang back into the same crossed position from which it'd begun. With a perplexed look, she again reached out and picked up his hand, only to release it immediately and watch it again curiously spring back into place. Her second attempt to pull him up was observed by a horrified visiting family member who rushed up to me and declared in an urgent, hushed whisper, "David, someone needs to stop Hannah; look what she's doing!"

I looked toward the casket just in time to observe Hannah Joy make her third attempt to pull Caleb up by the hands. Now it obviously had become a game as I watched her pick the hands up and release them only to see them spring back several more times. Eventually, she tired of the game and left the casket to go find somewhere else to play.

I later reflected that we're all very much like the tent Hannah requested to call Caleb. We are all really nothing more than tents in which our real selves dwell while on this beautiful and excruciating earth. It's only when we learn to look beyond our tents that we can really see each other. An innocent six-year-old child is not only beautiful because her outward appearance is breathtaking, but rather, in her innocence she shines a light that sadly most adults have learned to dim, dull, or turn off entirely.

Jesus said, "Let the little children come to me, and do not hinder them, for the kingdom of God belongs to such as these. Truly I tell you, anyone who will not receive the kingdom of God like a little child will never enter it."[7]

We can learn much from children if we'll only cease seeing everything through our own rusty lenses.

In much the same manner as Hannah Joy manifested childlike simplicity, our nearly eight-year-old son, Andrew, sat contentedly with my brother, John. As they looked through family photo albums brought to the funeral home for the occasion, they discussed guy stuff as only an uncle and nephew can. Andrew later reveled with pride as he recalled several things Uncle John had discussed with him. He and Uncle John had similar personalities, sensitive but strong. Andrew identified more with his uncle's hands-on approach to life than with his father's more fuzzy word-oriented way.

The next day at Caleb's funeral, our former pastor gave a marvelous and sensitive eulogy. He reminded the mass of admirers that the small child simply fought the final fight and went on ahead, setting an example for the rest of us. We should be sure to do likewise when it was time.

I then gave a message of hope and challenge to all assembled. I thanked everyone for their love and support offered our family not only that day but also during the years of my son's short life. I mused that perhaps some wondered why I, the father of the deceased, would be bringing the main message while wearing his U.S. Air Force dress blues.

In that half my life had been spent serving in uniform and that Caleb had lived his entire life in a military family, it seemed fitting to wear the uniform for this occasion. I then quoted General Robert E. Lee: "Duty then, is the sublimest word in the English language; you can never do more; you should never wish to do less."[8] I explained that just as Jesus stood up in the synagogue one day and declared he was anointed to preach the good news, it was also my duty to preach the good news to all who would listen on this day.

I related that on numerous occasions my mother had observed our son singing the simple song, "God Has a Plan for My Life." She surmised that perhaps the small child somehow understood that although his life might not be long in human terms, it would have a long-lasting impact on the many he met and to whom he demonstrated his zest for living. Surely, part of God's plan for Caleb's life was for him to point others to the very God who loved him and gave him purpose.

During the seasons of our son's short life, there were many times when the sentiments of Proverbs 3:5-6 granted me a helpful, steadying compass: "Trust in the Lord with all your heart and lean not on your own understanding; in all your ways acknowledge him, and He will make your paths straight."

During many of the trying times as we managed our son's extreme medical needs, our challenge was to trust God's purpose would prevail. Now, if I could not reconcile my great disappointment and sorrow in his death, how could I still trust that His purpose would prevail?

Could I, would I, dare to trust God when I could not come to terms and understand the why questions? Why did my son have to be infected with HIV? Why did my son have to die? In that these questions are incomprehensible, I realized I could not lean on my own understanding. The God in whom I'd placed my trust and hope during Caleb's life was the very same God in whom I'd have to trust, even in the despair of burying my son. Only then would God's purpose prevail.

I reminded the congregation of the importance of acknowledging God in all our ways. Because Caleb's very life was from God, we were to thank Him and acknowledge His working in our precious son's life all the many times he amazed the doctors. I reminded the audience that the neonatologists expected Caleb would not live beyond just a few days. He not only long outlived that expectation but also often thrived despite his many medical challenges. For more than two years, he kept the dreaded AIDS virus at bay—never plagued with a deadly opportunistic infection despite his decimated immune system.

I expressed the bittersweet sentiment of knowing our son had died in my arms but was immediately delivered into his Savior's arms. It was bitter in that his father's arms no longer hold him nor feel his touch but sweet because, not only do his Savior's arms now hold him, but also will those same arms one day embrace me as well. These are the arms of the Savior whose heart burst for Caleb and all mankind.

I recounted the story Irvin's wife, Terry, shared wherein she saw a number of sick children dying a slow and agonizing death in a hospital on life support. In stark contrast, she then saw our son boldly and in a flash leave his earthly father's arms for his Heavenly Father's arms. I challenged those present to follow my son's example and like his namesake, Caleb of old, boldly stand on their feet and thereby declare their intentions to approach God through faith in Jesus Christ—the Savior whose heart burst for them.

Several days later, I reflected in my journal.

. . . .

Thursday, 21 Sep: On Saturday during Caleb's funeral, eight individuals stood at my invitation to acknowledge Jesus Christ as their Savior and Lord, thereby receiving the gift of eternal life. Among those who made this decision was my very own mother. The next day, after attending the church that hosted us for the funeral, I asked my mother what her standing at the funeral meant. With tears in her eyes she proclaimed, "It was time."

. . . .

The Sunday following our son's funeral, many from our extended family, including my mother, attended the service at the church that hosted Caleb's ceremony the previous day. After the church service, we caravanned to the cemetery to visit Caleb's burial site. During the short drive, I described to my wife the conversation I'd just had with my mother.

As I parked our car right behind my mother's, I looked across the front seat and observed my wife in an anguished, silent cry. "Kathy, what is it?" I inquired. Kathy turned her tear-filled eyes from mine to the vehicle in front of us.

"Your mother," she sobbed, "if it took the death of our son to bring her to the Lord, then so be it!"

I was as breathless as speechless at her faith-filled declaration. I was not yet ready to admit such a willingness to sacrifice our son. Nevertheless, I was humbled by my wife's stance. Thus, if for nothing else, Caleb's life had counted for eternity, for my mother's sake.

Following the funeral, we spent a few blurry days visiting family before packing up and driving the eight hours to O'Fallon, Illinois, where our former church hosted a memorial service.

The service was a time of deep reflection. We remembered Caleb's life with our close friends and church family as well as associates and friends from my former office at Scott Air Force Base. Likewise, many of our precious Bosnian friends came and joined us from St. Louis. These dear friends deeply loved our Caleb.

Our dearest Bosnian friend, Elvir, brought a video, a moving tribute he'd made from pictures taken only one month earlier while visiting us in Washington, D.C. What a marvelous gift of love Elvir presented to us at the ceremony. We were as surprised as we were pleased at the tender, respectful tribute to our son's short life.

It had rained much of the day of the memorial ceremony in Fairview Heights, Illinois. Just before the service was to begin, amidst the last-minute commotion, an usher found me and excitedly implored me to come outside and see the awesome rainbow.

As we stepped out the side door of the church, he motioned with his hand and there before me appeared a glorious double rainbow, glistening in the sky. After catching my breath, I marveled that just as the rainbow's time in the sky is short-lived, so was our son's life, but it was lived to the full and was likewise a thing of beauty.

CHAPTER 34

To Live Again

The first Wednesday after Caleb's death saw Kathy and me in a fever of planning and organizing. Kathy's friend, Carleen, took our older children to church to attend their regular classes. Meanwhile, Kathy and I busied ourselves planning a two week trip to Michigan and Illinois for our son's funeral and memorial ceremony.

In the midst of our various tasks, we suddenly heard a car pull up. Notably earlier than expected, we looked up just in time to see Carleen jump out of her vehicle.

She dashed in, urgently imploring, "Come get Andrew!" I ran outside to see what was going on. As I approached the minivan, I heard Andrew anguishing in pain. I observed him holding his knees to his chest in a vice-like grip as he moaned and shrieked in obvious excruciating pain. His bulging bloodshot eyes screamed intolerable agony! I gathered the balled up child and immediately transferred him to my vehicle to take him straight to the emergency room.

As I laid him in our minivan, I breathed a prayer for comfort for my son. Minutes later as I turned into the ER parking lot,

"Can't you hear my son screaming? He's writhing in pain. He needs help immediately. What if his appendix has burst?"

Andrew began screaming even louder than before—amazing it was possible. I tried to comfort him, but he couldn't hear me over his own deafening shrieks. Into the ER I carried my balled up boy, who was poised to cannonball into the deep end of a pool as he tightly grasped his knees to his chest. Only, we weren't at a pool, and Andrew was in no condition to jump into deep water. Disheartened in that I observed a full house, I made eye contact with another father who quickly and unhesitatingly vacated his seat so I could set down my pained son. After lowering his quivering body onto the vinyl seat, I scampered to the check-in counter.

Much to my surprise, the ER front desk clerk not only failed to acknowledge my presence but also continued to ignore me until I spoke up and demanded, "Can't you hear that screaming? My son needs immediate help!"

In slow motion the civilian clerk merely held out a clipboard with a pen tethered by dingy medical tape.

Without looking up he calmly directed in a remarkably unconcerned nasal tone, "Please complete this form and have a seat."

Unable to contain my incredulity and impatience, I exploded, "Can't you hear my son screaming? He's writhing in pain. He needs help immediately. What if his appendix has burst?"

To my urgent demand, without so much as looking up, the disinterested attendant limply advised as he spoke to his clipboard, "I'm sorry, but I'm not qualified to diagnose that, Sir."

I had to exercise every ounce of self-control to resist the overwhelming urge to lunge over the counter and grab this impudent attendant by the collar and drag him over to look my agonizing son directly in the eye.

The attendant mechanically advised, "Sir, if you think you have an urgent emergency, you're welcome to dial 911."

"May I borrow your phone?" I asked with shock and incredulity.

"Certainly, it's right over there."

For the first time since our interaction began, the clerk looked up and motioned toward the ER phone that sat at the far end of the counter. I stepped to my right two side steps, picked up the phone, and punched 9-1-1. Within seconds I heard a voice acoustically as well as electronically.

The echoing voice declared, "911, state your emergency and location please."

"My seven-year-old son is experiencing excruciating abdominal pain, and I'm standing at the Andrews Air Force Base ER check-in counter!"

To this the startled voice gaffed, "Wha'..."

Suddenly, an incredulous ER nurse leaned out from behind the wall with a phone at his ear and a coiled cord pulling from its base, attached to the opposite wall.

With a shocked look of disbelief, he asked as he pointed back and forth from himself to the phone to me and asked, "Wha...ah...i...is this you?"

"Yes, it is," I resolutely replied.

The nurse immediately dropped the phone, bounded over the counter, and ran to my son who was still screaming and writhing in pain. The no-nonsense nurse deftly gathered Andrew in his arms and smoothly galloped over the furniture like an Olympic hurdler. Within moments we were in an examination room where the nurse proceeded to query Andrew of the intensity and source of his pain. Andrew described his pain as a nine on a scale of one to ten, ten being the worst possible pain. As the examination progressed and the more personal and complex the questions became, the quieter Andrew grew.

Finally, after about fifteen minutes, a number of questions, and various pokes and prods by the nurse, Andrew peacefully quieted himself as well as relaxed his legs as he released his clenched fists and vice-like grip on his knees. When he had completely relaxed his legs, I asked if his pain was totally gone.

He unhesitatingly declared, "Yes, my pain is all gone, Dad."

With this intriguing news, I stole a knowing glance at the nurse, who was busily writing orders for abdominal testing to be conducted the following day. I took the opportunity to advise the nurse that Andrew had undergone abdominal tests a couple of years ago at the Scott AFB Clinic. All results were negative. Formerly, his abdominal discomfort had never reached such an extreme level. The insightful nurse inquired to know if there had been any recent, unusual stressors in Andrew's life.

"Well, yes, as a matter-of-fact, Andrew's three and a half year old brother died on Sunday."

"Three days ago?" the suddenly incredulous nurse inquired.

"Yes, three days ago."

This medical professional took the information in stride, demonstrating just the right amount of concern. He indicated that Andrew surely had a valid stressor to cause such intense psychosomatic pains given his brother's sudden death, but he would not assume there was no organic cause without first conducting tests.

Given our imminent travel plans, I asked the nurse to hold the testing should we decide at some later date to re-engage the matter.

He readily agreed. With that Andrew and I strolled to our car and happily drove home.

As far as I know, not since that day has Andrew experienced these same or any other peculiarly indeterminate abdominal pains. His source of anxiety and inexplicable pain vanished along with his brother.

As Kathy and I considered the frequency of Andrew's strange abdominal pains, it occurred to us that they nearly always corresponded to when his younger brother was about to undergo major surgery. Therefore, we surmised the likely source of our son's pain was neither the loss of his brother nor the sorrow of missing him. Rather the source was most likely that of uncertainty.

Uncertainty is the cause of much of our stress in life—even for a child. But a child has not the wherewithal to understand the relationship of his pain to his fear of the unknown. We could only imagine the agonizing questions that must have plagued Andrew's mind each time his brother disappeared for weeks on end. Whether he was consciously aware, Andrew must have wondered: When will my little brother come home? Will my brother ever come home? If my brother never comes back, will I disappear too?

Andrew's concept that his brother was now in Heaven likely mitigated his fear. Although Andrew would miss his brother in that he wasn't coming home, Andrew also understood—as well as any seven-year-old could understand—Caleb was now in a safe place. Andrew didn't have to fret about Caleb's future anymore. Now that the origin of Andrew's excruciating pain had disappeared, so did his pain. Although Andrew's pain had ended, mine had not. My pain was just beginning.

About six weeks later, again on a Wednesday evening, my family was headed to church. After dropping off my wife and children at the front door, instead of parking our car in the church lot and also going in, I turned out onto the street and aimlessly drove to a restaurant five minutes away. I parked, walked in, and ordered a coffee, which I didn't drink.

As I sat in eerie silence, hearing no sound except the hushed voices of other patrons and the occasional clink of their utensils, a roaring volcano of maddening dread erupted in my mind: It's not right. It's not fair. My son should not be dead. I want my son back—now!

Suddenly aware my phone was ringing, I mechanically answered and recognized the familiar voice of my faithful friend Woody, who'd served alongside me in our church on Okinawa.

"David, you know you are going to see Caleb again someday," he began.

"Woody, that doesn't mean anything to me right now," I protested. "I don't want to see him again, someday. I want to see him now."

I don't remember if Woody said anything else nor how much longer we spoke, if at all. At that time I wanted to be, even tried to be, offended he should be so brash as to interrupt my agonizing sorrow with his trite exhortation that I'd see Caleb again someday. I didn't want to hear that I'd see my son again, someday; I wanted to see him right then, at that moment—but he was dead and I could not.

About three months after my son died, I happened to be riding with a fellow squadron pilot and friend in his car. We were driving north on I-295 from Washington DC to Baltimore, making typical small talk when he suddenly turned to me and asked, "How long are you going to continue grieving for your son?"

Without hesitation, I surprised myself by unthinkingly replying, "As long as he's still dead." My friend drew a sharp breath and without a word looked straight forward. Neither of us said another word all the way to Baltimore.

For months, I struggled with discouragement as I pensively contemplated the time that had elapsed since my son's death. I didn't want time to pass. I didn't want time to create distance between my thoughts of my son and me. I had a fear that the more time passed, the easier it would become to go on living without him. This thought was exceedingly stressful for I didn't want to go on without him. I was fearfully afraid of forgetting him. I had a recurring nightmare wherein I realized, in a sudden panic, I'd forgotten what he looked like.

I wanted to long for him with as much inconsolable passion as I had at the beginning. I wanted to miss him with as much mental paralysis as I had immediately after his death. Ironically, it was as though I wanted to be as overwhelmed with grief and despair as I had been soon after his death. I wanted the deliciousness of despair, I'd known, to continue surrounding me in its sinister cloak, for its numbing darkness was somehow strangely comforting—shielding me from the reality of my gnawing sorrow and unending pain.

It occurred to me that the more time passed since my son's death, the longer it'd been since I held him. The more time passed since my son's death, the longer it'd been since I felt his soft cheek against mine. The more time passed since his death, the longer it'd been since I'd read to him before bed. The more time passed since his death, the longer it'd been since I changed his colostomy bag. Logic would dictate I shouldn't miss that messy duty, but I did.

The more time passed since his death, the longer it'd been since I carried him in my arms. Ah, carrying him in my arms. That's perhaps how I remember him most. I have so many fond memories but that one tops them all. I remember tenderly holding and rocking him many times, with the myriad of medical tubes and wires attached to him, just hours after surgery. I remember pushing his stroller into countless doctors' offices. I likewise remember carrying him in my arms into the laboratory where his blood was so frequently drawn, proudly declaring that the fighter had arrived.

Often when I dreaded my son was gone and beyond my reach, Woody's words would haunt me. Although there were many days wherein I longed to remain in the despair of my immobilizing grief, I could not help but remember Woody's indelible reminder that I would see Caleb again, someday.

Not that I wanted such grief to keep me in despair. Quite the contrary, I wanted my son to live. I worked so hard to promote his life; I couldn't understand how he could be gone.

During his life I never knew how long he would live or what his limitations might be. Such questions caused me no end of uncertainty. Nevertheless, I would prefer the stress and uncertainty of caring for Caleb in life to the frequent pain of despairing his absence in death—for then I had hope to drive me.

As long as he was alive, I had hope that he would grow up to be a sensitive young man whose inspirational, overcoming faith and unflappable smile would not fade. As long as he was alive, I had hope that he would mature into a leader who understood trials and could encourage others to go on when it seemed hopeless. When he died, my hopes for him likewise died—but now, I faced a choice. Would I emotionally die with him? Or would I, as I believe he does, live again? I had to decide.

Eventually, it occurred to me I could change my perspective. I could consider that as time passed, I'm not moving chronologically farther from my son but rather moving closer to him. With each passing day, I could chose to look forward, anticipating the day when I would, as Woody's haunting words so often reminded me, see him again, someday.

It also occurred to me I was privileged to have experienced such passionate yearning for my son. I had come to realize that is precisely what God desires for each of His children. He longs for them to yearn for Him as I yearned for my son.

In considering this perspective for the first time since my son's death, I no longer possessed a defeatist, noncommittal attitude toward heaven and walking with God. Suddenly, I desired to live again in such a way that Jesus would be proud to welcome me into heaven and introduce me to His Father.

I decided to live again.

Even when my energy was again and again sapped by overwhelming grief, and my zest for living diminished, I determined I would yet choose to live again.

CHAPTER 35

To Glorify God

During his short three and a half years, Caleb taught me several lessons. He taught me that it's not only 70-year-old men who have heart disease, but it's also sometimes young children. He also taught me that it's not only homosexuals and drug addicts who are HIV-positive, but it's also sometimes young children. Although the 37-year-old male who donated his HIV-contaminated blood likely understood he would be endangering another's life, I learned that with God's help I could forgive the man of this misdeed. Although his action was inexcusable, it was forgivable.

While I was saddened by the untimely death of my son, I was thankful his life and death reminded me that God was also father of a son who suffered and died at the hands of men—and yet He forgave them. I was thankful for the many things for which God had forgiven me and likewise thankful that His forgiveness gave me strength to forgive.

With his carefree manner and unflappable, crooked smile, Caleb also taught me that when inconceivable and incomprehensible pain, heartache, and sorrow bury me in their weight, I can yet stand if I determine to let my Father carry the burden on my behalf. As surely as I did all I could to carry my son's burdensome challenges, my Heavenly Father will carry mine if I'll allow Him.

While I sometimes feel as though I am now maimed with scars from having been wounded, I am glad for having suffered because despite the fact that with my new gait I carry a distinct limp, I feel stronger. I am emboldened to confront difficulties and can rejoice in a purer joy than I'd known before. I rejoice not that my son is dead, but I have learned to rejoice in my newfound perspective with which I draw strength to live with renewed passion.

Furthermore, the experience of losing my son affected my faith by fostering an increased genuineness. A friend told me several years after my son died, "I like you better now. You're less pretentious." I learned through experience that pride evaporates when in the pit of despair. Not that I claim to have wrestled with God, but I can identify with Jacob in that as a result of my struggle, I'll certainly walk with a limp the rest of my life.[11]

I do not hold to the commonly held philosophy that says the difficulties we encountered during Caleb's life and beyond were divinely purposed. I do not believe God purposed for us to have a son born with multiple congenital anomalies, not the least of which was a gravely serious heart defect. I do not believe God purposed Caleb to endure ten major surgeries of which five were open-heart, months in and out of hospitals, a blood transfused HIV infection, and endless days of uncertainty, followed by his sudden, unexpected, and untimely death. Nevertheless, He allowed all these sufferings for some unknown and unknowable reason.

> Evidence of true faith is the determination to trust God when that which He allows makes no sense—and is utterly disagreeable.

Therefore, I must say with Job, "Shall we accept good from God, and not trouble? Though He slay me, yet will I hope in Him..."[9] Although the reason God would allow such unmitigated suffering is incomprehensible, He surely knows why He allowed it. Even though I cannot reconcile it, in the final analysis, God knows. As Job further pronounced, "To God belong wisdom and power; counsel and understanding are His."[10]

In other words, I do not hold that God intended but rather that for some inexplicable reason allowed this trouble to come upon our son as well as his parents and siblings. Although I neither understand nor like it, in my honest anger I can say nothing other than I do not know why God allowed it even though He had the power to stop it.

There have been many days wherein I was inclined to ask or even scream, "Why?" But I knew no reply except a deafening silence. Even in the excruciating silence, I nonetheless determined not to angrily disavow God's love. Whereas I believe God did not intend the calamity of my son's suffering and death, I likewise believe He could have acted to avert it—yet He did not.

Nevertheless, I refuse to turn from faith in Him. This is the stuff of which faith is really made. Evidence of true faith is the determination to trust God when that which He allows makes no sense—and is utterly disagreeable.

Of all the questions asked concerning lessons learned as a result of the tumultuous birth, life struggles, and untimely death of our son, the most common is simply, "Why was Caleb born this way?"

I reflect that when a soldier is in a heated, dangerous battle, he has not the luxury of contemplating the reasons the leaders of his country and those of his enemy are at odds with each other. He has no time for such ponderings. He can only consider how to perform his duty and accomplish his mission while seeking to protect his fellow soldiers and himself in the face of significant challenges and imminent danger.

Similarly, Caleb demonstrated an uncanny appreciation that he was to live with joy and enthusiasm even in the midst of intense suffering. He seemed to somehow understand he didn't have time to waste wallowing in self-pity. He had a job to do. He had a life to live and did not have time to waste whining and wondering why. He had to get on with living. He had books to read. He had games to play. And he had swings and slides on which to glide.

Many people, when encountering the inevitable trials and suffering life brings, seem absorbed and controlled by insisting on figuring it all out.

"Why did this happen to me?" they insist on asking. "What can we do to avoid the pain this suffering brings?"

Still others are more concerned with trying to be fulfilled and satisfied, attempting to discover the secret to living a life free from agony and distress. While seeking to avoid discomfort and disappointment is natural, a life free from pain is unrealistic.

I agree with Eugene Peterson when he says, "We need to know that suffering is part of what it means to be human and not something alien."[12]

We cannot always avoid heartache. Learning to acknowledge and live with suffering, sorrow, and pain yet, nevertheless, finding joy through an overcoming spirit is the only way to peace and fulfillment that lasts.

Our son knew he didn't have time to waste. He had a job to do and little time in which to do it. He needed to get on with it. Caleb never struggled with the question of why he was born this way. He simply sought to live—and live his life to the fullest. In so doing, he lived as he was born—to glorify God.

Epilogue

BY KATHLEEN M. INGERSON

I love the early morning when the entire world seems asleep and quiet reigns in my generally rambunctious household. During these still hours, shortly before the sun makes its glorious appearance and graciously greets me for the day, I enjoy a cup of strong coffee, read the Scriptures, pray, listen, journal, and perhaps complete an unfinished project before my family rises and busyness ensues.

I am not sure if my early morning ritual began as a result of my trying to find some amount of calm while raising young children, or I simply learned to follow what was patterned for me by my dairy farming father, who dutifully rose before dawn each day to complete his morning chores. Even so, I cherish this time of day.

It was during these early morning hours, at a quiet anniversary getaway in quaint Old Alexandria, Virginia, when I found myself silently pondering the years we had affectionately dubbed, the Caleb years. As David slept, I tearfully recounted a few of my most vivid memories from these years.

With bittersweet remembrance, I recalled Caleb's second open-heart surgery at Mott Children's Hospital in Michigan. Caleb's anticipated ten-day hospital stay agonizingly stretched into more than two months, largely due to post-operative complications.

Pleural effusion and a collapsed right upper lung made it difficult for Caleb to maintain sufficient oxygen levels.

During this time my mother-in-law cared for our three older children at our home in Illinois while David returned to duty at Scott Air Force Base. I stayed night and day at Caleb's bedside, relieved by my gracious mother now and then.

Caleb was a trooper as he tolerated unending breathing treatments, painful chest percussion (thumping his tiny chest around his still tender incision site), and cumbersome chest tubes, which had been thrust for a second time between his ribs and into his chest cavity. Not surprisingly, Caleb quickly learned to identify the respiratory personnel as they entered his room to perform the necessary and painful treatments; it broke my heart to watch him whimper and whine as he attempted to squirm out of their reach. Although this therapy continued for more than 40 days, progress was quite slow in that severe gastric reflux further complicated his recovery.

Around day 60, I decided I'd had enough of hospital life and desperately desired to go home. I missed my husband and my other children. I wanted to be home to celebrate our family's October birthdays—but mostly, I wanted to return to some kind of normal. As I sat in the chair next to Caleb's hospital crib, I poured out my frustration in a whispered tirade.

"So, God, why does Caleb—and consequently his parents—have to endure all these complications? A damaged lymph node and damaged nerve in his diaphragm? A collapsed lung? Fluid around his lungs? Breathing difficulties? Low oxygen levels? And now, severe gastric reflux—that awful retching—which puts further stress on his heart? Why the additional gastrointestinal complications?

"In fact, why was Caleb born with so many life-threatening birth defects in the first place? Wouldn't one have been enough? Isn't heart disease enough? And not just any heart disease—a severe and rare heart disease wherein the left side of his heart is virtually useless. After all, other children with this same heart defect do not suffer from these additional congenital problems like Caleb. It's just not fair," I lamented.

In a fit of frustration, like a small child shaking her fist and stomping her feet, I demanded an answer, but received none.

After some time, I quieted my mind and reigned in my discontent. As I softened my stance, I pleaded, "Oh Father, I'm sorry. Please help me."

Moments later, God, in His amazing grace, gently spoke to my burdened heart. *Kathy, my child, be thankful. Learn to be thankful. Caleb's gastrointestinal anomalies indicated additional defects. The doctors [in Okinawa] then knew to look for further problems. Without the imperforate anus you would not have known about the heart disease. You would have taken Caleb home, a seemingly healthy pink baby, only for him to struggle and die days later, a blue baby.*

Stunned, I humbly sank to my knees in tears. "God, You are right. I am sorry. Please help me be thankful," I weakly replied.

Although this medical perspective was not new to me, I had never considered being thankful for such dire medical conditions. I had never thought to give thanks for a congenital anomaly, an imperforate anus? No doubt about it, the lack of an anal orifice and his other gastrointestinal abnormalities did save Caleb when he entered this world.

After further contemplation, I said more confidently and resolutely, "God, I choose to be thankful."

Two days later Caleb's lung finally re-inflated and his remaining complications subsided. After a gastric repair, his recovery progressed swiftly, and we drove home ten days later, just in time to celebrate all the October birthdays. "Thank You, God," I whispered.

Quickly, my mind fast-forwarded twelve months to a time when I felt totally undone and extremely heartbroken. Early one morning at my kitchen table in our Illinois home, I was overcome with the absurd and unreal news that Caleb had been infected with HIV. There are no words to adequately describe the horror I felt, the sheer shock, anger, fear, and anguish that enveloped my heart, my mind, and my entire being.

In despair and confusion, with tears streaming down my face, I wailed, "How can this be? Statistically this is like winning the lottery, and we did not buy a ticket. How can Caleb possibly be positive for HIV? Really, God?"

It just did not make any sense. For months we had fought and sacrificed, scratched and kicked when necessary, and fought some more, in an attempt to save Caleb's life—and now this. I had been kicked in the gut and was not able to catch my breath. While gasping for air, I tried to make sense of the senseless situation.

Sometime later, in the midst of my desperate agony, God intervened and again spoke to my weary heart. *Kathy, be thankful,* He reminded me.

"Be thankful? Be thankful for what?" Dumbfounded, I asked, "What can I possibly be thankful for in this situation?"

You and David are HIV free. I am protecting you. Be thankful.

As Caleb's primary caregivers, David and I daily came in contact with his body fluids, even blood, when changing his colostomy bag. The irony of this situation was that as a home health care nurse working in the St. Louis area, I protected myself by wearing gloves each time I cared for my clients, especially when drawing blood. All the while, for nine months, I did not know my own son was inflicted with HIV. I certainly had not worn gloves while caring for him.

After Caleb's HIV status confirmed positive, David and I were immediately tested at the infectious disease specialist's recommendation. Although the medical community assured us our risk for HIV infection was extremely low, almost nonexistent, I feared the worst. I feared that David or I or both of us had been infected.

During one of my weekly commissary runs with children in tow, I set Caleb in the top seat of the grocery cart and bent down to speak eye-to-eye with him about some matter. As Caleb enthusiastically answered my question, he spewed a mouthful of spit directly into my eyes. "Wow," I exclaimed. "If Caleb were ever to infect me with HIV, it would be now."

Although I knew both tears and saliva contain negligible amounts of virus, I was afraid. Although there existed to date no known or reported cases of HIV infection transmitted via saliva, fear and uncertainty gripped my mind. The unexpected, the unimaginable, the unthinkable had already occurred: my son had been infected with HIV. I couldn't help but wonder if I would become infected as well.

As I continued my shopping, I quickly muttered a desperate prayer. "God, You said You are protecting me. I need to trust You. Please help me trust You."

I began to understand why God admonished me to be thankful. Thankfulness guards the heart. It shields one from the insidious nature of ingratitude. A contented, grateful heart will not surrender to resentment and self-pity, nor will it plummet into the muck of bitterness and unforgiveness. It simply is not possible to

Thankfulness opens the door and ushers in peace and joy like a blessed breeze on a hot and humid Louisiana summer day.

be both grateful and bitter. Truly, there is a protective nature to thankfulness.

Thankfulness is a necessary response to God's goodness. I began to be thankful in all things. I sought to not only recognize but also acknowledge God's hand—His blessings—in all my circumstances, especially the most difficult. Furthermore, I began to understand that even when I do not feel grateful, I can nonetheless choose to be thankful. When I so do, I reap an abundant harvest of not only peace that dispels my anxious thoughts and desperate fears but also joy that strengthens and allows me to persist even in the midst of sorrow and suffering.

Thankfulness opens the door and ushers in peace and joy like a blessed breeze on a hot and humid Louisiana summer day. The oppressive heat and humidity just won't subside, but the welcome breeze helps one to endure the unwelcome and unkind heat.

Hesitantly, my mind returned to the days immediately following the busyness of planning for and traveling to Caleb's funeral in Michigan and memorial service in Illinois. As we returned to our home in Maryland, the protective shock surrounding his death diminished. I was left with grief that was unspoken and pain that was acute. I knew I needed to grasp onto something, Someone—for I was slowly drowning in my own unshed tears of grief and sorrow.

God gently pursued me. He continually reminded me to be grateful. His words, *Kathy, be thankful,* echoed through my mind.

Finally, on one very lonely day, I intentionally chose not to dwell on that which caused me such anguish. Instead, I chose to be thankful.

"God, I am not thankful for the death of my son—that I will never hold him or see his precious smile again while on this earth—but I am thankful I will see him again in Heaven. I am grateful he did not die alone or in someone else's care. I am thankful we were together as a family and surrounded by people who love and care for us. I am thankful Caleb did not suffer while dying but spent his last hours playing, with his daddy by his side.

"I am grateful that I am surrounded by some of my very best friends to support me during this time—unusual considering our transient Air Force lifestyle. I am thankful for my husband and our stable marriage. I still hear his startling words: 'Kathy, if I have to suffer through the death of a child, there is no one else with whom I would rather go through it than you.'

"God, I am grateful for my remaining children. They are so young. Please help me to mother them. I am thankful for my parents as well as my mother-in-law and her new found faith in You. God, I am thankful for...."

The longer my list grew, the more grateful I became and the lighter my burdened heart felt. My inward focus and self-pity gradually faded as I grew increasingly mindful of God and His goodness.

Like that blessed breeze on a hot and humid still summer day, thankfulness brought a welcome relief to my heavy heart, even though I could not change the circumstances regarding Caleb—even though I could not bring back my son. My situation had not changed but my perspective had.

As my mind returned to the present, to our anniversary getaway in our Old Alexandria hotel suite, I cried out, "Thank You, God, for the gift of gratefulness. Without Your intervention, I would still be wallowing in self-pity and unforgiveness.

"Father, I am truly thankful for the three and a half years I had with Caleb. I know that if Your hand had not miraculously held him in my womb, I would not have had even those years.

"Yet, my mind still wonders and my heart still yearns to understand why Caleb's life had to end as it did. Certainly, he would have lived longer without the HIV infection. Certainly, You could have extended his life."

As the tears spilled down my face, I asked the questions which had plagued me for months. "God, why did my son have to become infected with HIV? Why did my son have to die because of the offense of another?"

As salty as the tears that stung my eyes, God's words pierced my heart. *Kathy, Kathy, my child, I know and understand your pain. My beloved Son, also, had to die because of the offense of another. He had to die—for your sin.*

In that moment I understood. In that moment, I was overwhelmed by God's absolute love for me. The Creator of the heavens and earth, God Most High, God Almighty owes me absolutely nothing but has given me everything, all that I need, in and through the ultimate gift of grace—the sacrifice of His Son.

Humbled, my why questions no longer seemed so important or necessary. I was no longer plagued by my anxious need to understand. I would trust the One who had sacrificed all for me.

Awakened from my contemplation by a sudden, swift movement from within me, I was immediately reminded of the baby in my womb and instinctively ran my hand over my ever-protruding belly.

After Caleb died, I was afraid to have any more children and told God as much: "No more children. It's just too painful!" I did everything within my power, short of a permanent fix, to prevent a pregnancy.

But now, I smiled as I felt Deborah moving and kicking, acknowledging that God often knows better than me. Deborah is a child of promise, the Lord's gift to us. She won't replace Caleb, yet she too will be a mighty reflection of His goodness.

I then raised my eyes, just in time to see the sun's majestic rays peek over the horizon. It was a glorious sight. It was a new day. Hope sprang afresh in me as I realized there would finally, once again, be shouts of joy and peals of laughter in our home.

> Yet this I call to mind and therefore I have hope:
> Because of the LORD's great love
> we are not consumed,
> for His compassions never fail.
> They are new every morning;
> great is Your faithfulness.
> —Lamentations 3:21-23

NOTE TO READER

In as much as our son's life hung in the balance from the moment of his birth due to the serious heart condition and other congenital anomalies with which he was born, we cannot say enough about the high quality urgent care provided him by the staff of the Neonatal Intensive Care Unit (NICU) at the Camp Lester Naval Hospital in Okinawa, Japan. Furthermore, not only to the Lester NICU but also to the doctors and the staff at Moffit Children's Hospital, University of California San Francisco; the Children's Hospital at Washington University in St. Louis, Missouri; and Mott Children's Hospital at the University of Michigan in Ann Arbor, we extend our most humble and heartfelt thanks for your commitment and service to our little fighter.

We also extend our deep appreciation to the military medical community from the general pediatrics and cardiology departments to the pharmacies as well as the infectious disease and gastroenterology staff at Travis Air Force Base (AFB) Hospital near Sacramento, California; Scott AFB Clinic near Belleville, Illinois; Andrews AFB Hospital near Washington, D.C.; and Walter Reed Army Medical Center in Bethesda, Maryland.

In that there was nearly no end to the vast number of doctors, nurses, pharmacists, surgical aides, respiratory therapists, nurses' aides, medical technicians, physicians' coordinators, social workers, and others within the medical community who served our little fighter so well, we offer a hearty thanks to all!

Without their continuing professionalism and attentive care, our son Caleb would not have enjoyed the high quality of life he did for his three and a half years. From the bottom of our heart, we deeply thank them.

ABOUT THE AUTHOR

David P. Ingerson is an exciting communicator who has spoken to audiences around the world. During his twenty years as a U.S. Air Force officer and pilot, he has traveled extensively and lived abroad with his family. From the time he served as an ordained teacher and evangelist in Okinawa, Japan, he has trained and led teams on short-term missions to the Philippines and Cambodia. Having suffered his own share of trials and setbacks as an entrepreneur, he encourages both employees and customers to rise above life's difficulties.

David is genuine and passionate as he encourages his listeners to honestly admit their challenges and disappointments. Through his story of triumph through tragedy, he spurs others to rise above life's frustrations and overcome in spite of intimidating obstacles.

David and his wife, Kathleen, are the parents of five children and make their home in Shreveport, Louisiana.

To contact the author, please visit his website:

www.thecalebyears.com

ENDNOTES

1   Page 100: Eugene Peterson, *A Long Obedience in the Same Direction,* Intervarsity Press, P.O. Box 1400, Downers Grove, IL 60515-1426, 2nd edition Copywrite 2000 by Eugene Peterson, 1st edition Copyright 1980 by Inter-Varsity Fellowship of the United States, used by permission.

2   Ibid; page 144; Peterson.

3   Used by permission: Copyright © 1992 Integrity's Hosanna! Music (ASCAP) (adm. at CapitolCMGPublishing.com) All rights reserved. Used by permission.

4   Page 44: Used by permission from "The Hiding Place," by Corrie Ten Boom, 35th Anniversary Edition, copyright 1971 and 1984 by Corrie ten Boom and Elizabeth and John Sherrill, and 2006 by Elizabeth and John Sherrill, Published by Chosen Books, a division of Baker Publishing Group.

5   James 4:14

6   John 17:3 (6)

7   Luke 18:16-17

8   Commonly attributed to General Robert E. Lee, Public Domain

9   Job 2:10; 13:15

10   Job 12:13

11   Jacob's story, from Genesis 32:22-32: [22]That night Jacob got up and took his two wives, his two female servants and his eleven sons and crossed the ford of the Jabbok. [23]After he had sent

them across the stream, he sent over all his possessions. [24]So Jacob was left alone, and a man wrestled with him till daybreak. [25]When the man saw that he could not overpower him, he touched the socket of Jacob's hip so that his hip was wrenched as he wrestled with the man. [26]Then the man said, "Let me go, for it is daybreak." But Jacob replied, "I will not let you go unless you bless me." [27]The man asked him, "What is your name?" "Jacob," he answered. [28]Then the man said, "Your name will no longer be Jacob, but Israel,[a] because you have struggled with God and with humans and have over-come." [29]Jacob said, "Please tell me your name." But he replied, "Why do you ask my name?" Then he blessed him there. [30]So Jacob called the place Peniel,[b] saying, "It is because I saw God face to face, and yet my life was spared." [31]The sun rose above him as he passed Peniel,[c] and he was limping because of his hip. [32]Therefore to this day the Israelites do not eat the tendon attached to the socket of the hip, because the socket of Jacob's hip was touched near the tendon.

[12] Ibid; page 144; Peterson.